The 150 best
Slow Cooker
recipes

The 150 best
Slow Cooker
recipes

Judith Finlayson

Robert
ROSE

For complete cataloguing information, see page 248.

Disclaimer
The recipes in this book have been carefully tested by our kitchen and our tasters. To the
best of our knowledge, they are safe and nutritious for ordinary use and users. For those
people with food or other allergies, or who have special food requirements or health issues,
please read the suggested contents of each recipe carefully and determine whether or not
they may create a problem for you. All recipes are used at the risk of the consumer.

We cannot be responsible for any hazards, loss or damage, which may occur as a result
of any recipe use.

For those with special needs, allergies, requirements or health problems, in the event
of any doubt, please contact your medical advisor prior to the use of any recipe.

Design & Production: PageWave Graphics Inc.
Editor: Carol Sherman
Copy Editor: Bernice Eisenstein
Photography: Mark T. Shapiro
Food Stylist: Kate Bush
Prop Stylist: Charlene Erricson
Color Scans & Film: Colour Technologies

Cover image: Turkey Chili with Black-Eyed Peas (*see recipe, page 64*)
Photo page 2: Succulent Succotash (*see recipe, page 76*)

We acknowledge the financial support of the Government of Canada through the
Book Publishing Industry Development Program (BPIDP) for our publishing activities.

Canadä

Published by: Robert Rose Inc.
120 Eglinton Ave. E., Suite 1000, Toronto, Ontario, Canada M4P 1E2
Tel: (416) 322-6552 Fax: (416) 322-6936

Printed in Canada

3 4 5 6 7 8 9 10   BP   09 08 07 06 05 04 03 02

To Bob and to Meredith
The best asset a cook can have — an appreciative and discerning audience.

Acknowledgements

In my experience, cookbooks, more than any other type of book, are a collaborative effort. From the initial concept, through recipe development and testing, editing, design, food styling and photography, it takes a dedicated team to produce a first-class book. I am very fortunate in those who have helped in so many ways to give this project life.

I owe my first thanks to my husband, Bob Dees, who persuaded me to write this book. Although I began my journalistic career as a food writer, restaurant reviewer and recipe developer and have maintained an active interest in food and cooking over the years, my reputation as a writer was established in other areas. Without his encouragement and support, I would likely have missed the enriching experience of working once again as a professional in a field that I love. Writing this book has been a pleasurable and creatively stimulating experience for which I have him to thank.

I deeply enjoy puttering in the kitchen, experimenting with ingredients and techniques, but the truth is that recipe development is often a hit-and-miss affair. I owe a great debt of appreciation to my family, friends and neighbors who gallantly sampled their share of less than successful dishes, often rising to the occasion to provide constructive suggestions for improving an idea that missed the mark. So, too, those who shared recipes with me or suggested dishes that might work well in the slow cooker. Some performed so far beyond the call of duty that they deserve special mention: my husband Bob and daughter Meredith, Margaret Hovanec and Peter Warrian, Audrey King and Scott Wilson and their children, Anna and Matthew, and Susan Meredith and Brian Harvey. I'd also like to thank recipe tester Jennifer Mackenzie for her exemplary enthusiasm and thoroughness.

The Robert Rose creative group is an author's dream team. Prop stylist Charlene Erricson helped to set the stage with her impressive knowledge of napkins, tableware and cutlery, and Kate Bush, food stylist extraordinaire, worked her magic to ensure that the food looked delicious. Then photographer Mark Shapiro focused his lens and brilliantly captured our collective vision on film, turning it into a reality that all can share. Special appreciation is due to designer Andrew Smith for creating the best-looking slow cooker book in the world and to my editor, Carol Sherman, whose keen eye and delightful personality took the pain out of the usually fretful editorial process.

Thanks to you all.

Contents

Introduction

To me, it makes perfect sense that the slow cooker, invented in the 1970s as an appliance for making baked beans, is enjoying a lively revival in the early years of the new millennium. Not only is it an invaluable tool for helping busy people manage their complex lives, it enables us to prepare delicious food with a minimum of attention and maximum certainty of success. Since discovering the slow cooker, I wouldn't make pot roast, beef brisket or short ribs and many kinds of stew any other way. Slow, moist cooking breaks down the tough connective tissue of less tender cuts of meat and allows the seasonings in complex sauces to intermingle without scorching. Moreover, the appliance does its work with virtually no assistance from me once I've prepared and assembled the ingredients and turned it on.

During the week, when we're often under pressure to meet the demands of scheduled evening activities, the slow cooker enables us to enjoy hot home-cooked meals just like those my mother used to make. The aromatic soups and stews that simmered on her stovetop are my idea of comfort food and they are deeply connected to my sense of family and home. I also love making steamed puddings and other old-fashioned desserts such as cobblers or "betty's" in my slow cooker. Not only are the results superb, it's unlikely the desserts will burn and I don't have to worry that the water bath required for many custards will evaporate, which happens all too easily in the oven.

As a convert to slow cooking, I decided to write a cookbook for a number of reasons, all of which revolve around my desire to communicate its potential to produce great-tasting food that people with even the most discriminating palates will savor. Naturally, I wanted to stress the slow cooker's value as an appliance that allows today's busy families to create nutritious and satisfying home-cooked food by sharing my recipes for everyday favorites, such as *Shepherd's Pie with Creamy Corn Filling*, *Hot Italian Meatball Sandwiches* and *Pineapple Upside-Down Spice Cake*. But once I discovered that my slow cooker was a great tool for entertaining, I also felt compelled to highlight its value as a hostess' helper, particularly since the appliance is so heavily identified with family-style cooking. Because I can get the preparation done for some dishes early in the day — or even the night before — the slow cooker also frees me up to entertain more often, including the occasional weeknight. For special occasions, I've made *East-West Pot Roast with Shiitake Mushroom Gravy* or *Osso Buco with Lemon Gremolata*. More relaxed evenings have produced dishes such as *Southwestern Turkey Pot Pie with Cornbread Cheddar Crust* or *Great Goulash with Potato Dumplings*. Since they are so easy to make, it's hard not to finish the meal off with a warm dessert such as *Delectable Apple-Cranberry Coconut Crisp* or *Old-Fashioned Gingerbread*.

Although I love my slow cooker as a helpmate, I also wanted to write a cookbook that would appeal to contemporary tastes by broadening the range of flavors and ingredients traditionally associated with slow cookers. Today, many food products, such as dried mushrooms, balsamic vinegar, Dijon mustard, coconut milk, curry powder and different varieties of chili peppers, are sold in most supermarkets. Not only can these ingredients enhance the flavor of slow-cooked foods, they also broaden the range of dishes that can be successfully prepared in the slow cooker, allowing for recipes with an international flair such as *Caribbean Pepper Pot Soup*, *Pork Roast with Chili-Orange Sauce*, *Turkey Breast Madras* and *Thai-Style Coconut Flan*. Since many contemporary consumers are trying to reduce the quantity of meat they consume, for health and other reasons, I've also used a wider range of principal ingredients, such as fish, seafood and vegetables, found in recipes such as *Snapper Vera Cruz* and *Eggplant and Tomato Gratin*. Given the healthful properties of legumes, I've also expanded the range of recipes using dried beans and lentils beyond the traditional bean pot to include Indian, Middle Eastern and Italian influences, among others, in recipes such as *Split Pea and Lentil Curry with Crispy Onions*, *Savory Chickpea Stew with Roasted Red Pepper Coulis* and *Tuscan-Style Beans with Rosemary*.

Not surprisingly, since it has traditionally been associated with making soups, stews and beans, the slow cooker is usually linked with "winter" food. While it does a great job with these dishes, I've also found the slow cooker to be of value in warm weather, when turning on the stove and heating up the kitchen has no appeal. In the summer, when we're usually grilling meat or fish on the barbecue, I most often use my slow cooker to prepare a flavorful cold soup, such as *Pumpkin Soup with Shrimp and Lime*, or an extra vegetable, such as *Cumin Beets* or *Creamy Mexican Beans*, which is a great accompaniment to grilled steak. It's also wonderful for making desserts that are prepared ahead and thoroughly chilled, such as *Crunchy Almond Crème Caramel* or *Chocolacinno Cheesecake*.

In writing this book, I've tried to include a wide range of recipes that will appeal to many tastes and requirements — from great family food to more sophisticated recipes for entertaining. I hope you will try the recipes and that you will enjoy them as much as I — and my family and friends — have. Happy cooking!

– Judith Finlayson

Using Your Slow Cooker

Slow Cooker Basics

About six million slow cookers are sold every year, making it one of our most popular appliances, which isn't surprising since it is also one of the easiest to use. Once the food is in the slow cooker, you can usually turn it on and forget about it until it's ready to serve.

Slow cookers are generally round or oval in shape and range in size from 1 to 7 quarts. The small round ones are ideal for dips and fondues, as well as some soups, main courses and desserts. The larger sizes, usually oval in shape, are necessary to cook whole roasts or chickens and desserts that need to be cooked in a dish or pan which fits into the stoneware. Once you begin using your slow cooker, you will soon get a sense of what your model does best.

Slow cookers work by cooking foods very slowly — from about 200°F (90°C) on the Low setting to 300°F (150°C) on High. They have crockery inserts and a heat source that surrounds the stoneware. All the recipes in this book were tested in either a round 3½-quart slow cooker, or an oval 6-quart slow cooker with a timing device. The advantage to the slow cooker with a timer is that it allows you to set the cooking time and temperature, and automatically switches to the Warm setting when the food is cooked. This is particularly helpful when cooking poultry or pork chops, which become overcooked if cooked for too long a time, even at a Low temperature.

Some manufacturers sell a "slow cooker," which is actually a multi-cooker. These have a heating element at the bottom and, in my experience, they cook faster than traditional slow cookers. Also, since the heat source is at the bottom, scorching is a possibility if the food is not stirred during the long cooking time.

Your slow cooker should come with a booklet that explains how to use the appliance. I recommend that you read this carefully and/or visit the manufacturer's web site for specific information on the model you purchased. I've cooked in a variety of slow cookers and have found that cooking times can vary substantially from one to another. Although it may not seem particularly helpful if you're just starting out, the only firm advice I can give you is: Know your slow cooker. After trying a few of these recipes, you will get a sense of whether your slow cooker is faster or slower than the ones I use and you will be able to adjust the cooking times accordingly.

Other variables that can affect cooking time are extreme humidity, power fluctuations and high altitudes. Be extra vigilant if any of these circumstances affect you.

Ensuring Food Safety

Slow cooker manufacturers have designed the appliance to ensure that bacterial growth is not a concern. According to the U.S. Department of Agriculture, bacteria in food is killed at a temperature of 165°F (74°C). So long as the lid is left on and the food is cooked for the appropriate length of time, that temperature will be reached quickly enough to ensure food safety. Most of the ingredients in my recipes are warm when added to the slow cooker (the meat has been browned and the sauce has been thickened on the stovetop), which adds a cushion of comfort to any potential concerns about food safety.

The following tips will help to ensure that utmost food safety standards are met:
- Do not allow ingredients to rise to room temperature before cooking.
- Do not refrigerate uncooked meat or poultry in the slow cooker stoneware as the insert will become very cold, which will slow the cooking process.
- Do not partially cook meat or poultry and refrigerate for subsequent cooking.
- If preparing ingredients in advance of cooking, refrigerate in separate containers and assemble when ready to cook.

- Pay attention to the make-ahead instructions for those recipes that can be partially prepared in advance of cooking as they have been developed to address the latest thinking in food safety.
- If cooking a large cut of meat, such as a pot roast, which has been added to the stoneware without being browned, set the temperature at High for 2 hours to accelerate the cooking process. Then reduce to Low for the duration of the cooking time.
- Thaw frozen food before adding to slow cooker. If added in a frozen state, it will significantly increase the time required for the temperature to reach the "safe zone," which inhibits bacteria growth. Frozen fruits and vegetables should be thawed under cold running water to separate before being added to recipes.
- When cooking whole poultry, which requires a longer cooking time in order for a safe temperature to reach the bone, test doneness by inserting an instant-read thermometer inside the thigh to ensure that the temperature has reached 170°F (77°C).
- Don't lift the lid while food is cooking. Each time the lid is removed it takes approximately 20 minutes to recover the lost heat. This increases the time it takes for the food to reach the "safe zone."
- Do not reheat food in the slow cooker.

Maximizing Convenience

Your slow cooker is one of the most effective time management tools available. Once the ingredients are assembled in the stoneware, you just select the appropriate temperature and get on with the rest of your life. Because the slow cooker does its work unattended, you can be away from the kitchen all day and return to a hot, delicious meal.

A little advance preparation can make your slow cooker an even more effective helpmate. If I have to be out of the house all day, I prepare my ingredients to the cooking stage the night before I intend to cook the dish so I have a minimum amount of work to do in the morning. Sometimes, I cook a recipe overnight in my slow cooker and refrigerate until I'm ready to serve. Where appropriate, all my recipes contain a make-ahead tip to help you maximize the convenience your slow cooker can bring to your home.

Preparing Great-Tasting Food

I was a latecomer to the joys of slow cooking. For many years, I shunned the appliance because I equated it with unappetizing food. Most of the recipes I came across in cookbooks or magazines confirmed my prejudice. Ingredients were simply combined in the stoneware, the appliance was turned on and the cook hoped for the best. When I finally acquired a slow cooker of my own, a gift from my husband, I decided to try this technique, against my better judgment, in the wild hope that there was some magic component to slow cooking that escaped my notice. No such luck! My beef stew consisted of chunks of unappealing meat in a flavorless, watery sauce, which was just about what I had expected in my more rational moments.

Despite my disappointment, even then I could see the slow cooker's potential as a device for tenderizing tough, but flavorful cuts of meat and for making succulent chilies and stews that didn't stick to the bottom of the pot. I decided to experiment by applying basic techniques of good cooking I had learned over the years. Soon I was turning out some delicious renditions of traditional slow cooker dishes. Gradually, I began to move farther afield, using unusual ingredients and seasonings, again with favorable results. Eventually, I concluded there is no great mystery to preparing fabulous food in the slow cooker. Success is the combined result of employing tried-and-true cooking techniques, old-fashioned common sense and careful observation to spot the occasional curveball the slow cooker will throw you, such as ingredients that don't respond well to long, slow cooking.

Slow Cooker Tips

Brown Meats and Soften Vegetables

There isn't a good cook in the world who won't sing the virtues of browning. Browning does much more than add color to ingredients. It initiates something called the Maillard reaction, which breaks down the natural sugars in foods, releasing sweet, complex flavors. This process of caramelization increases the flavor of dishes by extracting the fat soluble components of foods that enrich the taste. After browning, the fat can be emulsified by adding flour, cooking it briefly, then stirring in liquid that will thicken into a rich, homogeneous gravy when cooked. Although these steps take a few minutes at the front end of a recipe, I believe they balance out overall. Most of the recipes in this book can be served directly from the slow cooker. There are no extra steps required to reduce and/or thicken the liquid, which has usually cooked to a nice consistency.

Reduce and Concentrate Liquid

As you use your slow cooker, one of the first things you will notice is that it generates a tremendous amount of liquid. Because slow cookers cook on Low heat, tightly covered, liquid doesn't evaporate as it does in the oven or on top of the stove. As a result, food made from traditional recipes will be watery. So the second rule of successful slow cooking is to reduce the amount of liquid in recipes. Naturally, you don't want to reduce the flavor, so I suggest using concentrated broth, undiluted, whenever possible. The liquid generated as the dish cooks will thin the broth to its expected strength.

Cut Root Vegetables into Thin Slices or Small Pieces

Perhaps surprisingly, root vegetables — carrots, turnips and particularly potatoes — cook even more slowly than meat in the slow cooker. As a result, root vegetables should be thinly sliced or cut into small pieces no larger than 1-inch (2.5-cm) cubes. I have found the mandoline, a device for cutting fruits and vegetables, to be particularly useful for producing thinly sliced potatoes for use in some recipes.

Pay Attention to Cooking Temperatures and Times

To achieve maximum results, less tender cuts of meat should be cooked as slowly as possible at the Low setting. Expect to cook whole cuts of meat such as roasts for 10 hours on Low and give brisket 12 hours on Low to become truly succulent. If you're short of time and at home during the day, cook whole cuts of meat or whole chicken on High for 1 to 2 hours before switching the temperature to Low. As noted in Ensuring Food Safety (see page 10), if adding cold ingredients, particularly large cuts of meat, to the slow cooker, set on High for 2 hours before lowering the temperature.

Many desserts, such as those containing milk, cream or some leavening agents, need to be cooked on High. In these recipes, a Low setting is not suggested as an option. For recipes that aren't dependent upon cooking at a particular temperature, the rule of thumb is that 1 hour of cooking on High equals 2 to $2\frac{1}{2}$ hours on Low.

Take Extra Care with Some Ingredients

Although slow cooking reduces your chances of overcooking food, it is still not a "one size fits all" solution to meal preparation. If you want your slow cooker to cook while you are away, you should plan your day carefully if you have pork chops or chicken in the pot. It is very easy to overcook poultry, particularly chicken breasts, in the slow cooker, and unless you're cooking a whole chicken, poultry shouldn't require more than 6 hours on Low. If cooking white meat, which dries out easily, I recommend leaving the skin on, which helps to maintain precious moisture and flavor. Remove the skin when serving, if desired. Because legs and thighs stand up well in the slow cooker, remove the skin before cooking, which helps to reduce the fat content in the sauce.

Pork chops are usually cooked in 5 hours on Low. Some ingredients, such as zucchini, peas, snow peas, fish, seafood, milk and cream (which will curdle if cooked too long), should be added during the last 30 minutes of cooking.

Use Peppers Appropriately

In my experience, several kinds of peppers (notably fresh green bell peppers and dried red peppers) become bitter if cooked for too long. The same holds true for cayenne pepper or hot pepper sauces such as Tabasco. For that reason, I add fresh green bell peppers to recipes during the last 30 minutes of cooking, use cayenne in small quantities and add hot pepper sauce after the dish is cooked. I have also found that several varieties of dried peppers, such as New Mexico chilies, which become bitter if added to the slow cooker when dry or not fully rehydrated, work well if they are thoroughly soaked in boiling water for 30 minutes before being added to slow cooker recipes. All the recipes in this book address these concerns in the instructions.

Whole Leaf Herbs and Spices

For best results, use whole rather than ground herbs and spices in the slow cooker. Whole spices, such as cumin seed and cracked black peppercorns, and whole leaf herbs, such as dried thyme and oregano leaves, release their flavors slowly throughout the long cooking period, unlike ground spices and herbs which tend to lose flavor during slow cooking. If you're using fresh herbs, add them, finely chopped, during the last hour of cooking unless you include the whole stem (this works best with thyme and rosemary).

Using Dishes and Pans in the Slow Cooker

Some dishes, notably puddings and custards, need to be cooked in an extra dish which is placed in the slow cooker stoneware. Not only will you need a large oval slow cooker for this purpose, finding a dish or pan that fits into the stoneware can be a challenge. I've found that the standard 7-inch (17.5-cm) square, 4-cup (1-L) and 6-cup (1.5-L) ovenproof baking dishes are the best all-round dishes for this purpose and I've used them to cook most of the custardlike recipes in this book. A 7-inch (17.5-cm) springform pan, which fits into a large oval slow cooker, is also a useful purchase as it allows you to make perfectly formed cheesecakes in your slow cooker.

Before you decide to make a recipe requiring a baking dish, ensure that you have a container that will fit into your stoneware. I've noted the size and dimensions of the containers used on all relevant recipes. Be aware that varying the size and shape of the dish is likely to affect cooking times.

Pantry Ingredients

A well-stocked refrigerator or kitchen cupboard will prove to be particularly helpful in turning out great-tasting and innovative slow cooker food. Here are some of the ingredients I recommend keeping in your pantry:

Chili Peppers

Chili peppers are an invaluable asset in any kitchen. In addition to piquancy, chilies add complexity to sauces and their judicious use can easily transform a recipe from run-of-the-mill to delicious. Now widely available in supermarkets and specialty stores, chilies come in a diverse range of temperatures and flavors. Some are only mildly hot, others are incendiary and their tastes range from smoky and nutty to fruity.

Reading my recipes, you may notice that unlike some cooks, I don't seed chili peppers before chopping. This is simply my preference. Contrary to conventional wisdom, the "heat" in hot peppers is not concentrated in the seeds. I don't mind having pepper seeds in my food, but if this bothers you, by all means seed your peppers before chopping.

The following are chili peppers I have used to add zest to recipes in this book:

Scotch Bonnets

Reputedly the hottest pepper in the world, Scotch bonnets are named for their odd rounded shape and slightly rumpled-looking skin. Usually available in West Indian markets, they have a unique smoky flavor. They are interchangeable with Habanero chilies, but if you can't find either, substitute serrano or Thai chilies.

Thai or "Bird's Eye"

The smallest chilies, red or green Thai chilies, are extremely hot. Tiny and elongated, they have a slightly nutty flavor. Available mainly in Asian groceries, they are a bit harder to find than serrano chilies, which are an appropriate substitution.

Serrano Chilies

Larger, elongated and slightly less hot than "bird's eye" chilies, these red or green chilies are probably the most versatile member of the chili family. Often available in supermarkets, they can also be found in Asian groceries. They are commonly used in Indian or Mexican cooking and can be substituted for most other chilies.

Jalapeño Chilies

Probably the most common chili in North America, medium-hot jalapeños are the basis for many dishes with a Tex-Mex and occasionally South American flavor. They are usually available in the produce section of supermarkets. In my opinion, their unique flavor limits their use mainly to dishes inspired by North and South American cuisine.

New Mexico Chilies

These long pointed chilies are larger and milder than most and have a slightly smoky flavor that imparts a Southwestern tang to soups and stews. Like many more "exotic" chilies, they are now available in dried form in the produce section of many supermarkets. If the dried chilies are not thoroughly rehydrated for 30 minutes in boiling water, I've found that they impart a bitter flavor to recipes. If you can't find New Mexico chilies, I recommend adding a mild smoky hot pepper sauce, to taste, after the dish is cooked.

Dried Mushrooms

The widespread availability of many varieties of dried mushrooms is a boon to slow cooking. Dried mushrooms that have been rehydrated hold up well in the slow cooker and, along with their aromatic soaking liquid, add unique flavor and depth to many soups, stews and sauces. The recipes in the book use dried shiitake, morel, chanterelle or porcini mushrooms. Shiitake mushrooms, which are Asian in origin, are quite different from the other three and should only be used when recipes specifically call for them.

Dijon Mustard

No kitchen should be without a large jar of Dijon mustard, which is much more pungent than the "ballpark" variety. It's great for adding flavor to dips, spreads, stews and sauces and is available in supermarkets.

Worcestershire Sauce

This kitchen staple is made from a secret recipe originating in the 1840s. It contains onions, garlic and tamarind, among other ingredients, which are aged in fermented vinegar. All it takes is a spoonful to enliven even the blandest sauce.

Curry Powder

This prepared mixture is likely to include coriander, cumin, mustard and turmeric, among other spices. Although most Indian cooks mix their own, I often use curry powder because it's so easy. I prefer Madras curry powder, which I purchase in Asian grocery stores, because it has more flavor than the supermarket variety.

Cracked Black Peppercorns

I recommend the use of cracked black peppercorns rather than ground pepper in many of my recipes because they release flavor slowly during the long cooking process. "Cracked pepper" can be purchased in the spice sections of supermarkets, but I like to make my own in a mortar with a pestle. A rolling pin or even a heavy can on its side will also break up the peppercorns for use in slow-cooked dishes. If you prefer to use ground black pepper, use one quarter to one half the amount of cracked black peppercorns called for in the recipe.

Balsamic Vinegar

Balsamic is the Rolls-Royce of vinegar. Made from *must*, the juice extracted during the wine-making process, balsamic is aged for decades, sometimes centuries, until it achieves the desired result. It ranges widely in quality, and in Modena, Italy, where it is made, some of the finest examples are drunk, like liqueur. I always have two bottles of balsamic on hand — a house brand I buy at the supermarket for flavoring soups and stews, and a richer, denser (and more expensive) version which I save for more refined tasks such as embellishing fresh fruit.

Coconut Milk

Often used in Asian cooking, coconut milk is now widely available in North American supermarkets. It is not the liquid found inside coconuts, but the rich juice extracted from the flesh of a ripe coconut. It can add wonderful flavor to many soups, stews and desserts. Like many canned products imported from Asia, the coconut milk purchased here suffers from a lack of standardization. For simplicity, I've designated the can size as 14 oz (398 mL), but you may find that your supplier carries can sizes that vary slightly from that. So long as the difference does not exceed 1 oz (28 mL), feel free to substitute a different sized can. Otherwise, measure out $1\frac{3}{4}$ cups (400 mL) of liquid to substitute for one can.

Sambal Oelek

Although I've only suggested the use of sambal oelek in two recipes in this book, I'm such a fan of this condiment that I want to promote its use. An uncooked chili sauce made by crushing chilies with salt, lemon or lime juice or vinegar, it adds a zesty finish to many recipes. I rank it, along with mayonnaise and Dijon mustard, as my favorite condiment. If you can't find sambal oelek, hot pepper sauce makes an acceptable substitute.

Non-Standard Can Sizes

In today's global economy, it's not uncommon for food products, widely available in North American supermarkets, to be imported from distant locales and packaged or canned in non-standard sizes. As a result, you may find that the can sizes I give for ingredients such as canned shrimp, coconut milk and tomatoes are slightly different from those you purchase. I've bought canned shrimp in both $3\frac{3}{4}$ oz (106 g) and 4.2 oz (120 g) sizes, and, as noted, coconut milk in 14 oz (398 mL) or 13.5 oz (400 mL) sizes. Feel free to use any of these can sizes for those specified in the recipes. Canned tomatoes may create another problem. Large cans of tomatoes come in 28 oz (796 mL) to 35 oz (980 mL) sizes. I've used the 28 oz (796 mL) size in all my recipes. If using a 35 oz (980 mL) can, drain off 1 cup (250 mL) of liquid.

Dried Beans and Lentils

Dried beans and lentils come in many different shapes, sizes and colors — from yellow chickpeas, to red or white kidney beans, to multi-colored lentils. Loaded with vitamins and fiber, these legumes are one of our most healthful edibles. But they can also be tough and flavorless, unless they are properly prepared. Since slow cookers were developed as an appliance for making baked beans, it's not surprising that most recipes featuring legumes execute very well in the slow cooker.

Preparing Dried Beans
Soaking
When preparing dried beans, the first step is to replace the water which has been lost in the drying process. In a colander, rinse dry beans thoroughly under cold running water. In a large pot or bowl, combine one part beans with three parts water. Soak overnight or bring to a boil. Boil for 3 minutes, turn off heat and allow to sit for one hour. Whether beans are soaked overnight or "quick soaked," drain and rinse thoroughly under cold running water before cooking.

Cooking
In slow cooker, combine 2 cups (500 mL) presoaked beans and 6 cups (1.5 L) water. Season with garlic, bay leaves or a bouquet garni made from your favorite herbs tied together in a cheesecloth, if desired. Add salt, to taste. Cook on Low for 10 to 12 hours or overnight. The beans are now ready for use in your favorite recipe.

Lentils
Lentils are thin lens-shaped seeds that are always dried. Like dried beans, lentils, particularly those sold in bulk, need to be picked over carefully to remove any foreign matter or imperfect seeds. Spread the seeds out on a platter and pick through them, discarding any extraneous matter.

Unlike dried beans, lentils usually do not need to be presoaked. In a colander or sieve, rinse under cold water until the water runs clear and the legumes are thoroughly washed. To ensure proper cooking time, follow the recipes in this book.

Storing Legumes
Dried beans and lentils should be stored in a dry, airtight container at room temperature. Since they lose their moisture over time, they are best used within a year. Not only do old beans take longer to soak and to cook, they are likely to be tougher than beans that have been stored for only a few months. Because packaged legumes do not contain a "sell-by" date, it is difficult to tell their age from observation. However, according to some recent testing done by *Cook's Illustrated* magazine, dried beans are past their prime if their skins shrivel up when they are soaked. Fully hydrated and cooked beans should be plump with taut skin.

Once cooked, legumes should be covered and stored in the refrigerator where they will keep for four to five days. Cooked legumes can also be frozen. Packaged in an airtight freezer-friendly container, they will keep frozen for up to six months.

Substitutions
Canned beans are a quick and easy substitute for cooked dried beans. For 2 cups (500 mL) of cooked beans, use a standard 19-oz (540-mL) can. Rinse well under cold running water before adding to your recipe.

Appetizers and Fondues

Sumptuous Spinach and Artichoke Dip

Although spinach and artichoke dip has become a North American classic, its roots lie in Provençal cuisine, where the vegetables are usually baked with cheese and served as a *gratin*. This chunky dip, simplicity itself, always draws rave reviews and disappears to the last drop. • *SERVES 6 TO 8*

• **WORKS BEST IN A SMALL (MAXIMUM 3½ QUART) SLOW COOKER**

1 cup	shredded mozzarella cheese	250 mL
8 oz	cream cheese, cubed	250 g
¼ cup	grated Parmesan	50 mL
1	clove garlic, minced	1
¼ tsp	freshly ground black pepper	1 mL
1	tin (14 oz/398 mL) artichokes, drained and finely chopped	1
1 lb	fresh spinach leaves or 1 package (10 oz/300 g) spinach, stems removed, washed and finely chopped	500 g
	Tostadas or tortilla chips	

Tip

If you prefer a smoother dip, place spinach and artichokes in a food processor, in separate batches, and pulse until desired degree of fineness is achieved. Then combine with remaining ingredients in slow cooker stoneware.

1. Combine ingredients in slow cooker stoneware. Cover and cook on **High** for 2 hours, until hot and bubbling. Stir well and serve with tostadas or other tortilla chips.

Chilly Dilly Eggplant

This is a versatile recipe, delicious as a dip with raw vegetables or on pita triangles, as well as a sandwich spread on crusty French bread. It also makes a wonderful addition to a mezes or tapas-style meal. Although it is tasty warm, the flavor dramatically improves if it is thoroughly chilled before serving. • *SERVES 8 TO 10*

• **WORKS BEST IN A SMALL (MAXIMUM 3½ QUART) SLOW COOKER**

2	large eggplants, peeled, cut into 1-inch (2.5-cm) cubes and drained of excess moisture (see Tip, right)	2
2 to 3 tbsp	olive oil	25 to 45 mL
2	medium onions, chopped	2
4	cloves garlic, chopped	4
1 tsp	dried oregano leaves	5 mL
1 tsp	salt	5 mL
½ tsp	freshly ground black pepper	2 mL
1 tbsp	balsamic or red wine vinegar	15 mL
½ cup	chopped fresh dill	125 mL
	Dill sprigs (optional)	
	Finely chopped black olives (optional)	

1. In a skillet, heat 2 tbsp (25 mL) oil over medium-high heat. Add eggplant, in batches, and brown. Transfer to slow cooker stoneware.

2. In same pan, using more oil, if necessary, cook onions on medium heat, until soft. Add garlic, oregano, salt and pepper and cook for 1 minute. Transfer to slow cooker and stir to combine thoroughly. Cover and cook on **Low** for 7 to 8 hours or on **High** for 4 hours, until vegetables are tender.

3. Transfer contents of slow cooker (in batches, if necessary) to a blender or food processor work bowl. Add vinegar and dill and process until smooth, scraping down sides of bowl at halfway point. Taste for seasoning and adjust. Spoon into a small serving bowl and chill thoroughly. Garnish with sprigs of dill and chopped black olives, if using.

Make ahead

You'll achieve maximum results if you make this a day ahead and chill thoroughly before serving, or cook overnight, purée in the morning and chill.

Tip

Although eggplant is delicious when properly cooked, some varieties tend to be bitter. Since the bitterness is concentrated under the skin, I peel eggplant before using. Sprinkling the pieces with salt and leaving them to "sweat" for an hour or two also draws out the bitter juice. If time is short, blanch the pieces for a minute or two in heavily salted water. In either case, rinse thoroughly in fresh cold water and, using your hands, squeeze out the excess moisture. Pat dry with paper towels and it's ready for cooking.

Bubbling Bacon and Horseradish Dip

There's nothing like a good dollop of horseradish to add zest to a dish. On a cold winter's day, I can't think of anything more inviting than a bubbling pot of this savory blend. Open a big bag of potato chips and have some ready for après-ski or, for a more elegant presentation, serve on crisp spears of Belgian endive. • *SERVES 6*

• **WORKS BEST IN A SMALL (MAXIMUM 3½ QUART) SLOW COOKER**

2	slices bacon, finely chopped	2
1	package (8 oz/250 g) cream cheese, softened	1
¼ cup	sour cream	50 mL
2 tbsp	mayonnaise	25 mL
2 tbsp	prepared horseradish	25 mL
2 tbsp	finely chopped green onion	25 mL
1	clove garlic, minced	1
¾ cup	shredded Cheddar cheese, preferably old	175 mL
¼ tsp	freshly ground black pepper	1 mL
	Potato chips (optional)	
	Belgian endive (optional)	

Tip

If you want to avoid stirring the dip after an hour, place all the ingredients in a food processor and pulse two or three times until well blended. Transfer to slow cooker stoneware and cook on **High** as directed.

1. In a skillet, over medium-high heat, cook bacon until crisp. Remove with a slotted spoon and drain thoroughly on paper towel.

2. In slow cooker stoneware, combine ingredients. Stir well. Cover and cook on **High** for 1 hour. Stir again and cook on **High** for an additional 30 minutes, until hot and bubbly. Serve immediately or set temperature at **Low** until ready to serve.

Zesty Crab Spread

Serve this bubbling hot, with celery or carrot sticks, or spread it on crackers or melba toast. Make enough for leftovers as it reheats well and is a nice treat to have on hand for after-school snacks. If you prefer a spicy dip, add ½ tsp (2 mL) finely chopped chili pepper or 1 tsp (5 mL) of an Asian chili sauce such as *sambal oelek*, a bottled chili paste easily identified by its bright red color. It's very hot, but absolutely delicious and is a handy tool for embellishing many dishes. • *SERVES 6*

• **WORKS BEST IN A SMALL (MAXIMUM 3½ QUART) SLOW COOKER**

1	package (8 oz/250 g) cream cheese, softened	1
¼ cup	tomato-based chili sauce	50 mL
1 tsp	Dijon mustard	5 mL
2 tbsp	grated onion	25 mL
1	clove garlic, minced	1
¼ tsp	salt	1 mL
¼ tsp	freshly ground black pepper	1 mL
1	can (6 oz/170 g) crabmeat, drained	1
	Paprika, to taste	

1. In slow cooker stoneware, combine all ingredients, except paprika. Stir well. Cover and cook on **High** for 1 hour. Stir again and cook on **High** for an additional 30 minutes, until hot and bubbly. Sprinkle with paprika and serve. Or set temperature to **Low** until ready to serve.

Tip

If you want to avoid stirring the dip after an hour, place all the ingredients, except crab and paprika, in a food processor and pulse two or three times until well blended. Add crab and pulse once or twice more. Transfer to slow cooker and cook on **High** as directed.

Sizzling Shrimp and Dill Pickle Dip

This is a great all-season dip, which works well with both light and regular cream cheese and mayonnaise. Serve with celery or carrot sticks, spears of Belgian endives, crackers, biscuits, melba toast or potato chips and refrigerate any leftovers for future snacks. It keeps well and reheats nicely in the microwave. • *SERVES 6*

• WORKS BEST IN A SMALL (MAXIMUM 3½ QUART) SLOW COOKER

1	package (8 oz/250 g) cream cheese, softened and cut into cubes	1
¼ cup	mayonnaise	50 mL
1 tbsp	Dijon mustard	15 mL
1	can (3¾ oz/106 g) shrimp, drained (see Tip, right)	1
¼ cup	finely chopped dill pickle	50 mL
2 tbsp	finely chopped green onion	25 mL
2 tbsp	chopped fresh dill	25 mL

1. In slow cooker stoneware, combine cream cheese, mayonnaise and mustard. Cover and cook on **Low** for 2 hours or on **High** for 1 hour.

2. Add shrimp, dill pickle, green onion and dill and stir well to combine. Cover and cook on **Low** for 1 hour or on **High** for 30 minutes until bubbling.

Tip

Because much of the canned shrimp sold in North America is processed in Asia, the can sizes are not standard. I've used cans labeled 3¾ oz (106 g) for the recipes in this book, but you may find that the cans you are using vary slightly in size. So long as the difference is not dramatic, feel free to substitute a can that is sized slightly differently from those I've specified. You'll want about ½ cup (125 mL) shrimp for this recipe.

Hot Roasted Nuts

I completely agree with Elizabeth David, the late food writer, who wrote: "Nothing yet invented so sets the gastric juices to work as the sight of a plateful of freshly roasted and salted almonds." Little did she know how easy it is to make this superb treat and other hot roasted nuts in the slow cooker. When entertaining in winter, I like to light a fire and place small bowls full of these tasty nibblers around the living room. Pour everybody drinks and let people help themselves as conversation begins to flow. • *SERVES 6 TO 8*

• **THESE RECIPES WORK BEST IN A SMALL (MAXIMUM 3½ QUART) SLOW COOKER**

Salty Almonds with Thyme

2 cups	unblanched almonds	500 mL
½ tsp	white pepper	2 mL
1 tbsp	fine sea salt, or more to taste	15 mL
2 tbsp	extra-virgin olive oil	25 mL
2 tbsp	fresh thyme leaves	25 mL

1. In slow cooker stoneware, combine almonds and white pepper. Cover and cook on **High** for 1½ hours, stirring every 30 minutes (see Tip, right), until nuts are nicely toasted.

2. In a mixing bowl, combine salt, olive oil and thyme. Add to hot almonds in stoneware and stir thoroughly to combine. Spoon mixture into a small serving bowl and serve hot or allow to cool.

Spicy Cashews

2 cups	raw cashews	500 mL
1 tsp	chili powder	5 mL
½ tsp	cayenne pepper	2 mL
¼ tsp	ground cinnamon	1 mL
2 tsp	fine sea salt (see Tip, right)	10 mL
1 tbsp	extra-virgin olive oil	15 mL

1. In slow cooker stoneware, combine cashews, chili powder, cayenne and cinnamon. Stir to combine thoroughly. Cover and cook on **High** for 1½ hours, stirring every 30 minutes, until nuts are nicely toasted.

2. In a small bowl, combine sea salt and olive oil. Add to nuts in slow cooker and stir to thoroughly combine. Transfer mixture to a serving bowl and serve hot or allow to cool.

Variation

Sweet and Spicy Cashews: Substitute 1 tbsp (15 mL) butter for the olive oil and add along with 2 tbsp (25 mL) brown sugar.

Tip

For a holiday gift, make up a batch or two and package in pretty jars. If well sealed, the nuts will keep for 10 days.

Tip

I recommend using a small slow cooker for these recipes, as the nuts are less likely to burn. If you use a large slow cooker (5 or 6 quarts), watch carefully and stir the nuts every 15 minutes, as they will cook quite quickly (just over an hour) since almost all will come in contact with the hot crockery.

Tip

Sea salt is available in most supermarkets. It is much sweeter than table salt and is essential for these recipes as table salt would impart an unpleasant acrid taste to the nuts.

Classic Swiss Fondue

This is the mother of all fondues — thick and luscious cheese with an intriguing hint of kirsch, an aromatic cherry *eau de vie*. It's wonderfully welcoming after a day in the cold. If you live in an area that receives lots of snow, think about initiating a tradition of serving fondue on the day of the first snowfall, as some of our friends do. • *SERVES 6 TO 8 AS AN APPETIZER*

- WORKS BEST IN A SMALL (MAXIMUM 3½ QUART) SLOW COOKER
- FONDUE FORKS

1	clove garlic, split	1
1 lb	Swiss Emmenthal cheese, shredded	500 g
2 tbsp	all-purpose flour	25 mL
2 cups	dry white wine	500 mL
¼ cup	kirsch	50 mL
	Freshly grated nutmeg	
	Sliced baguette	

1. Rub slow cooker stoneware with garlic. Cover and turn heat to **High**.

2. On a large plate or platter, combine cheese and flour, using your hands to ensure that flour is distributed as evenly as possible. Set aside.

3. In a saucepan, over medium heat, bring wine to a rapid boil (see Tip, right). Pour into slow cooker stoneware. Add cheese mixture in handfuls, stirring to thoroughly combine after each addition. When all the cheese has been added, cover and cook on **High** for 30 minutes, until cheese is melted and mixture is hot. Add kirsch and stir to combine. Grate fresh nutmeg over mixture and turn heat to **Low**.

4. Break baguette slices into halves or quarters and, using fondue forks, dip into the hot cheese.

Tip

One secret to getting a Swiss fondue to work in a slow cooker is to ensure that the wine is boiling before you add the cheese. Benefits to making a fondue in the slow cooker are that it keeps the mixture at the right temperature and eliminates concern about keeping a flame lit, often a problem with traditional fondue pots.

Creamy Italian Fondue

Although Swiss Fondue has become the standard against which others are measured, other countries have their own techniques for making delicious dips with hot melted cheese. One of my favorites is Fonduta, a particularly rich and creamy fondue which comes from the Piedmontese region of Italy. I like to serve this with chunks of focaccia, a crusty Italian bread, but any crusty white bread will do. Since the sauce is runny — part of its unctuous charm — pass napkins or small plates to catch drips. You can also serve this as a sauce over slices of grilled polenta, which turns it into a plated appetizer eaten with forks. • *SERVES 6 TO 8*

- **WORKS BEST IN A SMALL (MAXIMUM 3½ QUART) SLOW COOKER**
- **FONDUE FORKS**

3 cups	shredded Fontina cheese	750 mL
¾ cup	half-and-half cream	175 mL
1 tbsp	unsalted butter, melted	15 mL
½	small clove garlic, put through a press (see Tip, right)	½
2	egg yolks	2
2 tbsp	hot milk	25 mL
¼ tsp	freshly ground black pepper	1 mL
	Chunks of crusty bread	

Tip

Because this fondue doesn't cook for a long time, I prefer to put the garlic through a press rather than mincing to ensure that the flavor is fully integrated into the cheese mixture. If you don't have a garlic press, a fine mince will do.

1. In slow cooker stoneware, combine cheese and cream. Cover and cook on **Low** for 1 hour. Increase heat to **High**.

2. In a small bowl, combine melted butter and garlic. Pour mixture into cheese mixture, stirring well, until thoroughly combined and the cheese is completely melted.

3. In a bowl, beat egg yolks with hot milk. Add to cheese mixture, stirring to thoroughly combine. Add pepper and stir.

4. Spear bread with fondue forks and dip in sauce, ensuring that guests have napkins or plates to catch any dripping sauce.

Hot Anchovy-Garlic Dunk

Traditionally, this is served with celery or carrot sticks, or broccoli or cauliflower florets, but almost anything tastes good in the ambrosial brew. One evening, when I didn't like the look of most vegetables at the supermarket, I cooked some beautiful little Brussels sprouts to the point where they were just slightly underdone. My guests speared them on fondue forks and dunked them in the hot bath. Even one who is usually no fan of Brussels sprouts, loved them. Crisp leaves of baby bok choy and Belgian endive also work well. For an even more luscious version, enrich the sauce with whipping cream, in which case cook for a few minutes on Low to allow the cream time to incorporate into the sauce. • *SERVES 6 TO 8*

• **WORKS BEST IN A SMALL (MAXIMUM 3½ QUART) SLOW COOKER**
• **FONDUE FORKS**

1	clove garlic, put through a press	1
¾ cup	extra-virgin olive oil	175 mL
2 tbsp	unsalted butter	25 mL
8	anchovy fillets, finely chopped (see Tip, right)	8
⅛ tsp	freshly ground black pepper	0.5 mL
¼ cup	whipping cream (optional)	50 mL
	Crudités (see Introduction, above)	

Tip

For a smoother blend, put the anchovies through a garlic press before adding to the stoneware.

1. In slow cooker stoneware, combine garlic, olive oil, butter, anchovies and pepper. Cover and cook on **High** until mixture is hot and anchovies have begun to dissolve, about 30 minutes. Stir well to incorporate anchovies into sauce. Add cream, if using, and turn heat to **Low**.

2. Arrange crudités on a serving plate or platter. Give each guest a plate and fondue fork and allow them to help themselves.

Nippy Cheddar Rabbit

When I was growing up, my mother's Welsh rarebit was one of my favorite treats. Now that I'm a mother myself, I still think it's yummy, and so does my family. Made with beer, this slightly adult version is a great predinner nibbler for guests. It also doubles as a light luncheon dish served, like mom's, over hot toast. • *SERVES 6*

- **WORKS BEST IN A SMALL (MAXIMUM 3½ QUART) SLOW COOKER**
- **FONDUE FORKS**

8 oz	old Cheddar cheese, shredded	250 g
1 cup	beer	250 mL
2	egg yolks, beaten	2
¼ tsp	dry mustard	1 mL
1 tsp	Worcestershire sauce	5 mL
1 tsp	packed brown sugar	5 mL
Pinch	cayenne pepper	Pinch
	White bread, crusts removed, cut into 1-inch (2.5 cm) cubes and lightly toasted under broiler	

Tip

I always keep a bottle of Worcestershire sauce in the pantry as just a spoonful of this venerable concoction (it was created over a century and a half ago) adds welcome zest to many gravies and sauces.

1. In slow cooker stoneware, combine cheese and beer. Cover and cook on **Low** for 30 minutes, or until cheese melts.

2. In a bowl, whisk together eggs, mustard, Worcestershire sauce, brown sugar and cayenne. Pour mixture into slow cooker stoneware and stir until thickened.

3. Spear toasted bread with fondue forks and dip in cheese, ensuring that guests have napkins or plates to catch any dripping sauce.

Kids' Favorite Fondue

Thanks to my dear friend, Marilyn Linton, writer, editor and volunteer extraordinaire, for this oh-so-easy "fondue." Creamy and delicious, it is a great hit with adults as well as kids. Give everyone their own fondue fork and serve with thick slices of French baguette, quartered, celery sticks or slices of green pepper. • *SERVES 6*

- **WORKS BEST IN A SMALL (MAXIMUM 3½ QUART) SLOW COOKER**
- **FONDUE FORKS**

1	large can (28 oz/796 mL) tomatoes, including juice (see Tip, right)	1
1 tsp	dried oregano leaves	5 mL
1 tsp	salt	5 mL
¼ tsp	freshly ground black pepper	1 mL
3 cups	shredded Cheddar cheese	750 mL
	Sliced baguette	
	Celery sticks	
	Sliced green pepper	

1. In a food processor or blender, process tomatoes until relatively smooth. Transfer to slow cooker stoneware. Add oregano, salt and pepper and cook on **High** for 1 hour, until tomatoes are bubbling hot.

2. Add cheese to slow cooker in handfuls, stirring to combine after each addition. Reduce heat to **Low** and serve, or cover and keep on **Low** until ready to serve. Using fondue forks, dip bread or vegetables into fondue.

Tip

If you're in a hurry, bring the tomatoes to a boil on top of the stove after they have been processed. Then transfer to the slow cooker.

Tip

Large cans of tomatoes come in 28 oz (796 mL) and 35 oz (980 mL) sizes. For convenience, I've called for the 28 oz (796 mL) size in my recipes. If you're using the 35 oz (980 mL) size, drain off 1 cup (250 mL) liquid before adding to recipe.

Soups

Classic French Onion Soup

On a chilly day, there's nothing more appetizing than a bowl of steaming hot onion soup, bubbling away under a blanket of browned cheese. Normally, caramelizing the onions for this masterpiece is a laborious process that can easily involve an hour of almost constant stirring. Fortunately, your slow cooker can now do most of this tiresome work for you. • *SERVES 6*

- 6 OVENPROOF SOUP BOWLS
- PREHEATED BROILER

2 to 3 lbs	sliced onions	1 to 1.5 kg
2 tbsp	melted butter	25 mL
1 tbsp	granulated sugar	15 mL
8 cups	good quality beef stock (see Tip, right)	2 L
1 tsp	salt	5 mL
1 tsp	cracked black peppercorns	5 mL
2 tbsp	brandy or cognac	25 mL
12	slices baguette, about ½ inch (1 cm) thick	12
2 cups	shredded Swiss or Gruyere cheese	500 mL

1. In slow cooker stoneware, combine onions and butter. Cover and cook on **High** for 2 hours.

2. Add sugar and stir well. Place two clean tea towels, each folded in half (so you will have four layers), over top of stoneware, to absorb the moisture. Cover and cook on **High** for 4 hours, stirring two or three times to ensure that onions are browning evenly, replacing towels each time.

3. Add beef stock, salt, pepper and brandy or cognac. Remove towels, cover and cook on **High** for 2 hours.

4. Preheat broiler. Ladle soup into ovenproof bowls. Place 2 slices baguette in each bowl. Sprinkle liberally with cheese and broil until top is bubbly and brown, for 2 to 3 minutes. Serve immediately.

Tip

Since it's important that the stock for this soup be top quality, I recommend using good quality homemade stock or enhancing canned beef stock. To improve 8 cups (2 L) canned beef stock, combine in a large saucepan with 2 carrots, peeled and coarsely chopped, 1 tsp (5 mL) celery seed, 1 tsp (5 mL) cracked black peppercorns, ½ tsp (2 mL) dried thyme, 4 parsley sprigs, 1 bay leaf and 1 cup (250 mL) white wine. Bring to a boil, simmer, covered, for 30 minutes and strain.

Savory Cheddar Cheese Soup

This hearty meal-in-a-bowl makes a great weeknight dinner or doubles as a starter to a traditional dinner such as roast beef with Yorkshire pudding. My family likes to scoop up the vegetables on thick slices of country bread, but if you're serving this to guests, puréeing mixture in a food processor before adding the cream and cheese produces a more polished result. • *SERVES 4 TO 6 AS A LIGHT MEAL OR 8 AS A STARTER*

1 tbsp	butter	15 mL
1	leek, white part with just a bit of green, cleaned and finely chopped (See Tip, page 212)	1
2	medium carrots, finely chopped	2
3	stalks celery, peeled and finely chopped	3
1 tsp	dry mustard	5 mL
½ tsp	salt	2 mL
½ tsp	freshly ground black pepper	2 mL
2 tbsp	all-purpose flour	25 mL
2	cans (10 oz/284 mL) condensed beef consommé (undiluted)	2
3 cups	water	750 mL
1 tbsp	Worcestershire sauce	15 mL
1	bay leaf	1
½ cup	whipping cream	125 mL
3 cups	shredded Cheddar cheese	750 mL
	Hot pepper sauce to taste (optional)	

Make ahead

This dish can be assembled the night before it is cooked but without adding the cream, cheese and hot pepper sauce, if using. Complete Step 1 and refrigerate overnight. The next day, continue cooking as directed in Step 2.

1. In a large skillet, over medium heat, melt butter. Add leeks, carrots and celery. Turn heat to low, cover and cook for 10 minutes, until vegetables are soft. Add dry mustard, salt, pepper and flour to pan and cook, stirring, for 1 minute. Add consommé, water, Worcestershire sauce and bay leaf and cook until slightly thickened.

2. Transfer mixture to slow cooker stoneware. Cover and cook on **Low** for 8 to 10 hours or on **High** for 4 to 5 hours. Discard bay leaf. If desired, transfer solids plus 1 cup (250 mL) liquid to a food processor and process until smooth, then return mixture to slow cooker.

3. Add cream and cheese, cover and cook on **High** for 15 minutes, until cheese is melted and mixture is bubbling. Ladle into individual serving bowls and pass the hot pepper sauce.

Split Green Pea Soup with Tarragon Cream

Not only is this soup delicious and elegant, it's extremely easy to make. If you grow tarragon or mint in your garden, or on your windowsill, it can be made from pantry ingredients. The addition of tarragon cream provides a nice finish, and if you prefer a richer soup, you can add additional cream, to taste, before serving. • *SERVES 6 TO 8*

1 cup	dried split green peas, soaked, rinsed and drained (see Soaking, page 17)	250 mL
1	large onion, chopped	1
2	cloves garlic, chopped	2
3	stalks celery, peeled and thinly sliced	3
4	sprigs tarragon	4
1 tsp	salt	5 mL
¼ tsp	freshly ground black pepper	1 mL
6 cups	chicken or vegetable stock	1.5 L

Tarragon Cream

¼ cup	whipping cream	50 mL
¼ cup	sour cream	50 mL
1 tbsp	finely chopped tarragon	15 mL

Make ahead

Cook soup overnight in slow cooker without adding the tarragon cream. Purée in morning and refrigerate until ready to serve. In a pot, bring to a boil on stovetop and simmer for 5 to 10 minutes. Continue with Steps 3 and 4.

1. In slow cooker stoneware, combine peas, onion, garlic, celery, tarragon, salt, pepper and stock. Cover and cook on **Low** for 10 to 12 hours or on **High** for 5 to 6 hours, until vegetables are tender.

2. In a blender or food processor, purée soup in batches. Set aside.

3. To make Tarragon Cream: In a bowl, whisk cream until thick. Add sour cream and tarragon and blend well.

4. Ladle soup into individual bowls and garnish with Tarragon Cream.

Variation

Split Green Pea Soup with Mint Cream: Substitute fresh mint for the tarragon.

Luscious Fish Chowder

This recipe makes a nicely peppery chowder, but if you're heat averse, omit the cayenne. Although you can make an acceptable soup using water, clam juice or a good fish stock produce better results. I make mine with whipping cream, but I've had requests for an even richer chowder. If that appeals to you, finish with 3 cups (750 mL) whipping cream and reduce the quantity of cooking liquid by 1 cup (250 mL). • *SERVES 6 TO 8*

2	slices bacon, chopped	2
3	leeks, white part only, cleaned and thinly sliced (see Tip, page 212)	3
3	stalks celery, peeled and thinly sliced	3
½ tsp	dried thyme leaves	2 mL
2 tbsp	all-purpose flour	25 mL
4 cups	fish stock or water or 2 cups (500 mL) clam juice diluted with 2 cups (500 mL) water	1 L
1	bay leaf	1
1	medium potato, cut into ½-inch (1-cm) cubes	1
2 cups	milk or whipping cream	500 mL
¼ tsp	cayenne pepper, or to taste	1 mL
2 lbs	firm white fish fillets, such as halibut or snapper, cut into 1-inch (2.5-cm) cubes	1 kg
	Finely chopped parsley or chives	

Make ahead

Cook soup overnight in slow cooker, without adding the milk or cream, cayenne pepper or fish fillets. Refrigerate until almost ready to serve. In a pot, bring to a boil on stovetop. Add cream, cayenne and fish and simmer until fish is cooked through, about 15 minutes. Alternately, complete Steps 1 and 2 the night before serving. Cover and refrigerate overnight. The next day, continue cooking as directed in Step 3.

1. In a skillet, over medium-high heat, cook bacon until crisp. Remove with a slotted spoon to a paper-towel-lined plate and set aside.

2. Drain all but 1 tbsp (15 mL) fat from pan. Reduce heat to medium. Add leeks and celery and cook until soft. Add thyme and bacon and stir. Add flour, stir and cook for 1 minute. Add stock, water or clam juice and bay leaf and cook, stirring, until slightly thickened.

3. Transfer mixture to slow cooker stoneware. Add potato and stir. Cover and cook on **Low** for 8 to 10 hours or on **High** for 4 to 5 hours, until vegetables are tender.

4. In a saucepan, bring milk or cream to a boil, watching carefully to ensure it doesn't boil over the pot. Stir in cayenne. Add mixture to slow cooker stoneware along with fish. Cover and cook on **High** for 30 minutes, or until fish is cooked through. Discard bay leaf. Ladle into individual bowls and garnish with finely chopped parsley or chives.

Seafood Gumbo

Gumbo is a classic of Creole cooking and there are many different opinions about what it should contain, okra or filé powder (made from dried sassafras leaves) being the only constants. This version, although simple, is unconventional since it is not thickened with a well-cooked *roux*. It is absolutely delicious nonetheless. My family likes this degree of richness, but if you're concerned about cholesterol, increase stock to 2 cups (500 mL) and reduce cream to 1 cup (250 mL). • *SERVES 6 TO 8*

1	small onion, finely chopped	1
2	stalks celery, peeled and finely chopped	2
2	cloves garlic, minced	2
1 tbsp	fresh thyme leaves or 1 tsp (5 mL) dried thyme leaves	15 mL
½ tsp	dry mustard	2 mL
1	bay leaf	1
1 tsp	salt	5 mL
½ tsp	freshly ground black pepper	2 mL
1 tbsp	Worcestershire sauce	15 mL
1	can (28 oz/796 mL) tomatoes, including juice, coarsely chopped (see Tip, page 32)	1
1 cup	vegetable, chicken or fish stock or ½ cup (125 mL) clam juice diluted with ½ cup (125 mL) water	250 mL
2 cups	okra, cut into ¼-inch (0.5-cm) slices (See Tip, right)	500 mL
1	green bell pepper, cut into ¼-inch (0.5-cm) dice	1
1 to 2	chili peppers, (serrano or finger), finely chopped (see Tip, page 138)	1 to 2
8 oz	cooked crabmeat	250 g
12	large shrimp, cooked, deveined and shells removed, cut in thirds	12
2 cups	whipping cream	500 mL

1. In slow cooker stoneware, combine onions, celery, garlic, thyme, dry mustard, bay leaf, salt, pepper, Worcestershire sauce, tomatoes and stock. Cover and cook on **Low** for 8 to 10 hours or on **High** for 4 to 5 hours, until vegetables are tender.

2. Add okra, green pepper, chili pepper, crabmeat, shrimp and cream. Cover and cook on **High** for 30 minutes, or until okra and peppers are tender. Spoon into individual bowls and serve piping hot.

Make ahead

This dish can be partially assembled the night before it is cooked. Combine ingredients in Step 1 and refrigerate overnight. The next day, continue with Step 1 as directed. For added convenience, prepare the okra, green pepper and chili peppers. Combine in a bowl, cover and refrigerate overnight. Cook, devein and cut the shrimp and refrigerate, covered, in a separate bowl, until ready to use.

Tip

Okra, a tropical vegetable, is a great thickener for broths and sauces, but becomes unpleasantly sticky when overcooked. Choose young okra pods, 2 to 4 inches (5 to 10 cm) long, that don't feel sticky to the touch, which means they're too ripe. Gently scrub the pods, cut off the top and tail and slice, if desired.

Pumpkin Soup
with Shrimp and Lime

Although pumpkin is normally associated with Thanksgiving pie, in many other cultures it is used more innovatively as a vegetable or in richly flavored sauces. This soup, which is delicious hot or cold, has its origins in both French provincial and Latin American cuisine. It's breathtakingly easy and makes an elegant start to any meal. If pumpkin is unavailable, substitute any orange-fleshed squash, such as acorn or butternut. • *SERVES 6 TO 8*

6 cups	peeled pumpkin, cut into 2-inch (5-cm) cubes	1.25 L
3	leeks, white part only, cleaned and coarsely chopped (see Tip, page 212)	3
4 cups	chicken or vegetable stock	1 L
1 tsp	salt	5 mL
¼ tsp	freshly ground black pepper	1 mL
	Zest and juice of 1 lime	
Pinch	cayenne pepper	Pinch
1 cup	whipping cream	250 mL
8 oz	cooked salad shrimp or 2 cans (3¾ oz/106 g) shrimp, rinsed and drained	250 g
6 to 8	cherry tomatoes, halved	6 to 8
2 tbsp	toasted pumpkin seeds (optional) (see Tip, right)	25 mL
	Finely chopped chives or cilantro	

1. In slow cooker stoneware, combine pumpkin, leeks, stock, salt and pepper. Cover and cook on **Low** for 8 to 10 hours or on **High** for 4 to 6 hours, until pumpkin is tender.

2. Strain vegetables, reserving stock. In a blender or food processor, purée vegetables with 1 cup (250 mL) reserved stock until smooth.

3. If serving hot, return soup to slow cooker, add remaining stock, lime zest and juice, cayenne, cream and shrimp and cook on **High** for 20 minutes, or until shrimp are heated through. If serving cold, combine ingredients in a large bowl and chill thoroughly.

4. When ready to serve, ladle soup into individual bowls and garnish with cherry tomatoes, pumpkin seeds, if using, and chives or cilantro.

Make ahead

This soup can be made a day ahead, refrigerated overnight and served cold or reheated. It can also be cooked overnight, puréed and chilled. To serve hot: Refrigerate puréed soup until ready to serve. In a pot, bring to a boil on the stovetop and simmer for 5 to 10 minutes. Add lime zest and juice, cayenne, cream and shrimp and cook until heated through. Continue with Step 4. To serve cold: Add lime zest and juice, cayenne, cream and shrimp after the mixture is puréed and refrigerate. When ready to serve, complete Step 4.

Tip

If using pumpkin seeds, panfry in a dry, hot skillet until they are lightly browned and puffed. When purchasing pumpkin seeds, taste first, as they tend to go rancid quickly. Store in the freezer until ready for use.

Vichyssoise

Although named in honor of Vichy, a town in France, this wonderfully refreshing chilled soup was actually invented in America by Louis Diat, a French-born chef, at New York's Ritz Carlton Hotel. On a hot summer day, there's nothing better — and with the slow cooker, you don't even turn on the stove. • *SERVES 6 TO 8*

3	leeks, white part only, cleaned and coarsely chopped (see Tip, page 212)	3
1	onion, chopped	1
2	cloves garlic, chopped	2
5	medium potatoes, peeled and cut into 1/2-inch (1-cm) cubes	5
5 cups	chicken stock	1.25 L
1 tsp	salt	5 mL
1/4 tsp	freshly ground black pepper	1 mL
1 cup	whipping cream	250 mL
2 tbsp	finely chopped chives	25 mL

1. In slow cooker stoneware, combine leeks, onion, garlic, potatoes, stock, salt and pepper. Cover and cook on **Low** for 8 to 10 hours or on **High** for 4 to 6 hours, until vegetables are tender.

2. In a blender or food processor, purée soup in batches. Transfer to a large bowl and chill thoroughly, preferably overnight.

3. Before serving, stir in cream. Spoon into individual soup bowls and garnish with chives.

Variations

Watercress Vichyssoise: Add one bunch watercress to mixture when puréeing. Serve soup garnished with chopped watercress.

Leek and Potato Soup with Stilton: The English have their own version of this classic soup — a quintessential winter dish topped with a dollop of rich blue-veined Stilton cheese. Add about a heaping tablespoonful (15 mL) cheese to each serving of steaming hot soup. If you can't find Stilton, substitute Danish Blue or French Roquefort, but be aware that the results won't be as memorable.

Make ahead

To serve cold: Cook Vichyssoise overnight in slow cooker. Purée in morning and chill until ready to serve. Continue as directed. To serve hot: Prepare Leek and Potato Soup, without adding the Stilton. Chill until ready to serve. In a pot, bring to a boil on stovetop and simmer for 5 to 10 minutes. Continue as directed.

Cranberry Borscht

Served cold in chilled bowls, this fresh, fruity soup is one of my favorite preludes to an outdoor dinner on a warm night. My friend, Margaret Hovanec, calls this a summer borscht, made without meat from garden-fresh beets, and I thank her for the idea of enhancing the broth with beet leaves. Many years ago, I learned about adding cranberries to borscht from a recipe created by New York restaurateur George Lang. Their fruity tang provides just enough tartness to round out the soup. For a vegetarian version, substitute concentrated vegetable stock for the beef broth. This soup is also good served hot. • *SERVES 6 TO 8*

6	medium beets, peeled and cut into ½-inch (1-cm) cubes	6
	Leaves from the beets, washed, coarsely chopped and set aside in refrigerator	
4	cloves garlic, chopped	4
1	can (10 oz/284 mL) condensed beef broth (undiluted)	1
4 cups	water	1 L
1 tsp	salt	5 mL
½ tsp	freshly ground black pepper	2 mL
1 cup	cranberries	250 mL
2 tbsp	granulated sugar	25 mL
	Zest and juice of 1 orange	
	Sour cream	
	Chopped dill (optional)	

Make ahead

This dish can be assembled the night before it is cooked but without adding the cranberries, sugar, orange juice and zest and beet leaves. Follow preparation directions and refrigerate overnight in a large bowl. The next day, continue cooking as directed in Step 1. Or the soup can be cooked overnight in the slow cooker, finished the next morning and chilled during the day.

1. In slow cooker stoneware, combine beets, garlic, beef stock, water, salt and pepper. Cover and cook on **Low** for 8 to 10 hours or on **High** for 4 to 5 hours, until vegetables are tender.

2. Add cranberries, sugar, orange zest and juice and beet leaves. Cover and cook on **High** for 30 minutes or until cranberries are popping from their skins.

3. In a blender or food processor, purée soup in batches. If serving cold, transfer to a large bowl and chill thoroughly, preferably overnight.

4. When ready to serve, spoon into individual bowls, top with sour cream and garnish with dill, if using.

Sophisticated Mushroom Barley Soup

Dried wild mushrooms give this soup a rich flavor and sophisticated flair. At the same time, it's hearty enough to make an ideal pick-me-up after a busy day. Spiff it up by adding ½ cup (125 mL) sherry or Madeira just before serving. For a vegetarian version, use 7 cups (1.75 L) vegetable stock and omit the extra cup (250 mL) water. • *SERVES 6 TO 8*

1	cup boiling water	250 mL
1	package (½ oz/14 g) dried wild mushrooms, such as porcini	1
2 tbsp	butter, divided	25 mL
3	onions, finely chopped	3
6	cloves garlic, minced	6
1 tsp	salt	5 mL
1 tsp	cracked black peppercorns	5 mL
1½ lbs	button mushrooms, sliced	750 g
⅔ cup	pearl barley	150 mL
6 cups	beef stock	1.5 L
1 cup	water	250 mL
1	bay leaf	1
¼ cup	soya sauce	50 mL
	Finely chopped green onions or parsley (optional)	

Make ahead

This dish can be assembled the night before it is cooked. Follow preparation directions in Steps 1 and 2 and refrigerate overnight. The next day, transfer to slow cooker stoneware and continue cooking as directed in Step 3.

1. In a heatproof bowl, combine boiling water and dried mushrooms. Let stand for 30 minutes, then strain through a fine sieve, reserving liquid. Chop mushrooms finely and set aside.

2. In a skillet, over medium heat, melt 1 tbsp (15 mL) butter. Add onions and cook until soft. Add garlic, salt and pepper and cook for 1 minute. Transfer mixture to slow cooker stoneware. In same pan, melt remaining butter and cook button mushrooms over medium-high heat until they begin to lose their liquid. Add dried mushrooms, toss to combine and cook for 1 minute. Transfer mixture to slow cooker stoneware. Add barley, reserved mushroom soaking liquid, stock, water, bay leaf and soya sauce.

3. Cover and cook on **Low** for 6 to 8 hours or on **High** for 3 to 4 hours. Discard bay leaf. Ladle into individual bowls and garnish with chopped green onions or parsley, if using.

Sumptuous Celery Soup

Celeriac, or celery root, a knobby brown root, now widely available in North American supermarkets, is often used raw, as a salad, in France and Italy. It is actually a type of celery, with crispy white flesh that is slightly peppery. Since it will keep for a week or longer in the refrigerator, it makes an excellent winter vegetable. This simple cream soup has a lovely sweet, yet piquant flavor, which is complimented with the addition of dill. Serve it as a starter to an elegant dinner or as a weekday meal with crusty bread and salad. • *SERVES 6 TO 8*

1 tbsp	butter	15 mL
1	medium onion, chopped	1
1	clove garlic, minced	1
½ tsp	salt	2 mL
¼ tsp	freshly ground black pepper	1 mL
1	large celery root, peeled and shredded (see Tip, right)	1
1	large potato, peeled and cut into ½-inch (1-cm) cubes	1
4 cups	chicken or vegetable stock	1 L
1 cup	whipping cream	250 mL
Pinch	ground nutmeg	Pinch
¼ cup	chopped fresh dill	50 mL

1. In a skillet, over medium heat, melt butter. Add onions and cook until soft. Add garlic, salt and pepper and cook for 1 minute. Add celery root and potato, stirring to combine. Pour stock over mixture.

2. Transfer to slow cooker stoneware. Cover and cook on **Low** for 8 to 10 hours or on **High** for 4 to 5 hours, until vegetables are tender.

3. Using a slotted spoon, transfer solids plus 1 cup (250 mL) liquid to a blender or food processor and process until smooth. Return to slow cooker, add cream and nutmeg. Cover and cook on **High** for 15 minutes. Ladle soup into bowls and garnish with dill.

Make ahead

This soup can be assembled the night before it is cooked, but without adding the cream, nutmeg and dill. Follow preparation directions in Step 1 and refrigerate overnight. The next day, transfer to slow cooker stoneware and continue cooking as directed in Step 2.

Tip

Since celery root oxidizes quickly on contact with air, be sure to use as soon as it is shredded.

Southwestern Corn and Roasted Red Pepper Soup

Although the roots of this soup lie deep in the heart of Tex-Mex cuisine, it is elegant enough for even the most gracious occasion. Serve it as a starter or add canned crab (see Variation) for a deliciously different meal-in-a-bowl. Hot sourdough bread makes a perfect accompaniment. • *SERVES 6*

2	red bell peppers, roasted and cut into ½-inch (1-cm) cubes (see Tip, page 70)	2
1	dried New Mexico chili (optional) (see Tips, right)	1
1 cup	boiling water	250 mL
1	large onion, diced	1
6	cloves garlic, minced	6
1 tbsp	cumin seeds	15 mL
1 tbsp	chopped rosemary, dried or fresh	15 mL
1	bay leaf	1
1 tsp	salt	5 mL
½ tsp	freshly ground black pepper	2 mL
4 cups	corn kernels, thawed if frozen	1 L
6 cups	chicken or vegetable stock	1.5 L
2 cups	whipping cream	500 mL
	Finely chopped parsley or cilantro	

1. In a heatproof bowl, soak chili pepper in boiling water for 30 minutes. Drain.

2. In a blender or food processor, purée chili, onion, garlic, cumin seeds and rosemary with ½ cup (125 mL) stock. Add to slow cooker stoneware along with remaining stock, bay leaf, salt, black pepper and corn.

3. Cover and cook on **Low** for 6 to 8 hours or on **High** for 3 to 4 hours.

4. Add roasted pepper and whipping cream. Cover and cook on **High** for 15 to 20 minutes, until heated through. Discard bay leaf. Spoon into individual bowls and garnish with parsley or cilantro.

Variation

Corn and Roasted Red Pepper Soup with Crab: For a more substantial soup, add 2 cans (6 oz/170 g) drained crab meat along with the corn and pepper.

Make ahead

This dish can be assembled the night before it is cooked but without adding the roasted pepper and whipping cream. Complete Steps 1 and 2 and refrigerate. The next day, continue with Step 3.

Tip

Dried chilies that are not properly reconstituted impart a bitter taste to slow cooker recipes. In my experience, they require a full 30-minute soak in boiling water. With larger chilies, make sure the entire pepper is submerged throughout the process.

Tip

Dried New Mexico chilies are now available in most supermarkets. Their smoky flavor adds a nice note to this soup, but you can omit them and add a smoky hot pepper sauce, such as one made with chipotle peppers, to taste, after soup is cooked.

Peppery Cream of Turnip Soup

This soup, French in origin, makes an elegant starter to any meal. It must be made with white turnips — the more pungent yellow rutabagas, although delicious in their own right, just won't do. The amount of hot pepper sauce makes a nicely piquant version — vary the quantity depending upon your preference. For an added touch, sprinkle with Garlic Croutons (see recipe, below). • *SERVES 6 TO 8*

9	small white turnips, cut into ½-inch (1-cm) cubes, about 6 cups (1.5 L)	9
2	potatoes, peeled and cut into ½-inch (1-cm) cubes	2
3	onions, diced	3
½ tsp	ground nutmeg	2 mL
½ tsp	granulated sugar	2 mL
1 tsp	salt	5 mL
¼ tsp	freshly ground black pepper	1 mL
6 cups	chicken stock	1.5 L
1 cup	whipping cream	250 mL
1 tsp	hot pepper sauce, such as Tabasco	5 mL
	Finely chopped parsley or chives	

Garlic Croutons (optional)

2 tbsp	olive oil	25 mL
1	clove garlic, put through a press or finely minced	1
2 cups	white bread, crusts removed, cut into ¼-inch (0.5-cm) cubes	500 mL

Make ahead
This dish can be assembled the night before it is cooked but without adding the cream and hot pepper sauce. Complete Step 1 and refrigerate overnight. The next day, continue cooking as directed in Step 1. Or cook the soup overnight in the slow cooker, purée and refrigerate. When ready to serve, bring to a boil in a pot on stovetop and simmer for 5 to 10 minutes before serving. Stir in cream and hot pepper sauce.

1. In slow cooker stoneware, combine turnips, potatoes, onions, nutmeg, sugar, salt, pepper and chicken stock.

2. Cover and cook on **Low** for 8 to 10 hours or on **High** for 4 to 5 hours, until vegetables are tender.

3. In a blender or food processor, purée soup in batches. Stir in cream and hot pepper sauce. Spoon into individual soup bowls and garnish with parsley or chives or garlic croutons, if using.

4. To make Garlic Croutons: Preheat oven to 375°F (190°C). In a small bowl, combine olive oil and garlic. Place bread cubes in a large bowl. Pour olive-oil mixture over bread cubes and toss to combine. Arrange bread on a baking sheet in a single layer. Toast until golden, turning once, about 10 minutes.

Caribbean Pepper Pot Soup

This delicious vegetable soup is a meal in itself and it's so good, you'll want seconds. I particularly like the way the sweetness of the brown sugar and the coconut milk combines with the heat of the chilies. • *SERVES 6*

1 tbsp	vegetable oil	15 mL
2	onions, finely chopped	2
3	cloves garlic, minced	3
1 tbsp	minced gingerroot	15 mL
2 tbsp	chili powder	25 mL
½ to 1	chili pepper, preferably Scotch bonnet, finely chopped (see Tip, right)	½ to 1
1 tsp	whole coriander seeds	5 mL
1 tsp	celery seeds	5 mL
1 tsp	salt	5 mL
1 tsp	cracked black peppercorns	5 mL
1 tbsp	packed brown sugar	15 mL
4 cups	acorn or butternut squash, peeled and cut into ½-inch (1-cm) cubes, or 4 cups (1 L) carrots, peeled and thinly sliced	1 L
1	can (19 oz/540 mL) kidney beans, rinsed and drained, or 2 cups (500 mL) cooked and drained dried kidney beans	1
1	can (28 oz/796 mL) tomatoes, including juice, chopped (see Tip, page 32)	1
4 cups	chicken or vegetable stock	1 L
1	can (14 oz/398 mL) coconut milk (see page 16)	1
	Finely chopped parsley or cilantro (optional)	

1. In a large skillet, heat oil over medium heat. Add onions and cook until soft. Add garlic, gingerroot, chili powder, chili pepper, coriander seeds, celery seeds, salt and pepper and cook, stirring, for 1 minute. Add sugar and stir to combine. Add squash or carrots, kidney beans, tomatoes and stock.

2. Transfer to slow cooker stoneware. Cover and cook on **Low** for 8 to 10 hours or on **High** for 4 to 5 hours, until vegetables are tender.

3. Add coconut milk. Cover and cook on **High** for another 15 to 20 minutes, until heated through. Garnish with parsley or cilantro, if using.

Make ahead

This soup can be assembled in advance of serving, but without adding the coconut milk. Complete Step 1 and refrigerate overnight. The next day, continue cooking as directed in Step 2.

Tip

Although any chili pepper will provide the appropriate degree of heat, only Scotch bonnet peppers, available in West Indian markets, truly capture the spirit of the Caribbean. Short, squat and slightly wrinkled and ranging in color from yellow to red to green, Scotch bonnets have a unique smoky flavor. Be particularly cautious when handling them, as they are reputedly the world's hottest pepper.

Pasta and Chickpea Soup with Garlic-Almond Picada

This Italian classic makes a great one-dish meal or a delicious lunch. I like to make a batch and refrigerate it so that people can reheat individual servings themselves. The *picada*, a mixture made from ingredients such as garlic, olive oil, ground herbs and nuts, which is used to flavor and thicken dishes, adds a Spanish touch and zest to the soup but it isn't essential. The more traditional accompaniment of freshly grated Parmesan cheese also works very well. • *SERVES 6 TO 8*

2 tbsp	olive oil	25 mL
2	onions, finely chopped	2
4	cloves garlic, minced	4
1 tbsp	dried Italian herb seasoning	15 mL
¼ tsp	cayenne pepper	1 mL
1 tsp	salt	5 mL
1 tsp	cracked black peppercorns	5 mL
1	can (28 oz/796 mL) tomatoes, including juice, coarsely chopped (see Tip, page 32)	1
2	cans (19 oz/540 mL) chickpeas, drained and rinsed, or 2 cups (500 mL) cooked and drained chickpeas	2
6 cups	chicken or vegetable stock	1.5 L
1 cup	macaroni or other small pasta	250 mL
1 lb	fresh spinach leaves or 1 package (10 oz/300 g) spinach, stems removed, washed and coarsely chopped	500 g

Garlic-Almond Picada (optional)

2 tbsp	olive oil	25 mL
¼ cup	blanched almonds	50 mL
3	cloves garlic, minced	3
¼ cup	chopped parsley	50 mL
¼ tsp	salt	1 mL
¼ tsp	black pepper	1 mL
2	slices white bread, about ½ inch (1 cm) thick, crusts removed, cut into 2-inch (5-cm) cubes	2
3 tbsp	freshly grated Parmesan cheese	45 mL

Make ahead

This dish can be assembled the night before it is cooked but without adding the pasta and spinach. Complete Step 1 and refrigerate overnight. The next day, continue cooking as directed in Step 2. Or cook the soup overnight. Complete Step 3 in the morning, cover and refrigerate. When you're ready to serve, bring to a boil in a pot on stovetop and simmer for 5 to 10 minutes. Then continue as directed.

1. In a skillet, heat oil over medium heat. Add onion and cook until soft. Add garlic, Italian seasoning, cayenne, salt and pepper and cook, stirring, for 1 minute. Add tomatoes and chickpeas and bring to a boil.

2. Transfer mixture to slow cooker stoneware. Add chicken or vegetable stock, cover and cook on **Low** for 8 to 10 hours or on **High** for 4 to 5 hours.

3. In a large pot of boiling salted water, cook pasta until tender but firm. Drain well and add to slow cooker along with spinach. Stir well. Cover and cook on **High** for 20 minutes, or until spinach is cooked.

4. To make Garlic-Almond Picada: In a skillet, heat oil over medium heat. Add almonds and cook, stirring, until nicely browned. Remove with a slotted spoon and place in a food processor.

5. Add garlic, parsley, salt and pepper to pan and cook, stirring, for 1 minute. Add bread, adding more oil, if required, and cook, turning, until nicely browned on all sides. Transfer to food processor. Add Parmesan and purée to a mealy consistency.

6. When ready to serve, spoon soup into individual bowls and pass the picada, allowing people to help themselves.

Minestrone with Garlic-Flavored Crostini

This hearty meal in a bowl is a classic of Italian cuisine. All you'll need for a satisfying dinner is a big green salad, preferably with lots of arugula, a sharply flavored green reminiscent of watercress, which often turns up in Italian kitchens. • SERVES 8

1 tbsp	olive oil	15 mL
3	leeks, white part only, cleaned and very thinly sliced (see Tip, page 212)	3
4	stalks celery, peeled and cut into ½-inch (1-cm) cubes	4
4	medium carrots, peeled and cut into ½-inch (1-cm) cubes	4
2	potatoes, peeled and shredded	2
4 cups	shredded cabbage	1 L
2	sprigs fresh rosemary or 2 tsp (10 mL) dried rosemary leaves	2
2	cloves garlic, minced	2
1 tsp	salt	5 mL
½ tsp	cracked black peppercorns	2 mL
1	can (28 oz/796 mL) tomatoes, including juice (see Tip, page 32)	1
6 cups	chicken or vegetable stock	1.5 L
1	can (19 oz/540 mL) white kidney beans, drained and rinsed, or 2 cups (500 mL) cooked and drained white kidney beans	1
1	small zucchini, cut into ½-inch (1-cm) cubes, sweated and rinsed (see Tip, right)	1
½ cup	green beans, cut into 1-inch (2.5-cm) lengths	125 mL
	Freshly grated Parmesan cheese	
	Crostini (see recipe, page 56)	

1. In a skillet, heat oil over medium heat. Add leeks, celery, carrots, potatoes and cabbage and stir to combine. Reduce heat to low, cover and cook for 10 minutes, or until vegetables are softened.

2. Increase heat to medium. Add rosemary, garlic, salt and pepper and cook, stirring for 1 minute. Add tomatoes and juice, breaking up with a spoon, and bring to a boil. Transfer mixture to slow cooker stoneware. Add chicken stock and white kidney beans and stir well to combine.

continued on page 56

Make ahead

This dish can be assembled the night before it is cooked but without adding the green beans and zucchini. Complete Steps 1 and 2 and refrigerate overnight. The next day, continue cooking as directed in Step 3. Or cook the soup overnight, complete cooking in the morning and refrigerate until you're ready to serve. In a pot, bring to a boil on stovetop and simmer for 5 to 10 minutes. Then continue with Step 5.

Tip

To sweat zucchini: Peel zucchini, cut or slice according to recipe instructions and place prepared pieces in a colander. Sprinkle with salt and let drain for at least 20 minutes. Rinse thoroughly under cold water.

3. Cover and cook on **Low** for 8 to 10 hours or on **High** for 4 to 5 hours.

4. Add sweated zucchini and green beans. Cover and cook on **High** for 20 minutes, or until vegetables are tender.

5. To make Crostini: Preheat broiler. Brush 8 baguette slices on both sides with garlic-infused olive oil mixture (see Recipe, right) and toast under broiler, turning once.

6. When ready to serve, place crostini in bottom of individual bowls, ladle soup over and lace liberally with Parmesan cheese.

Tip

Although you can buy garlic-flavored olive oil, it's easy to make your own – but use it immediately as infused oils are a favored medium for bacteria growth. Garlic-Infused Oil: In a clean jar or cruet, combine ½ cup (125 mL) extra-virgin olive oil with 4 cloves garlic put through a press. Cover and let steep at room temperature for several hours. Strain through a fine sieve or funnel lined with paper coffee filter and discard garlic.

South American Black Bean Soup

This mouthwatering combination of black beans, lime juice and cilantro with just a hint of hot pepper is one of my favorite one-dish meals. To jack up the heat, add a chopped jalapeño along with the garlic. The flavor of this soup actually improves if it is allowed to sit overnight and then reheated. • *SERVES 4 TO 6 AS A MAIN COURSE OR 6 TO 8 AS A STARTER*

6	slices bacon, chopped	6
2	onions, finely chopped	2
2	stalks celery, peeled and finely chopped	2
2	carrots, peeled and finely chopped	2
2	cloves garlic, minced	2
1 tsp	dried thyme leaves	5 mL
2 tbsp	cumin seeds	25 mL
1 tbsp	dried oregano leaves	15 mL
1 tsp	salt	5 mL
1 tsp	cracked black peppercorns	5 mL
¼ tsp	cayenne pepper	1 mL
2 tbsp	tomato paste	25 mL
6 cups	chicken stock	1.5 L
4	cans (19 oz/540 mL) black beans, rinsed and drained, or 4 cups (1 L) dried black beans, cooked and drained	4
⅓ cup	freshly squeezed lime juice	75 mL
	Finely chopped cilantro	
	Sour cream (optional)	
	Salsa (optional)	

Make ahead

This dish can be assembled the night before it is cooked but without adding the lime juice and garnishes. Complete Steps 1 and 2. Cover and refrigerate overnight. The next day, continue cooking as directed in Step 3. Or cook the soup overnight, cover and refrigerate. When you're ready to serve, bring to a boil in a pot on stovetop and simmer for 5 to 10 minutes. Then complete Step 4.

1. In a skillet, over medium-high heat, cook bacon until crisp. Remove with a slotted spoon to a paper-towel-lined plate and drain thoroughly. Set aside.

2. Drain all but 1 tbsp (15 mL) fat from pan. Reduce heat to medium. Add onions, celery and carrots and cook, stirring, until vegetables are softened, 4 to 5 minutes. Add garlic, thyme, cumin seeds, oregano, salt, pepper and cayenne and cook, stirring, for 1 minute. Add tomato paste and stir to combine thoroughly. Transfer contents of pan to slow cooker stoneware. Add bacon, stock and beans and stir to combine.

3. Cover and cook on **Low** for 8 to 10 hours or on **High** for 4 to 6 hours.

4. Before serving, stir in lime juice. In blender or food processor, purée soup in batches. Spoon into individual soup bowls and garnish with cilantro and/or sour cream and salsa, if using.

Beans, Lentils and Chilies

Texas-Style Chili Con Carne

Although I call this Texas-Style Chili — because it is made with chunks of beef rather than ground meat — it's not the real thing since it contains beans. I like to serve this with hot onion buns on the side, garnished with shredded Cheddar or Monterey Jack cheese, sour cream and finely chopped green onions. • *SERVES 6 TO 8*

1	dried New Mexico chili (optional) (see Tip, right)	1
1 cup	boiling water	250 mL
4	slices bacon, finely chopped	4
2 lbs	stewing beef, cut into 1-inch (2.5-cm) cubes	1 kg
2	onions, thinly sliced	2
	Vegetable oil, if necessary	
4	cloves garlic, minced	4
1 to 2	jalapeño peppers, finely chopped	1 to 2
1 tbsp	each cumin seeds and dried oregano leaves	15 mL
2 tsp	each salt and cracked black peppercorns	10 mL
1	can (28 oz/796 mL) tomatoes, coarsely chopped (see Tip, page 32)	1
1	can (10 oz/284 mL) condensed beef broth (undiluted)	1
1 cup	dry red wine	250 mL
1	can (19 oz/540 mL) red kidney beans, drained and rinsed, or 1 cup (250 mL) dried red kidney beans, cooked and drained	1

1. In a heatproof bowl, soak chili in boiling water for 30 minutes (see Tips, page 48). Drain and discard liquid. Pat dry with paper towel, chop finely and set aside.

2. In a skillet, over medium-high heat, cook bacon until crisp. Using a slotted spoon, transfer to paper towels to drain. Pour off all but 2 tbsp (25 mL) fat. Add beef to pan, in batches, and brown. Transfer to stoneware.

3. Add onions to pan and cook until soft. Add chili pepper, if using, garlic, jalapeño pepper, cumin seeds, oregano, black pepper and salt and cook, stirring, for 2 minutes. Stir in tomatoes, beef broth, wine and bacon and bring to a boil.

4. Pour mixture over beef. Add beans and stir well.

5. Cover and cook on **Low** for 8 to 10 hours or on **High** for 4 to 5 hours, until beef is very tender.

Variation

Party-Style Chili: Roast and peel 2 red bell peppers, 2 green bell peppers and 2 yellow banana peppers (see page 70). Chop coarsely, mix well and spread over top of the chili before serving.

Make ahead

This dish can be partially prepared ahead of time. Complete Steps 1 through 3, but omit browning the beef. Cover and refrigerate mixture overnight. The next morning, brown beef, if time permits combine with remaining ingredients and continue cooking as directed in Step 5. Alternately, the chili may be cooked overnight in the slow cooker, then refrigerated and reheated later on the stovetop. In a Dutch oven, bring to a boil and simmer for 5 to 10 minutes before serving.

Tip

Round steak also works well in this recipe, but since it is thinner than stewing beef when cut, the meat won't make cubes.

Tip

Instead of using New Mexico chili, add a smoky hot pepper sauce, such as one made with chipotle peppers, to taste, after the chili is cooked.

Best-Ever White Chili

This is my favorite white chili. I love the rich, creamy sauce and the way the ground chicken absorbs the flavors of the spices. Serve this with a good dollop of sour cream, your favorite salsa and a sprinkling of chopped cilantro. • *SERVES 4 TO 6*

2 tbsp	vegetable oil	25 mL
1 lb	ground chicken or turkey	500 g
2	onions, finely chopped	2
6	cloves garlic, minced	6
1 tbsp	cumin seeds	15 mL
1 tbsp	dried oregano leaves	15 mL
1 to 2	jalapeño peppers	1 to 2
1 tsp	each salt and cracked black peppercorns	5 mL
1	can (28 oz/796 mL) tomatoes, including juice, chopped (see Tip, page 32)	1
2 cups	chicken or vegetable stock	500 mL
1	can (19 oz/540 mL) white kidney beans, rinsed and drained, or 1 cup (250 mL) dried white kidney beans, soaked, cooked and drained	1
2	green bell peppers, thinly sliced lengthwise	2
1½ cups	shredded Monterey Jack cheese	375 mL
1	can (4½ oz/127 mL) diced mild green chilies, drained	1

Make ahead

This dish can be partially prepared the night before. Slice green peppers and shred cheese. Cover and refrigerate. Complete Steps 1 and 2, chilling meat and onion mixtures separately. Cover and refrigerate overnight. The next morning, continue cooking as directed in Step 3. Alternately, chili may be cooked overnight in slow cooker, finished the next morning and refrigerated for subsequent reheating on stovetop. In a Dutch oven, bring to a boil and simmer for 5 to 10 minutes before serving.

1. In a skillet, heat 1 tbsp (15 mL) oil over medium-high heat. Add ground chicken or turkey and cook, breaking up meat with a wooden spoon, until it is no longer pink. Remove with a slotted spoon to slow cooker stoneware. Drain and discard liquid.

2. Reduce heat to medium. Add remaining oil to pan. Add onions and cook, stirring, until softened. Add garlic, cumin seeds, oregano, jalapeño peppers, salt and pepper and cook, stirring, for 1 minute. Add tomatoes and broth and bring to a boil. Cook, stirring, until liquid is reduced by one third, about 5 minutes.

3. Add beans to stoneware and pour tomato mixture over them. Stir to combine. Cover and cook on **Low** for 6 to 8 hours or on **High** for 3 to 4 hours, until mixture is hot and bubbling.

4. Stir in green pepper, cheese and mild green chilies. Cover and cook on **High** for 20 to 30 minutes, until pepper is tender and cheese is melted. Ladle into bowls and top with sour cream, salsa and chopped cilantro.

Variation

White Vegetarian Chili: Omit the ground meat and add an extra can of beans. Use vegetable broth, rather than chicken.

Beef Chili with Cornbread Topping

Thanks to Marta Bozdeck for sharing her family's favorite chili recipe with me. Children, adults and teenagers all love this savory chili with its unusual cornbread topping. A great finish to a day of hiking or skiing, all it needs is a big salad and some robust red wine. Serve with plenty of your favorite salsa, sour cream and finely chopped red or green onion. • *SERVES 8 TO 10*

2 tbsp	vegetable oil	25 mL
1 lb	lean ground beef	500 g
2	onions, finely chopped	2
4	cloves garlic, minced	4
1 tbsp	cumin seeds	15 mL
1 tbsp	cracked black peppercorns	15 mL
1 tbsp	chili powder	15 mL
1 tsp	salt	5 mL
½ tsp	ground allspice	2 mL
¼ tsp	cayenne pepper	1 mL
2 tsp	unsweetened cocoa powder	5 mL
1 tbsp	cornmeal	15 mL
1 tbsp	Worcestershire sauce	15 mL
¼ cup	tomato paste	50 mL
2 cups	tomato sauce	500 mL
½ cup	condensed beef broth (undiluted)	125 mL
2	cans (10 oz/284 mL) corn kernels, drained, or 2 cups (500 mL) frozen corn kernels, thawed	2
1	can (19 oz/540 mL) red kidney beans, drained and rinsed, or 1 cup (250 mL) dried red kidney beans, cooked and drained	1
1 cup	pimento-stuffed olives, thinly sliced	250 mL
1	green bell pepper, cut into ½-inch (1-cm) cubes	1
	Hot pepper sauce, such as Tabasco, to taste (optional)	

Cornbread Topping

1 cup	all-purpose flour	250 mL
1 cup	cornmeal	250 mL
3 tbsp	granulated sugar	45 mL
2 tsp	baking powder	10 mL
¼ cup	melted butter	50 mL
1 cup	milk or buttermilk	250 mL
1	large egg, beaten	1
1 cup	grated Cheddar cheese	250 mL
1	can (4½ oz/127 mL) chopped green chilies, including juice (optional)	1
½ cup	finely chopped green onions (optional)	125 mL

Make ahead

This recipe may be partially prepared the night before it is cooked. Complete Steps 1 and 2, chilling cooked meat and onion mixture separately. Chop green pepper and cover. Refrigerate overnight. The next morning, combine beef and onion mixture and continue cooking as directed in Step 3.

Tip

This quantity of topping works best in a large, oval slow cooker. If you're using a tall, narrow slow cooker, make half the amount of batter.

1. In a skillet, heat 1 tbsp (15 mL) oil over medium-high heat. Add beef and cook, stirring and breaking meat up with the back of a spoon, until beef is no longer pink. Transfer to slow cooker stoneware. Drain off liquid in pan.

2. Reduce heat to medium and heat remaining oil in pan. Add onions and cook until softened. Add garlic, cumin seeds, pepper, chili powder, salt, allspice and cayenne and cook, stirring, for 1 minute. Add cocoa and cornmeal and stir well. Stir in Worcestershire sauce, tomato paste, tomato sauce and beef broth and bring to a boil.

3. Pour mixture into slow cooker stoneware. Add corn and beans and stir to combine. Cover and cook on **Low** for 8 to 10 hours or on **High** for 4 to 5 hours, until hot and bubbling.

4. Add olives and green pepper to slow cooker and stir well. Taste and adjust seasoning, adding hot pepper sauce if you prefer a spicier chili.

5. To make Cornbread Topping: In a bowl, combine flour, cornmeal, granulated sugar and baking powder. Add melted butter, milk or buttermilk and egg and stir well until ingredients are combined. Add grated Cheddar cheese and chopped green chilies, including juice, and green onions, if using, and stir well.

6. Drop cornbread batter, by spoonfuls, over the top of the mixture. Cover and cook on **High** for 30 to 40 minutes, until topping is set.

Turkey Chili with Black-Eyed Peas

This delicious chili is lighter than those made with red meat and it's a favorite with my family. I like to serve this (and almost any chili) with an Avocado Topping (see page 67). • *SERVES 6 TO 8*

1 tbsp	vegetable oil	15 mL
2 lbs	boneless, skinless turkey breast or thighs, cut into 1-inch (2.5-cm) cubes	1 kg
2	onions, finely chopped	2
3	cloves garlic, minced	3
2	jalapeño peppers, finely chopped	2
2 tbsp	chili powder	25 mL
1 tsp	dried oregano leaves	5 mL
1 tsp	ground coriander	5 mL
1 tsp	cumin seeds	5 mL
1	can (28 oz/796 mL) tomatoes, including juice, coarsely chopped	1
1	can (10 oz/284 mL) condensed chicken broth (undiluted)	1
2	cans (19 oz/540 mL) black-eyed peas, drained and rinsed, or 2 cups (500 mL) dried black-eyed peas, cooked and drained	2
2	green bell peppers, cut into thin strips	2
	Avocado Topping (see recipe, page 67) or grated Monterey Jack cheese	
	Sour cream	
	Finely chopped red onion	
	Finely chopped cilantro	

Make ahead

This dish can be partially prepared the night before it is cooked. Slice green peppers, cover and refrigerate. Complete Step 2, heating 1 tbsp (15 mL) oil before softening onions. Cover and refrigerate mixture overnight. The next morning, brown turkey (Step 1), or skip this step if you're pressed for time. Combine with black-eyed peas and refrigerated mixture and continue cooking as directed in Step 3. Alternately, chili may be cooked overnight in slow cooker, finished the next morning and refrigerated for subsequent reheating on the stovetop. In a Dutch oven, bring to a boil and simmer for 5 to 10 minutes before serving.

1. In a skillet, heat oil over medium-high heat. Add turkey, in batches, and brown. Transfer to slow cooker stoneware.

2. Reduce heat to medium. Add onions to pan and cook until soft. Add garlic, jalapeño peppers, chili powder, oregano, coriander and cumin seeds and cook, stirring, for 1 minute. Add tomatoes and chicken broth and bring to a boil.

3. Add peas to slow cooker stoneware. Pour tomato mixture over turkey and peas and stir to combine. Cover and cook on **Low** for 8 to 10 hours or on **High** for 4 to 5 hours, until turkey is no longer pink inside.

4. Stir in green bell peppers, cover and cook for 20 to 25 minutes. Spoon into individual bowls and top with any combination of grated Monterey Jack or Cheddar cheese, sour cream, chopped red onion and cilantro or with Avocado Topping.

Vegetarian Chili

Today, most people are trying to eat healthier foods and reduce their intake of fat. While this vegetarian chili qualifies on both counts, it also makes a delicious and satisfying meal. I like to serve this with Avocado Topping (see recipe, page 67), but it's also good with light sour cream, shredded cheese and chopped green onion. • *SERVES 6 TO 8*

1	dried New Mexico chili (optional) (see Tips, page 48)	1
1 cup	boiling water	250 mL
1 tbsp	vegetable oil	15 mL
2	onions, finely chopped	2
4	stalks celery, peeled and thinly sliced	4
2	medium carrots, peeled and thinly sliced	2
6	cloves garlic, minced	6
1 to 2	jalapeño peppers, finely chopped	1 to 2
2 tbsp	chili powder	25 mL
1 tbsp	cumin seeds	15 mL
2 tsp	dried oregano leaves	10 mL
1 tsp	dried thyme leaves	5 mL
1½ tsp	salt	7 mL
1 tsp	cracked black peppercorns	5 mL
1 tbsp	unsweetened cocoa powder	15 mL
1 tbsp	balsamic vinegar	15 mL
1 tbsp	packed brown sugar	15 mL
2	cans (10 oz/284 mL) corn kernels, drained, or 2 cups (500 mL) frozen corn kernels, thawed	2
1	can (28 oz/796 mL) tomatoes, including juice, coarsely chopped (see Tip, page 32)	1
2 cups	vegetable stock	500 mL
2 cups	yellow-fleshed squash, such as acorn or butternut, peeled and diced into ½-inch (1-cm) cubes	500 mL
1	can (19 oz/540 mL) red kidney beans, drained and rinsed, or 1 cup (250 mL) dried kidney beans, cooked and drained	1
2	green bell peppers, seeded and cut into thin strips	2
	Avocado Topping (optional)	
	Light sour cream	
	Shredded Cheddar or Monterey Jack cheese (optional)	
	Finely chopped green onion	

Make ahead

This chili can be assembled the night before it is cooked but without adding the green peppers and corn. Complete Steps 1 and 2 and refrigerate overnight. The next day, continue cooking as directed in Step 3.

1. In a heatproof bowl, soak chili in boiling water for 30 minutes, making certain that all parts of the pepper are submerged. Drain and discard liquid. Pat dry with paper towels, chop finely and set aside.

2. In a skillet, heat oil over medium heat. Add onions, celery and carrots and cook until soft. Add garlic, jalapeño pepper, chili powder, cumin seeds, oregano, thyme, salt, pepper and chili pepper and cook for 1 minute. Stir in cocoa, balsamic vinegar, brown sugar, corn, tomatoes and vegetable stock and bring to a boil. Transfer mixture to slow cooker stoneware. Add squash and kidney beans and stir to combine.

3. Cover and cook on **Low** for 8 to 10 hours or on **High** for 4 to 5 hours, until hot and bubbling.

4. Stir in green pepper. Cover and cook on **High** for 25 to 30 minutes. Ladle into bowls and top with sour cream, shredded cheese, if using, and green onions.

5. To make Avocado Topping: Chop 1 whole avocado into ½-inch (1-cm) cubes and toss with 1 tbsp (15 mL) lime juice, 2 tbsp (25 mL) finely chopped red onion and 2 tbsp (15 mL) finely chopped cilantro. Add salt and pepper to taste.

Tuscan-Style Beans with Rosemary

I love this simple combination of white kidney beans and pancetta, seasoned with vegetables and herbs. A perfect light evening meal, it also makes a great accompaniment to roasted poultry or meat. Make an effort to find pancetta, but if you're not successful, prosciutto can be substituted toward the end of the cooking time. Stir in 3 oz (75 g) prosciutto and cook on High for 30 minutes before serving the beans. • *SERVES 6 TO 8*

1 tbsp	olive oil	15 mL
3 oz	pancetta, finely chopped	75 g
1	large red onion, finely chopped	1
4	cloves garlic, minced	4
1	large potato, peeled and grated	1
2	sprigs fresh rosemary or 1 tbsp (15 mL) dried rosemary leaves	2
¼ cup	whole parsley leaves	50 mL
½ tsp	salt	2 mL
½ tsp	cracked black peppercorns	2 mL
1	can (28 oz/796 mL) tomatoes, including juice (see Tip, page 32)	1
2	cans (19 oz/540 mL) white kidney beans, drained and rinsed, or 2 cups (500 mL) dried white kidney beans, cooked and drained	2

1. In a skillet, heat oil over medium-high heat. Add pancetta and cook until it just begins to brown. Transfer to slow cooker stoneware.

2. Reduce heat to medium. Add onion to pan and cook, stirring, until softened. Add garlic, potato, rosemary, parsley, salt and pepper. Cook, stirring, for 1 minute. Stir in tomatoes and bring to a boil. Cook, stirring until liquid is reduced by approximately one third, about 2 minutes.

3. Add beans to slow cooker stoneware. Pour contents of pan over beans and stir well. Add water, barely to cover. Cover and cook on **Low** for 8 to 10 hours or on **High** for 4 to 5 hours, until hot and bubbly.

Make ahead

This dish can be partially assembled the night before it is cooked. Complete Steps 1 and 2, chilling pancetta and onion mixture separately. Refrigerate overnight. The next day, continue cooking as directed in Step 3. Alternately, beans may be cooked overnight in slow cooker, refrigerated the following morning and reheated later on the stovetop. In a Dutch oven, bring to a boil and simmer for 5 to 10 minutes before serving.

Old-Fashioned Pork and Beans

At least once every winter we love to have a Sunday dinner of home-cooked pork and beans, with a hot loaf of freshly baked whole wheat bread and coleslaw. For many years, I cooked my beans in an antique bean pot, which I found in a rural secondhand store. Although it was charming, I've become a convert to the more convenient slow cooker, which produces optimum results. • *SERVES 6 TO 8*

2 cups	dried navy beans, cooked and drained (see Preparing Dried Beans, page 17)	500 mL
½ lb	salt pork belly, thinly sliced	250 g
2	onions, thinly sliced	2
1	can (28 oz/796 mL) tomatoes, including juice, coarsely chopped (see Tip, page 32)	1
1 tbsp	cracked black peppercorns	15 mL
1 tsp	salt	5 mL
1 tsp	dry mustard	5 mL
½ tsp	dried thyme leaves	2 mL
¼ tsp	cayenne pepper	1 mL
Pinch	ground cloves	Pinch
¼ cup	molasses	50 mL

1. In slow cooker stoneware, place half the salt pork. Add half the onions, half the beans and half the tomatoes and their liquid. Repeat.

2. In a small bowl, combine pepper, salt, mustard, thyme, cayenne, cloves and molasses. Add ½ cup (125 mL) boiling water and stir to combine. Pour mixture over beans and add water, barely to cover.

3. Cover and cook on **Low** for 8 to 10 hours or on **High** for 4 to 5 hours, until beans are hot and bubbling.

Variation

Old-Fashioned Pork and Beans with Caramelized Apples: Thanks to Cinda Chavich, author of *The Wild West Cookbook*, for this idea. When beans are almost cooked, peel and core 4 apples, then slice them vertically into thin slices. In a skillet, over medium heat, melt 3 tbsp (45 mL) butter. Add ¼ cup (50 mL) brown sugar and cook, stirring, for about 2 minutes. Add apple slices and stir to coat with sugar mixture. Add ¼ cup (50 mL) rum. Increase heat to medium-high and cook, turning, until the liquid evaporates and the apples are tender. Arrange apple slices on top of beans, cover and cook on **High** for 1 hour.

Make ahead

This dish can be assembled the night before it is cooked. Complete Steps 1 and 2, allowing molasses mixture to cool before adding to beans, and refrigerate overnight. The next morning, continue with Step 3. Alternately, beans may be cooked overnight in slow cooker and refrigerated until you're ready to serve. In a Dutch oven, bring to a boil on stovetop and simmer for 5 to 10 minutes before serving.

Moors and Christians

Although I've come across several different versions of how this classic Cuban dish got its name, all lead back to the eighth century when Spain was invaded by their enemies, the Moors. For a genuine Cuban touch, spoon onto plates, top with a fried egg and accompany with Fried Plantains (see page 98). I guarantee you'll have requests for seconds. This dish is also delicious cold and makes a nice addition to a buffet as a rice salad. • *SERVES 8*

1	roasted red bell pepper, finely chopped (see Tip, right)	1
1 tbsp	vegetable oil	15 mL
2	medium onions, finely chopped	2
4	large cloves garlic, minced	4
2 tsp	dried oregano leaves	10 mL
2 tsp	cumin seeds	10 mL
1	medium tomato, peeled, seeded and chopped	1
1	can (19 oz/540 mL) black beans, rinsed and drained, or 1 cup (250 mL) dried black beans, cooked and drained	1
½ cup	condensed chicken broth (undiluted)	125 mL
2 cups	long-grain rice	500 mL
1	green bell pepper, finely chopped	1
2 tbsp	lemon or lime juice	25 mL
¼ cup	finely chopped cilantro	50 mL
4	green onions, white part only, finely chopped	4

1. In a skillet, heat oil over medium heat. Add onion and cook until soft. Add garlic, oregano and cumin seeds and cook for 1 minute. Stirring, add roasted red pepper, tomato, beans and chicken broth and bring to a boil. Transfer to slow cooker stoneware.

2. Cover and cook on **Low** for 8 to 10 hours or on **High** for 4 to 5 hours.

3. When bean mixture is cooked, make rice. In a heavy pot with a tight-fitting lid, combine rice with 4 cups (1 L) water. Cover, bring to a rapid boil, then turn off the heat, leaving the pot on the warm element. Do not lift the lid or move the pot until rice is ready, which will take about 20 minutes.

4. Meanwhile, add green pepper to contents of slow cooker and stir well. Cover and cook on **High** for 20 to 30 minutes, until pepper is tender.

5. Stir cooked rice into slow cooker. Add lemon or lime juice, cilantro and green onions and stir to combine thoroughly. Serve hot as a main course or cold as a salad.

Make ahead

This dish can be prepared the night before it is cooked but without adding the rice, green pepper, cilantro, green onions and lemon or lime juice. Complete Step 1 and refrigerate overnight. The next day, continue cooking as directed in Step 2.

Tip

To roast peppers: Preheat oven to 400°F (200°C). Place pepper(s) on a baking sheet and roast, turning two or three times, until the skin on all sides is blackened. (This will take about 25 minutes.) Transfer pepper(s) to a heatproof bowl. Cover with a plate and let stand until cool. Remove and, using a sharp knife, lift skins off. Discard skins and slice according to recipe instructions.

Creamy Mexican Beans

In the summer, on those evenings when we're eating outdoors and barbecuing steaks, I like to serve this as a side dish. The creamy sauce is great with steak and in the hot weather I enjoy not having to turn on the stove. Along with steak, I serve this with grilled zucchini, tossed with extra-virgin olive oil and fresh thyme. Because there are tomatoes in the sauce, which will toughen beans during cooking, dried lima beans should be cooked before being added to this recipe. • *SERVES 4 TO 6 AS A SIDE DISH*

• **WORKS BEST IN A SMALL (MAXIMUM 3½ QUART) SLOW COOKER (SEE TIP, BELOW)**

2	onions, finely chopped	2
4	cloves garlic, minced	4
2	jalapeño peppers, finely chopped	2
1 tsp	dried oregano leaves	5 mL
1 tsp	cracked black peppercorns	5 mL
1 tsp	salt	5 mL
1	can (19 oz/540 mL) tomatoes, drained and coarsely chopped	1
1 tbsp	oil-packed sun-dried tomatoes, finely chopped	15 mL
1 cup	chicken or vegetable stock or water	250 mL
1 cup	frozen lima beans, thawed, or ½ cup (125 mL) dried lima beans, cooked and drained	250 mL
4 oz	cream cheese, softened and cut into 2-inch (5-cm) squares	125 g

1. In a skillet, heat oil over medium heat. Add onions and cook, stirring, until softened. Add garlic, jalapeño pepper, oregano, peppercorns and salt and cook, stirring, for 1 minute. Stir in tomatoes, sun-dried tomatoes and stock or water and bring to a boil.

2. Place beans in slow cooker stoneware and pour vegetable mixture over.

3. Cover and cook on **Low** for 8 hours or on **High** for 4 hours. Stir in cream cheese, cover and cook on **High** for 15 minutes, until cheese is melted and mixture is hot and bubbling.

Make ahead

This dish can be assembled the night before it is cooked but without adding the cream cheese. Complete Steps 1 and 2 and refrigerate overnight. The next day, continue cooking as directed in Step 3. Alternately, beans may be cooked overnight, finished in the morning and refrigerated until you're ready to serve. In a Dutch oven, bring to a boil and simmer for 5 to 10 minutes before serving.

Tip

If making this quantity, cook in a tall, narrow slow cooker to ensure that there is enough liquid to cover the beans. To serve as a main course, double the quantities and cook in a large slow cooker.

Saucy Pinto Beans with Chorizo Sausage

Chorizo, a spicy sausage available in most supermarkets in either a soft or hard, cured version, gives this rustic dish an elegant touch. Serve this to guests with a basket of hot garlic bread, a big tossed salad and good Spanish wine, such as Rioja. Hot Italian sausage can be substituted for soft chorizo and cranberry or red kidney beans for pinto beans. • *SERVES 6 TO 8*

4 oz	bacon, cut into small cubes	100 g
2	onions, finely chopped	2
6	cloves garlic, minced	6
1 tsp	dried thyme leaves	5 mL
1 tsp	celery seeds	5 mL
1 tsp	cumin seeds	5 mL
2 tbsp	chili powder	25 mL
2 tbsp	balsamic vinegar	25 mL
1	can (5½ oz/156 mL) tomato paste	1
1	can (10 oz/284 mL) condensed beef broth (undiluted)	1
2 cups	dried pinto beans, cooked and rinsed (see Preparing Dried Beans, page 17), or 2 cans (19 oz/540 mL) pinto beans, drained and rinsed	500 mL
2 lbs	soft chorizo sausage	1 kg

Make ahead

This dish can be assembled the night before it is cooked but without adding the sausage. Complete Steps 1 and 2 and refrigerate overnight. The next day, continue cooking as directed in Step 3. Alternately, beans may be cooked overnight in slow cooker. Cover and refrigerate until you're ready to serve. In a Dutch oven, bring to a boil and simmer for 5 to 10 minutes. Add hot sausages when they are cooked (Step 4).

1. In a skillet, over medium-high heat, cook bacon until crisp. Remove with a slotted spoon and drain on paper towel. Pour off all but 1 tbsp (15 mL) of fat in pan.

2. Reduce heat to medium. Add onions to pan and cook until soft. Add garlic, thyme, celery seeds, cumin seeds, chili power and cook, stirring, for 1 minute. Add balsamic vinegar, tomato paste and beef broth. Pour mixture into stoneware. Add beans, bacon and water, barely to cover. Stir well.

3. Cover and cook on **Low** for 8 to 10 hours or on **High** for 4 to 5 hours, until hot and bubbly.

4. Forty-five minutes prior to serving, prick sausages all over with a fork and place in a large skillet. Cover with water, bring to boil and simmer for 10 minutes. Drain. Return sausage to pan and brown on all sides over medium-high heat. Cut into 2-inch (5-cm) lengths and add to beans. Cover and cook on **High** for 30 minutes, until mixture is hot and bubbling.

Gingery Chickpeas in Spicy Tomato Gravy

This zesty stew can be served as a vegetarian main course or as a rich side dish to accompany roasted meat or grilled fish. At our house, we like to eat it with hot naan or pita bread and a cool cucumber salad. • *SERVES 6 TO 8*

1 tbsp	vegetable oil	15 mL
2	onions, finely chopped	2
4	cloves garlic, finely chopped	4
2 tbsp	minced gingerroot	25 mL
2 tsp	ground coriander	10 mL
1 tsp	cumin seeds	5 mL
1 tsp	salt	5 mL
½ tsp	black pepper	2 mL
2 tsp	balsamic vinegar	10 mL
2 cups	coarsely chopped tomatoes, canned or fresh	500 mL
2	cans (19 oz/540 mL) chickpeas, rinsed and drained, or 2 cups (500 mL) dried chickpeas, cooked and drained	2
	Chopped green onion (optional)	

Make ahead

This dish can be completely assembled the night before it is cooked. Complete Step 1 and refrigerate overnight. The next day, continue cooking as directed in Step 2.

1. In a skillet, heat oil over medium heat. Add onions and cook, stirring, until they begin to brown, about 10 minutes. Add garlic, gingerroot, coriander, cumin seeds, salt and pepper and cook, stirring, for 1 minute. Add balsamic vinegar and tomatoes and bring to a boil. Place chickpeas in slow cooker stoneware. Pour tomato mixture over and stir well.

2. Cover and cook on **Low** for 6 to 8 hours or on **High** for 3 to 4 hours, until hot and bubbling. Garnish with chopped green onion, if using.

Savory Chickpea Stew with Roasted Red Pepper Coulis

I love this mixture of Mediterranean and Indian flavors, with a Red Pepper Coulis for a contemporary flair. • *SERVES 6 TO 8*

Stew

1	large eggplant, peeled, cut into 2-inch (5-cm) cubes and drained of excess moisture (see Tip, page 22)	1
1 tbsp	vegetable oil	15 mL
1	large onion, finely chopped	1
4	cloves garlic, finely chopped	4
2 tsp	cumin seeds	10 mL
1 tsp	dried oregano leaves	5 mL
½ tsp	turmeric	2 mL
1 cup	condensed chicken or vegetable broth (undiluted) (see Tip, right)	250 mL
1	can (28 oz/796 mL) tomatoes, including juice, coarsely chopped (see Tip, page 32)	1
2	large potatoes, cut into ½-inch (1-cm) cubes	2
1	can (19 oz/540 mL) chickpeas, rinsed and drained, or 1 cup (250 mL) dried chickpeas, cooked and drained	1

Red Pepper Coulis

2	roasted red bell peppers (see Tip, page 70)	2
3	oil-packed sun-dried tomatoes, chopped	3
2 tbsp	extra-virgin olive oil	25 mL
1 tbsp	balsamic vinegar	15 mL
10	fresh basil leaves (optional) (see Tip, right)	10

Make ahead

This dish can be completely assembled the night before it is cooked except for the Coulis. Complete Step 1 and refrigerate overnight. The next day, continue cooking as directed in Step 2. Alternately, the stew may be cooked overnight and refrigerated until you're ready to serve. In a Dutch oven, bring to a boil and simmer for 5 to 10 minutes before serving.

Tip

If you can't find condensed vegetable broth, make your own with a vegetable bouillon powder by doubling the recommended quantity of powder for a 1-cup (250-mL) quantity.

Tip

The basil adds a nice note to the Coulis, but if you can't get fresh leaves, omit it — the Coulis will be quite tasty, anyway.

1. In a skillet, heat oil over medium heat. Add onions and cook until soft. Add sweated eggplant and cook until it begins to brown. Add garlic, cumin seeds, oregano and turmeric and cook for 1 minute. Add broth and tomatoes, stirring and breaking up with a spoon. Bring mixture to a boil and cook, stirring, for 1 minute. In slow cooker stoneware, combine potatoes and chickpeas. Pour tomato mixture over and stir to combine.

2. Cover and cook on **Low** for 8 to 10 hours or on **High** for 4 to 5 hours, until potatoes are tender.

3. To make Red Pepper Coulis: In a food processor, combine roasted peppers, sun-dried tomatoes, oil, balsamic vinegar and basil, if using, and process until smooth.

4. Ladle stew into bowls and top with coulis.

Succulent Succotash

Made with freshly picked corn, succotash has become a late summer and autumn tradition. The idea of adding a topping of Sautéed Halibut, a surprisingly tasty accompaniment, came from Thomas Keller's *The French Laundry Cookbook*. I like to make a full recipe and add halibut to half the quantity. Then I refrigerate the rest for leftovers. • *SERVES 8 TO 10*

1 tbsp	vegetable oil	15 mL
2	onions, finely chopped	2
4	stalks celery, peeled and thinly sliced	4
2	large carrots, cut in quarters lengthwise, then thinly sliced	2
4	cloves garlic, minced	4
1 tbsp	paprika	15 mL
2	sprigs fresh rosemary or 1 tbsp (15 mL) dried rosemary leaves	2
1 tsp	each salt and cracked black peppercorns	5 mL
1	can (28 oz/796 mL) tomatoes, including juice, coarsely chopped (see Tip, page 32)	1
1	can (10 oz/284 mL) condensed chicken broth (undiluted)	1
2 cups	dried lima beans, cooked and drained, or 4 cups (1 L) frozen lima beans, thawed	500 mL
2 cups	corn kernels, thawed if frozen	500 mL
1 cup	whipping cream (optional)	250 mL
	Grated Parmesan cheese (optional)	
	Freshly grated nutmeg, to taste	

Make ahead

This dish can be assembled the night before it is cooked but without adding the cream and Parmesan. Complete Step 1 and refrigerate overnight. The next day, continue cooking as directed in Step 2. Alternately, Succotash can be cooked overnight and refrigerated until you're ready to serve. In a Dutch oven, bring to a boil and simmer for 5 to 10 minutes before serving.

Tip

One pound (500 g) of halibut is an appropriate quantity for half the recipe and feeds four people as a complete meal.

1. In a skillet, heat oil over medium heat. Add onions, celery and carrots and cook, stirring, until softened. Add garlic, paprika, rosemary, salt and pepper and cook, stirring, for 1 minute. Stir in tomatoes and stock and bring to a boil. Place beans and corn in stoneware. Add contents of pan and stir well.

2. Cover and cook on **Low** for 8 to 10 hours or on **High** for 4 to 5 hours, until hot and bubbling. Stir in cream and Parmesan, if using, and season with nutmeg, to taste.

Variation

Succotash with Sautéed Halibut: On a plate, mix together ¼ cup (50 mL) all-purpose flour, 1 tsp (5 mL) paprika, ½ tsp (2 mL) each salt and pepper. Debone 1 lb (500 g) halibut steak and cut into ½-inch (1-cm) cubes. Roll halibut in flour mixture until lightly coated. Discard excess flour. In a skillet, heat 1 tbsp (15 mL) oil over medium-high heat. Add dredged halibut and sauté, stirring, until fish is nicely browned and cooked to desired doneness. Spoon succotash into a serving dish and layer halibut on top.

Sausage and Lima Bean Stew

Nothing could be easier than this elementary stew, but don't be fooled by its simplicity. The results are delicious. Just add a green salad and crusty rolls for a complete meal. Since there is nothing in the stew to toughen beans (contrary to traditional wisdom, the latest thinking is that cooking dried beans with salt actually tenderizes them), for this recipe there's no need to precook dried beans as they cook very nicely in the stew. They, do, however, need to be soaked and rinsed beforehand. • *SERVES 6 TO 8*

2 lb	Italian sausage, hot or mild	1 kg
1 tbsp	vegetable oil	15 mL
4	onions, sliced	4
4	cloves garlic, minced	4
1 tsp	cracked black peppercorns	5 mL
¼ cup	all-purpose flour	50 mL
4 cups	chicken stock	1 L
2 cups	dried lima beans, soaked, or 4 cups (1 L) frozen lima beans, thawed, or 2 cans (19 oz/540 mL) lima beans, drained and rinsed	500 mL
2	green bell peppers, thinly sliced	2

Make ahead

This dish can be partially completed the night before it is cooked. Complete Steps 1 and 2, chilling meat and onion mixture separately. Slice green peppers and cover. Refrigerate overnight. The next morning, continue cooking as directed in Step 3.

1. Remove sausage meat from casing. In a skillet, over medium-high heat, cook meat, breaking up with a spoon, until it is no longer pink. Drain off liquid and transfer to slow cooker stoneware.

2. Reduce heat to medium. Heat oil, add onions and cook until soft. Add garlic and pepper and cook, stirring, for 1 minute. Sprinkle flour over sausage mixture and cook for 2 minutes. Add stock and cook, stirring, until thickened.

3. Place beans in slow cooker stoneware and pour sausage mixture over them. Cover and cook on **Low** for 8 to 10 hours or on **High**, 4 to 5 hours, until beans are tender.

4. Add green peppers. Cover and cook on **High** for 20 minutes, until peppers are tender. Ladle into individual bowls and serve.

Potato-and-Cauliflower Dal with Spicy Shallots

This simple vegetarian curry, made with yellow split peas, is both hearty and tasty. Stir in the Spicy Shallots so their flavor will disperse throughout. • *SERVES 6 TO 8*

1 cup	yellow split peas (chana dal), soaked, drained and rinsed (see Soaking, page 17)	250 mL
2 tbsp	clarified butter or vegetable oil	25 mL
2	onions, finely chopped	2
4	stalks celery, peeled and thinly sliced	4
4	cloves garlic, minced	4
1 tbsp	minced gingerroot	15 mL
1 tsp	curry powder	5 mL
1 tsp	salt	5 mL
½ tsp	black pepper	2 mL
¼ tsp	ground nutmeg	1 mL
3 cups	vegetable broth or water	750 mL
3	potatoes, peeled and cut into ½-inch (1-cm) cubes	3
1	small cauliflower, cut into florets, or 4 cups (1 L) frozen cauliflower, thawed	1

Spicy Shallots

2 tbsp	clarified butter or vegetable oil	25 mL
2	long French shallots, thinly sliced, or 8 green onions, white part only, thinly sliced	2
¼ to ½ tsp	finely chopped chili pepper	1 to 2 mL
1 tbsp	finely chopped cilantro	15 mL
2 tbsp	balsamic vinegar or lemon juice	25 mL

Make ahead

This dish can be assembled the night before it is cooked but without adding the shallots. Complete Step 1 and refrigerate overnight. The next day, continue cooking as directed in Step 2. Alternately, the dal may be cooked overnight and refrigerated until you're ready to serve. In a Dutch oven, bring to a boil and simmer for 5 to 10 minutes before serving.

1. In a skillet, heat clarified butter or oil over medium heat. Add onions and celery and cook until softened. Add garlic, gingerroot, curry powder, salt, pepper and nutmeg and cook, stirring, for 1 minute. Add vegetable broth or water and bring to a boil. Place potatoes, cauliflower and soaked peas in slow cooker stoneware. Pour onion mixture over and stir well.

2. Cover and cook on **Low** for 8 to 10 hours or on **High** for 4 to 5 hours, until vegetables are tender.

3. To make Spicy Shallots: In a skillet, heat clarified butter or oil over medium-high heat. Add shallots and cook, stirring, until crisp. Remove pan from heat. Stir in chilies, cilantro and balsamic vinegar or lemon juice. Transfer to a small bowl. Ladle dal into individual bowls, top with Spicy Shallots and stir well.

Split Pea and Lentil Curry with Crispy Onions

This Indian-style dish appeals to vegetarians and meat eaters alike. I like to serve it with a cucumber or tomato salad, steamed rice and hot naan, an Indian flat bread, for a delicious and nutritious meal. • *SERVES 4 TO 6*

1 cup	yellow split peas (chana dal), soaked, drained and rinsed (see Soaking, page 17)	250 mL
1 tbsp	vegetable oil	15 mL
1	onion, finely chopped	1
2	cloves garlic, minced	2
1 tbsp	grated gingerroot	15 mL
2 tsp	cumin seeds	10 mL
1 tsp	coriander seeds	5 mL
1 tsp	mustard seeds	5 mL
½ tsp	turmeric	2 mL
½ tsp	cayenne pepper	2 mL
½ tsp	ground cinnamon	2 mL
1 cup	brown lentils, picked over and rinsed	250 mL
4 cups	water or vegetable stock	1 L

Crispy Onion Topping

1 tbsp	clarified butter or vegetable oil	15 mL
2	onions, cut in half vertically, then cut into paper-thin slices	2

Make ahead

This dish can be assembled the night before it is cooked but without adding the Crispy Onion Topping. Complete Step 1 and refrigerate overnight. The next day, continue cooking as directed in Step 2. Alternately, curry may be cooked overnight and refrigerated until you're ready to serve. In a Dutch oven, bring to a boil and simmer for 5 to 10 minutes before serving.

1. In a skillet, heat oil over medium heat. Add onion and cook until soft. Add garlic, gingerroot, cumin seeds, coriander seeds, mustard seeds, turmeric, cayenne and cinnamon and cook, stirring, for 1 minute. Add yellow split peas, lentils and water or broth and stir to combine.

2. Transfer mixture to slow cooker stoneware, cover and cook on **Low** for 8 to 10 hours or on **High** for 4 to 5 hours, until peas and lentils are tender.

3. To make Crispy Onion Topping: In a skillet, heat clarified butter or oil over high heat. Add onions and cook, stirring constantly, until crisp and brown. Ladle curry into individual bowls and top with crispy onions.

Balsamic-Glazed Vegetables with Hearty Lentils

Rich, flavorful lentils combine with root vegetables and a balsamic-mustard glaze in this quintessential winter dish. The addition of fresh spinach or Swiss chard adds a refreshing bit of greenery. • *SERVES 6*

1 tbsp	vegetable oil	15 mL
2	onions or leeks, white part only, cleaned and finely chopped (see Tip, page 212)	2
6	stalks celery, peeled and thinly sliced	6
6	carrots, cut into ¼-inch (0.5-cm) dice	6
4	cloves garlic, minced	4
1 tbsp	tomato paste	15 mL
¼ cup	balsamic vinegar	50 mL
1 tbsp	Dijon mustard	15 mL
2	medium potatoes, peeled and very thinly sliced	2
2 cups	brown lentils, picked over and rinsed	500 mL
4 cups	water, chicken or vegetable stock	1 L
1 lb	fresh spinach leaves or Swiss chard leaves, stems removed, washed and coarsely chopped, or 1 package (10 oz/300 g) spinach, washed and stems removed and coarsely chopped	500 g

Make ahead

This dish can be assembled the night before it is cooked but without adding the spinach. Complete Steps 1 and 2 and refrigerate overnight. The next day, continue cooking as directed in Step 3. Alternately, dish may be cooked overnight, finished in the morning (Step 4) and refrigerated until you're ready to serve. In a Dutch oven, bring to a boil and simmer for 5 to 10 minutes before serving.

1. In a skillet, heat oil over medium heat. Add onions or leeks, celery and carrots and stir to combine. Cover, reduce heat to **Low** and cook until vegetables are softened, about 10 minutes.

2. Increase heat to medium. Add garlic to pan and cook, stirring, for 1 minute. Add tomato paste, balsamic vinegar and Dijon mustard and stir to combine thoroughly. Add potatoes and stir.

3. Place lentils in slow cooker stoneware. Add contents of pan, along with stock. Stir to combine thoroughly. Cover and cook on **Low** for 8 to 10 hours or on **High** for 4 to 5 hours, until lentils are tender.

4. Stir in spinach or Swiss chard. Cover and cook on **High** for 20 to 25 minutes, until spinach is cooked and mixture is hot and bubbling.

Beef and Veal

East-West Pot Roast with Shiitake Mushroom Gravy

Thanks to my friend Margaret Hovanec for the idea of making a classic pot roast with shiitake mushroom gravy. Not surprisingly, other Asian flavors such as gingerroot, soya sauce and hoisin sauce also complement the beef. Continuing the fusion theme, I like to serve this with hot noodles, tossed in extra-virgin olive oil and sprinkled with finely chopped green onion, although it's also delicious over fluffy white rice or mashed potatoes. • *SERVES 6*

1	package (½ oz/14 g) dried shiitake mushrooms	1
1 cup	boiling water	250 mL
1 tbsp	vegetable oil	15 mL
1	beef pot roast, blade or rump, about 3½ to 4 lbs (1.5 to 2 kg)	1
4	long French shallots, thinly sliced, or 8 small shallots	4
4	cloves garlic, minced	4
1 tbsp	minced gingerroot	15 mL
1 tsp	salt	5 mL
1 tsp	cracked black peppercorns	5 mL
8 oz	fresh shiitake mushrooms, stems removed	250 g
⅓ cup	vodka (optional)	75 mL
1	can (10 oz/284 mL) condensed beef broth (undiluted)	1
¼ cup	soya sauce	50 mL
2 tbsp	oyster sauce (see Tip, page 85)	25 mL
2 tbsp	hoisin sauce	25 mL
1 tsp	finely chopped chili pepper	5 mL
2 tbsp	corn starch dissolved in 2 tbsp (25 mL) cold water	25 mL
	Hot cooked rice or mashed potatoes (optional)	

1. In a heatproof bowl, soak mushrooms in boiling water for 30 minutes. Strain through a fine sieve, reserving liquid. Pat mushrooms dry with paper towel and chop finely. Set aside.

2. In a skillet, heat oil over medium-high heat. Add roast and brown on all sides. Transfer to slow cooker stoneware.

3. Reduce heat to medium. Add shallots to pan and cook until soft. Add garlic, gingerroot, salt, pepper and reserved mushrooms. Cook for 1 minute, stirring constantly. Add fresh mushrooms and cook, stirring, for 1 or 2 minutes. Add vodka, if using, and cook, stirring, for 1 minute. Add reserved mushroom soaking liquid and beef broth and bring to a boil.

Make ahead

This dish can be partially prepared the night before it is cooked. Complete Steps 1 and 3 in method, heating 1 tbsp (15 mL) oil in pan before softening shallots. Cover and refrigerate mixture overnight. The next morning, brown roast (Step 2), or if you're pressed for time, skip this step and place roast directly in stoneware. Continue cooking as directed in Steps 4 and 5. Alternately, this dish may be cooked overnight and refrigerated. When ready to serve, spoon off congealed fat. Remove roast from sauce and slice. Place meat and solids in an ovenproof serving dish, cover with aluminum foil and place in a warm oven at 325°F (163°C) for 15 to 20 minutes until meat is heated through. Meanwhile, complete Step 5.

4. Pour mixture over roast, cover and cook on **Low** for 8 to 10 hours or on **High** for 4 to 5 hours, until meat is tender. Transfer roast to a large platter. Using a slotted spoon, remove solids from cooking liquid and arrange around roast. Cover with foil and keep warm.

5. In a saucepan, over medium heat, bring cooking liquid to a boil. Add soya sauce, oyster sauce, hoisin sauce and chili pepper, if using. Cook for 5 minutes until liquid is reduced by one third. Stir in dissolved cornstarch and cook until sauce thickens. Pour over roast and mushrooms.

Tip

Oyster sauce and hoisin sauce are usually available in the Asian section of supermarkets. They are often used in Asian cooking to enhance the flavor in sauces.

Stuffed Pot Roast in Cumin-Flavored Gravy

Western European cooks have been using anchovies to enrich sauces since the eighteenth century. The olives, sun-dried tomatoes and cumin seeds add a distinctly Mediterranean touch. Serve with crisp roasted potatoes or rice to soak up the sauce. • *SERVES 6 TO 8*

1 cup	bread crumbs	250 mL
2 tbsp	chopped fresh parsley	25 mL
1 tbsp	lemon zest	15 mL
2 tbsp	lemon juice	25 mL
1 tbsp	finely chopped anchovies or 2 tbsp (25 mL) anchovy paste	15 mL
2 tbsp	finely chopped oil-packed sun-dried tomatoes	25 mL
2 tbsp	butter, melted	25 mL
1	beef pot roast, blade or rump, about 3 to 4 lbs (1.5 to 2 kg)	1
1 tbsp	vegetable oil	15 mL
2 cups	thinly sliced onions	500 mL
2 tsp	dried thyme leaves	10 mL
1½ tbsp	cumin seeds	20 mL
¼ tsp	cayenne pepper	1 mL
¼ cup	all-purpose flour	50 mL
1	can (10 oz/284 mL) condensed beef broth (undiluted)	1
½ cup	dry red wine	125 mL
1 cup	pitted green olives, sliced	250 mL

Make ahead

This dish can be partially prepared the night before it is cooked. Combine ingredients for stuffing. Cover and refrigerate. Complete Step 3, heating 1 tbsp (15 mL) oil in pan before softening onions. Cover and refrigerate mixture overnight. The next morning, stuff roast and brown (Steps 1 and 2), or if you're pressed for time, skip browning and place roast directly in stoneware. For food safety reasons, do not stuff roast the night before it is cooked. Continue cooking as directed (Step 4).

1. In a bowl, combine bread crumbs, parsley, lemon zest and juice, anchovies or paste, sun-dried tomatoes and butter. Mix well. With a long, sharp knife, make three deep slits in roast. Fill with stuffing, using your fingers to push mixture down into slits.

2. In a large skillet, heat oil over medium-high heat. Add roast and brown on all sides, being careful not to dislodge stuffing. Transfer to slow cooker stoneware.

3. Reduce heat to medium. Add onions to skillet and cook until softened. Add thyme, cumin seeds, cayenne and flour and cook for 1 more minute. Pour in stock and red wine, bring to boil and cook, stirring, until thickened.

4. Pour mixture over roast. Cover and cook on **Low** for 10 to 12 hours, until meat is tender. Increase heat to **High**, add olives and cook for another 15 minutes, until heated through.

Easy Pot Roast with Rich Tomato Gravy

There's no substitute for a simple old-fashioned pot roast — the kind my mother used to make. Its appetizing aromas, wafting through the house, are every bit as good as the meal itself. This easy-to-make version uses a can of tomato soup to create a rich sumptuous gravy. I've added a brown sugar and vinegar finish, which creates a subtle sweet-and-sour taste, but the gravy is delicious without this addition. Whichever version you prefer, serve this with plenty of mashed potatoes to soak up the sauce. • *SERVES 6 TO 8*

1	beef pot roast, cross rib or rump, about 3 to 4 lbs (1.5 to 2 kg)	1
1 tbsp	vegetable oil	15 mL
2	onions, thinly sliced	2
3	stalks celery, peeled and thinly sliced	3
3	large carrots, peeled and cut into ½-inch (1-cm) cubes	3
2	cloves garlic, minced	2
1 tsp	dry mustard	5 mL
½ tsp	dried thyme leaves	2 mL
1 tsp	salt	5 mL
¼ to ½ tsp	cracked black peppercorns	1 to 2 mL
2 tbsp	all-purpose flour	25 mL
1	can (10 oz/284 mL) condensed tomato soup	1
½ cup	condensed beef broth (undiluted)	125 mL
1 tbsp	Worcestershire sauce	15 mL
2 tbsp	packed brown sugar (optional)	25 mL
2 tbsp	balsamic or red wine vinegar (optional)	25 mL

1. Pat roast dry with paper towel. In a skillet, heat oil over medium-high heat. Add roast and cook, turning, until brown on all sides, about 7 to 10 minutes. Transfer to slow cooker stoneware.

2. Reduce heat to medium. Add onions, celery and carrots to pan and cook, stirring, until vegetables are softened. Add garlic, mustard, thyme, salt and pepper and cook, stirring, for 1 minute. Sprinkle mixture with flour and stir. Add tomato soup and beef broth and cook, stirring, until thickened. Stir in Worcestershire sauce.

3. Pour mixture over roast, cover and cook on **Low** for 10 to 12 hours or on **High** for 5 to 6 hours, until meat is very tender. Remove roast from slow cooker and place on serving platter. Stir in brown sugar and vinegar, if using, to pan juices. Pour sauce over roast or serve in a separate sauceboat. Serve piping hot.

Make ahead

This dish can be partially prepared the night before it is cooked. Complete Step 2, heating 1 tbsp (15 mL) oil in pan before softening onions, celery and carrots. Cover and refrigerate mixture overnight. The next morning, brown roast (Step 1), or if you're pressed for time, skip this step and place roast directly in stoneware. Continue cooking as directed in Step 3. Alternately, cook roast overnight. Stir in brown sugar and vinegar, if using. Cover and refrigerate. When ready to serve, spoon off congealed fat, remove meat from sauce and slice. Place sliced meat in a Dutch oven, cover with sauce and bring to a boil. Simmer, covered, for 10 minutes and serve.

Low Country Pot Roast with Gingersnap Gravy

I first tasted gingersnap gravy when we visited Charleston, South Carolina, for our nephew's wedding. On that trip, and on subsequent excursions through the "Low Country" area, we pursued the distinctive and delicious cuisine of this beautiful region, returning with many fond memories and unique culinary discoveries such as this snappy addition to a Sunday pot roast. • *SERVES 6 TO 8*

1	beef pot roast, cross rib or rump, about 3 to 4 lbs (1.5 to 2 kg)	1
1 tbsp	vegetable oil	15 mL
2	medium onions, finely chopped	2
2	stalks celery, peeled and thinly sliced	2
3	cloves garlic, minced	3
2 tbsp	minced gingerroot	25 mL
1 tbsp	chili powder	15 mL
½ tsp	ground nutmeg	2 mL
1 tsp	salt	5 mL
1 tsp	cracked black peppercorns	5 mL
¼ cup	all-purpose flour	50 mL
1 cup	condensed beef broth (undiluted)	250 mL
1 tbsp	balsamic or red wine vinegar	15 mL
½ cup	sour cream	125 mL
½ cup	gingersnap crumbs (see Tip, page 164)	125 mL
	Mashed potatoes or hot cooked rice	

1. Pat roast dry with paper towel. In a large skillet, heat oil over medium-high heat. Add roast and cook, turning, until brown on all sides, about 7 to 10 minutes. Transfer to slow cooker stoneware.

2. Reduce heat to medium. Add onions and celery to skillet and cook, stirring often, until softened. Add garlic, ginger, chili powder, nutmeg, salt and pepper and cook, stirring, for 1 minute. Sprinkle flour over mixture and cook, stirring, for 1 minute. Add beef broth and vinegar and cook until thickened.

3. Pour mixture over meat, cover and cook on **Low** for 10 to 12 hours, until meat is tender.

4. Add sour cream and gingersnaps and cook for 20 minutes on **High**, until hot and bubbling. Serve over mashed potatoes or rice.

Make ahead

This dish can be partially prepared the night before it is cooked. Complete Step 2, heating 1 tbsp (15 mL) oil in pan before softening vegetables. Cover and refrigerate mixture overnight. The next morning, brown roast (Step 1), or skip this step and place roast directly in stoneware. Continue cooking as directed in Steps 3 and 4. Alternately, cook the roast overnight. Cover and refrigerate. When you're ready to serve, spoon off congealed fat, remove roast from liquid and slice. Place meat in an ovenproof serving dish, cover with aluminum foil and place in a warm oven at 325°F (163°C) until meat is heated through. Meanwhile, in a pot, bring sauce to a simmer and complete Step 4. Pour over meat and serve.

Beef Noodle Casserole with Cheddar-Crumb Topping

This delicious comfort food dish is a favorite with kids and adults. There's something about the combination of well-seasoned beef, soft bland noodles and creamy cheese that is irresistible. I like to serve this with a big tossed salad — plenty of tomatoes, lots of Boston lettuce and a handful of mesclun greens in a pungent balsamic-mustard vinaigrette which I make by mixing 2 tbsp (25 mL) balsamic vinegar with 1 tsp (5 mL) Dijon mustard. Then I whisk in ¼ cup (50 mL) extra-virgin olive oil and season, to taste, with salt and pepper. Hope for leftovers as this casserole is delicious reheated. • *SERVES 4 TO 6*

- **LARGE (MINIMUM 5 QUART) OVAL SLOW COOKER**
- **LIGHTLY GREASED SLOW COOKER STONEWARE**

2 tbsp	vegetable oil, divided	25 mL
1 lb	lean ground beef	500 g
2	onions, finely chopped	2
4	stalks celery, peeled and thinly sliced	4
4	cloves garlic, minced	4
1 tsp	salt	5 mL
1 tsp	cracked black peppercorns	5 mL
2 tsp	dried oregano leaves	10 mL
1 tsp	dry mustard	5 mL
1	can (10 oz/284 mL) condensed beef broth (undiluted)	1
1	can (8 oz/250 mL) tomato sauce	1
4 oz	cream cheese, softened and cubed	125 g
8 oz	egg noodles, cooked and drained	250 g

Cheddar-Crumb Topping

1 cup	bread crumbs	250 g
2 tbsp	melted butter	25 mL
1 cup	shredded Cheddar cheese	250 mL

Make ahead

This dish can be partially prepared the night before it is cooked. Complete Steps 1 and 2, chilling cooked meat and onion mixture separately. Refrigerate overnight. The next morning, continue cooking as directed in Steps 3 and 4. To facilitate preparation, the night before you plan to cook this casserole, shred Cheddar cheese, cover and refrigerate.

1. In a skillet, heat 1 tbsp (15 mL) oil over medium-high heat. Add beef and cook, stirring and breaking up with the back of a spoon, until no longer pink, about 5 minutes. Remove with a slotted spoon and set aside. Drain off liquid in pan.

2. Add remaining oil to pan, return to element and reduce heat to medium. Add onions and celery and cook until softened. Add garlic, salt, pepper, oregano and mustard and cook, stirring, for 1 minute. Add beef broth, tomato sauce and cream cheese and cook, stirring, until cheese is melted.

3. To assemble casserole: Spoon ½ cup (125 mL) tomato-sauce mixture in bottom of slow cooker stoneware. Cover with a layer of meat, then noodles. Repeat, finishing with a layer of sauce. Cover and cook on **Low** for 8 to 10 hours or on **High** for 4 to 5 hours, until mixture is hot and bubbling.

4. To make Cheddar-Crumb Topping: In a bowl, combine bread crumbs and butter. Add cheese and stir to combine. Spread over casserole and cook on **High** for 30 minutes, until cheese is melted and top is bubbling.

Great Goulash with Potato Dumplings

I discovered the affinity between tomatoes and gin by accident, many years ago, while spending a weekend in the country. Our hostess offered to make Bloody Marys, then discovered there was no vodka. Since necessity is the mother of invention, she made the drinks with gin, which were every bit as tasty as the original. I don't know if that's the secret to this delicious goulash, but it always disappears to the last mouthful. The potato dumplings are a nice touch for presentation, but if you're short of time, serve the stew over mashed potatoes or hot buttered noodles. • *SERVES 6*

1 tbsp	vegetable oil	15 mL
2 lbs	stewing beef, cut into ½-inch (1-cm) cubes	1 kg
2	onions, finely chopped	2
4	cloves garlic, minced	4
2 tbsp	paprika	25 mL
1 tbsp	caraway seeds	15 mL
1 tsp	dried marjoram	5 mL
1 tsp	salt	5 mL
1 tsp	cracked black peppercorns	5 mL
¼ cup	all-purpose flour	50 mL
¼ cup	tomato paste	50 mL
¼ cup	gin (optional)	50 mL
1	can (10 oz/284 mL) condensed beef broth (undiluted)	1
	Zest of 1 lemon	
½ cup	sour cream	125 mL

Potato Dumplings

4	medium potatoes	4
½ cup	bread crumbs	125 mL
1	egg, lightly beaten	1
2 tbsp	milk	25 mL
1 tbsp	all-purpose flour, plus additional for dusting dumplings	15 mL
½ tsp	salt	2 mL
¼ cup	finely chopped parsley or chives	50 mL

1. In a skillet, heat oil over medium-high heat. Add beef, in batches, and brown. Transfer to slow cooker stoneware.

continued on page 94

Make ahead

This dish can be partially prepared the night before it is cooked. Cook potatoes and chill in skins. Complete Step 2, heating 1 tbsp (15 mL) oil in pan before softening onions. Cover and refrigerate mixture overnight. The next morning, brown beef (Step 1), or if you're pressed for time, skip this step and place meat directly in stoneware. Continue cooking as directed following Steps 3 through 6. Alternately, cook goulash overnight (Steps 1 through 3). Cover and refrigerate. When ready to serve, bring to a boil in a Dutch oven and simmer for 10 minutes, until mixture is hot and bubbling and meat is heated through. Add sour cream. Make dumplings and cook on stovetop for approximately 15 minutes (Steps 4 through 6).

2. Reduce heat to medium. Add onions to pan and cook until softened. Add garlic, paprika, caraway seeds, marjoram, salt and pepper and cook, stirring, for 1 minute. Add flour and cook, stirring, for 2 minutes. Add tomato paste and stir well. Add gin, if using, and cook, stirring, until almost all the liquid evaporates (this will only take a few seconds). Pour in beef broth and cook, stirring, until thickened. Stir in lemon zest.

3. Pour mixture over beef. Stir to combine. Cover and cook on **Low** for 8 to 10 hours or on **High** for 4 to 5 hours, until beef is tender.

4. To make Potato Dumplings: In a large pot of boiling salted water, cook potatoes in skins. Drain and allow to cool until they can be handled easily. Lift skins off and squeeze potatoes through a ricer, or mash with a potato masher until smooth. Set aside.

5. In a bowl, combine bread crumbs, egg, milk, flour, salt and parsley or chives. Add potatoes and mix well. Form mixture into balls approximately 2 inches (5 cm) in diameter. Sprinkle additional flour over a cutting board or plate. Roll dumplings in flour until they are lightly coated.

6. Stir sour cream into goulash. Add dumplings, spooning some sauce over them to ensure that they are well-coated with liquid. Cover and cook on **High** for 20 minutes, until mixture is bubbling. Serve immediately .

Greek Beef Stew with Onions and Feta Cheese

This robust stew, known as *Stiffado* in Greece, is different and delicious. The feta and vinegar add tartness, which is nicely balanced by a tiny bit of sugar, along with cinnamon and allspice. Use only good quality tomato sauce and serve as the Greeks do, with long strands of hot buttered macaroni, often known as bucatini (not the usual broken or stubby variety) or fluffy mashed potatoes. • *SERVES 6 TO 8*

1 tbsp	vegetable oil	15 mL
2 lbs	stewing beef, cut into 1-inch (2.5-cm) cubes	1 kg
3	large onions, finely chopped	3
4	cloves garlic, minced	4
½ tsp	ground cinnamon	2 mL
½ tsp	ground allspice	2 mL
3 tbsp	red wine vinegar	45 mL
1½ cups	tomato sauce	375 mL
1 tsp	sugar	5 mL
1	bay leaf	1
1 cup	crumbled feta cheese	250 mL
	Macaroni, noodles or mashed potatoes	

1. In a skillet, heat oil over medium-high heat. Brown beef in batches, adding more oil, if necessary, and transfer with a slotted spoon to slow cooker stoneware.

2. Reduce heat to medium. Add onions to pan and cook until soft. Add garlic, cinnamon and allspice and cook for 1 minute. Add vinegar, tomato sauce, sugar and bay leaf and stir to combine.

3. Pour mixture over meat and cook on **Low** for 8 to 10 hours or on **High** for 4 to 5 hours, until beef is tender.

4. Add feta cheese and cook on **High** for 10 minutes. Discard bay leaf. Spoon over hot buttered macaroni, noodles or mashed potatoes.

Variation

Party-Style Stiffado: For a special-occasion dish, substitute 2 lbs (1 kg) pearl onions for the chopped onions. To peel pearl onions, cut a small "x" in the bottom and drop in a pot of boiling water for 1 minute. Drain and rinse under cold running water. The skins will come off easily with a paring knife.

Make ahead

This dish can be partially prepared the night before it is cooked. Complete Step 2, heating 1 tbsp (15 mL) oil in pan before softening onions. Cover and refrigerate mixture overnight. The next morning, brown beef (Step 1), or if you're pressed for time, skip this step and add meat directly to stoneware. Continue cooking as directed in Steps 3 and 4. Alternately, cook stew overnight, completing Step 3. When you're ready to serve, bring to a boil in a Dutch oven and simmer for 10 minutes, until meat is heated through and sauce is bubbling. Complete Step 4 and serve.

Classic Boeuf Bourguignon

To the French, this is comfort food — a long-simmered dish that evokes warm memories of childhood. To North Americans, it's great bistro food — flavorful and hearty, perfectly suited to a full-bodied red wine and lively evenings with friends. Either way, it's perfect for the slow cooker and great as a leftover since it's even better reheated. Serve with new potatoes in their skins, buttered noodles or plain white rice and a simple green vegetable such as beans or broccoli. • *SERVES 8*

1 tbsp	vegetable oil	15 mL
4 oz	chunk of bacon or salt pork belly, cut into ½-inch (1-cm) cubes	125 g
2 lbs	stewing beef, cut into 1-inch (2.5-cm) cubes	1 kg
1 lb	mushrooms, whole or halved, depending on size	500 g
3	carrots, peeled and thinly sliced	3
2	onions, thinly sliced	2
2	cloves garlic, minced	2
1 tsp	dried thyme leaves or 2 sprigs fresh thyme	5 mL
1 tsp	salt	5 mL
½ tsp	black pepper	2 mL
½ cup	all-purpose flour	125 mL
½ cup	condensed beef broth (undiluted)	125 mL
2 cups	dry red wine	500 mL
1	bay leaf	1
	Zest of 1 orange	
	Chopped parsley	

1. In a large skillet, heat oil over medium-high heat. Add bacon or salt pork and cook until crisp. Remove with a slotted spoon and drain on paper towel. Drain off all but 2 tbsp (25 mL) fat in pan.

2. Add beef to pan, in batches, and brown. Transfer to slow cooker, using a slotted spoon.

3. Add mushrooms to pan and cook until tops are lightly browned. Using a slotted spoon, transfer to slow cooker stoneware. Reduce heat to medium-low. Add carrots and onion to pan. Cover and cook until vegetables are softened, about 10 minutes. Increase heat to medium. Add garlic, thyme, salt and pepper and cook, stirring, for 1 minute. Add flour and cook, stirring, for 1 minute. Add beef broth and wine and cook, stirring, until thickened. Stir in bacon or salt pork, bay leaf and orange zest.

4. Add mixture to slow cooker stoneware. Stir to thoroughly combine ingredients. Cover and cook on **Low** for 8 to 10 hours or on **High** for 4 to 5 hours, until beef is very tender. Discard bay leaf. Just before serving, garnish liberally with parsley.

Make ahead

This dish can be partially prepared the night before it is cooked. Complete Steps 1 and 3, stirring browned mushrooms into wine mixture. Cover and refrigerate mixture overnight. The next morning, brown beef (Step 2), or if you're pressed for time, skip this step and place beef directly in stoneware. Continue cooking as directed in Step 4. Alternately, cook beef overnight, following Steps 1 through 4. Cover and refrigerate. When ready to serve, bring to a boil in a Dutch oven and simmer for 10 minutes, until mixture is hot and bubbling and meat is heated through. Garnish with parsley.

Hearty Carbonnade

On a cold winter day, there is nothing more satisfying than the aroma of a hearty beef stew bubbling away. This classic Belgian dish, cooked in beer, is one of the best. Serve with mashed potatoes or hot buttered noodles and plenty of bread to soak up the luscious sauce. Occasionally, when I feel the need for spice, I add some finely chopped chili peppers just before serving. • *SERVES 6*

1 tbsp	vegetable oil	15 mL
4 oz	chunk of bacon or salt pork belly, cut into ¼-inch (0.5-cm) dice	125 g
2 lbs	stewing beef, cut into 1-inch (2.5-cm) cubes	1 kg
4	medium onions, thinly sliced	4
4	cloves garlic, minced	4
2 tsp	dried thyme leaves	10 mL
1 tsp	celery seeds	5 mL
1	bay leaf	1
1 tsp	salt	5 mL
1 tsp	cracked black peppercorns	5 mL
1 tbsp	granulated sugar	15 mL
¼ cup	all-purpose flour	50 mL
2 cups	beer	500 mL

1. In a skillet, heat oil over medium-high heat. Add bacon or salt pork and cook until crisp. Remove with a slotted spoon and drain on paper towel. Set aside. Drain off all but 1 tbsp (15 mL) fat in pan.

2. Over medium-high heat, brown meat in batches. Using a slotted spoon, transfer to slow cooker.

3. Reduce heat to medium. Add onions to pan and cook until soft. Add garlic, thyme, celery seeds, bay leaf, salt and pepper and cook for 1 minute. Sprinkle sugar over mixture and stir well. Add flour and cook, stirring, for 1 minute. Add bacon and beer and cook until mixture thickens.

4. Pour mixture over beef. Cover and cook on **Low** for 8 to 10 hours or on **High** for 4 to 5 hours, until meat is tender. Discard bay leaf. Serve immediately.

Make ahead

This dish can be partially prepared the night before it is cooked. Complete Steps 1 and 3. Cover and refrigerate mixture overnight. The next morning, heat 1 tbsp (15 mL) oil in pan and brown beef (Step 2), or skip this step and place meat directly in stoneware. Continue cooking as directed in Step 4. Alternately, cook Carbonnade overnight, following Steps 1 through 4. Cover and refrigerate. When ready to serve, bring to a boil in a Dutch oven and simmer for 10 minutes, until mixture is hot and bubbling and meat is heated through.

Cuban Picadillo
with Pimento-Stuffed Olives

This easy and delicious dish can best be described as a Cuban version of hash. We like to eat it topped with a fried egg and accompanied by Fried Plantains (see recipe, below). • *SERVES 6*

2 tbsp	vegetable oil, divided	25 mL
2 lbs	lean ground beef	1 kg
4	cloves garlic, minced	4
1	jalapeño pepper, finely chopped	1
2 tsp	dried oregano leaves	10 mL
1 tsp	salt	5 mL
½ tsp	black pepper	2 mL
¼ tsp	ground cinnamon	1 mL
2	whole cloves	2
1	bay leaf	1
1	can (5½ oz/156 mL) tomato paste	1
2 tbsp	red wine vinegar	25 mL
12	large pimento-stuffed olives, sliced	12

Fried Plantains

2 tbsp	butter	25 mL
4	plantains, thinly sliced	4
2 tbsp	lemon or lime juice	25 mL

Make ahead

This dish can be partially prepared the night before it is cooked. Complete Steps 1 and 2, chilling cooked meat and tomato mixture separately. Refrigerate overnight. The next morning, continue cooking as directed in Step 3.

Tip

This recipe is great as is, but if you want to dress it up for friends, add a chili-almond garnish. Melt 2 tbsp (25 mL) butter in a small saucepan over low heat. Add 1 tsp (5 mL) chili powder and cook for 1 minute. Add ¼ cup (50 mL) slivered almonds and cook, stirring, until they begin to turn brown. Spoon over the Picadillo.

1. In a skillet, heat 1 tbsp (15 mL) oil over medium-high heat. Add beef and cook, breaking up with a wooden spoon, until no longer pink. Using a slotted spoon, transfer to slow cooker stoneware. Drain off liquid from pan.

2. Reduce heat to medium. Add remaining oil to pan. Add garlic, jalapeño pepper, oregano, salt, black pepper, cinnamon, cloves and bay leaf and cook, stirring, for 1 minute. Stir in tomato paste and red wine vinegar and bring mixture to a boil.

3. Pour mixture over meat and stir well. Cover and cook on **Low** for 8 to 10 hours or on **High** for 4 to 5 hours, until mixture is hot and bubbling.

4. Stir in olives. Cover and cook on **High** for 20 minutes, until heated through. Serve immediately.

5. To make Fried Plantains: In a skillet, melt butter over medium heat. Add plantains and cook until brown. Pour lemon or lime juice over top and serve hot.

Braised Beef Curry with Fragrant Spices

In this Indian-inspired dish, chunks of beef cook in their own juices, seasoned with spices. You'll love the aroma wafting through your house as the beef cooks. Using whole spices such as cloves and coriander seeds and cinnamon sticks, rather than ground versions, improves the result since they release their flavor slowly as the curry cooks. Serve with lots of fluffy white rice and Indian bread such as naan to soak up the delicious sauce. • *SERVES 6*

1 tbsp	vegetable oil	15 mL
2 lbs	stewing beef, cut into 1-inch (2.5-cm) cubes	1 kg
2	medium onions, finely chopped	2
4	cloves garlic, minced	4
1 tbsp	minced gingerroot	15 mL
1 tbsp	coriander seeds	15 mL
1 tsp	turmeric	5 mL
½ tsp	fennel seeds	2 mL
1	2-inch (5-cm) piece of cinnamon stick	1
4	whole cloves	4
2	serrano chilies, finely chopped (see Tip, page 138)	2
1 tsp	salt	5 mL
1 tsp	cracked black peppercorns	5 mL
¼ cup	condensed beef broth (undiluted)	50 mL

1. In a skillet, heat oil over medium-high heat. Brown beef, in batches, and, using a slotted spoon, transfer to slow cooker stoneware.

2. Reduce heat to medium. Add onions to pan and cook until soft. Add garlic, ginger, coriander, turmeric, fennel, cinnamon, cloves, chili peppers, salt and pepper and cook, stirring, for 1 minute. Add beef broth and bring to a boil.

3. Pour mixture over beef. Cover and cook on **Low** for 8 to 10 hours or on **High** for 4 to 5 hours, until beef is tender. Serve immediately.

Make ahead

This dish can be partially prepared the night before it is cooked. Complete Step 2, heating 1 tbsp (15 mL) oil in pan before softening onions. Cover and refrigerate mixture overnight. The next morning, brown beef (Step 1), or skip this step and place meat directly in stoneware. Continue cooking as directed in Step 3. Alternately, cook beef overnight. Cover and refrigerate. When ready to serve, bring to a boil in a Dutch oven and simmer for 10 minutes, until mixture is hot and bubbling and meat is heated through.

South African Bobotie

Don't be fooled by the exotic name. A popular South African dish, *Bobotie* is a simple baked curry topped with an egg and milk sauce. This version uses beef and dried apricots and fits the bill if your tastebuds are desperately seeking new sensations. I've served Bobotie to a wide group of people, from sophisticated adults to picky teenagers, always with enthusiastic results. Serve with fluffy white rice, a bowl of good chutney and enjoy! • *SERVES 6 TO 8*

2 tbsp	vegetable oil, divided	25 mL
2 lbs	lean ground beef	1 kg
2	medium onions, finely chopped	2
4	cloves garlic, minced	4
2 tbsp	curry powder	25 mL
1 tsp	salt	5 mL
½ tsp	black pepper	2 mL
½ cup	dried apricots	125 mL
1 cup	bread crumbs	250 mL
2	eggs, beaten	2
½ cup	whipping cream	125 mL

Make ahead

This dish can be partially prepared the night before it is cooked. Complete Steps 1 and 2, chilling cooked meat and onion mixture separately. Refrigerate overnight. The next morning, continue cooking as directed in Steps 3 and 4.

1. In a skillet, heat 1 tbsp (15 mL) oil over medium-high heat. Add beef and cook, stirring often, until meat is no longer pink. Using a slotted spoon, transfer to slow cooker stoneware. Drain off liquid in pan.

2. Reduce heat to medium. Add remaining oil to pan. Add onions and cook until soft. Add garlic, curry powder, salt and pepper and cook for 1 minute. Remove from heat.

3. Add apricots and bread crumbs, combine well and transfer mixture to slow cooker stoneware. Mix well to integrate with meat mixture. Cover and cook on **Low** for 6 to 8 hours or on **High** for 3 to 4 hours, until mixture is hot and bubbling.

4. In a small bowl, combine eggs and cream. Mix well. Pour over meat mixture. Cover and cook on **High** for 30 minutes, until top is set.

Italian-Style Meat Loaf with Sage

The addition of fresh sage and pancetta makes this an especially succulent and flavorful meat loaf. Pancetta, Italian cured bacon, is available in most supermarkets or in specialty stores. Although it imparts a unique flavor to this dish, if you can't find it, use prosciutto instead. Serve this with mashed or baked potatoes and a green salad. • *SERVES 6*

2 lbs	lean ground beef	1 kg
2	onions, finely chopped	2
¼ lb	pancetta, finely chopped	125 g
15	fresh sage leaves, finely chopped (see Tip, right)	15
¼ cup	freshly grated Parmesan cheese	50 mL
2	eggs, lightly beaten	2
¾ cup	fine, dry bread crumbs	175 mL

1. Fold a 2-foot (60-cm) piece of aluminum foil in half lengthwise. Place on bottom and up the sides of slow cooker stoneware.

2. In a large bowl, combine ingredients and mix well. Shape into loaf and place in middle of foil strip on bottom of slow cooker. Cover and cook on **Low** for 8 to 10 hours or on **High** for 4 to 5 hours, until juices run clear when meat loaf is pierced with a fork or a meat thermometer reads 170°F (75°C). Lift loaf out using foil strip and, using a large lifter, transfer to a warm platter. Garnish with fresh sage leaves, if available. Pour juice into a sauceboat and serve alongside, with plenty of fluffy mashed potatoes.

Tip

To ease chopping, coarsely chop onions, sage and pancetta, then pulse in a food processor.

Tip

Fresh sage is a fundamental ingredient in Italian cooking, although it can be difficult to find in North American supermarkets. If you have a garden, it's an easy-to-grow perennial which is almost indestructible. In this recipe, you can substitute ½ cup (125 mL) chopped Italian parsley and ½ tsp (2 mL) dried sage for the fresh sage leaves.

Memories of Mortimer's Meat Loaf

Mortimer's, which no longer exists, used to be a restaurant on Manhattan's upper east side that specialized in serving comfort food to many of New York's rich and famous. Its meat loaf was particularly well loved by regulars, including designer Bill Blass who shared his recipe with readers of *Vogue* magazine many years ago. It has been a favorite at our house ever since. I love to serve this with that other ultimate comfort food — scalloped potatoes. The original version calls for strips of bacon to be layered over the loaf before it is baked. For the slow cooker version, I've incorporated cooked bacon into the loaf itself. • *SERVES 6 TO 8*

2	slices bacon, cooked to crisp, then crumbled	2
1 lb	lean ground beef	500 g
1 lb	lean ground pork	500 g
1 lb	ground veal	500 g
3	stalks celery, peeled and finely diced	3
½ cup	finely chopped parsley	125 mL
½ cup	tomato-based chili sauce (see Tip, right)	125 mL
2	eggs, lightly beaten	2
½ cup	fine, dry bread crumbs	125 mL
1 tbsp	Worcestershire sauce	15 mL
Pinch	dried marjoram	Pinch
1 tsp	salt	5 mL
½ tsp	black pepper	2 mL

Tip

Tomato-based chili sauce is the kind I grew up with — at our house we always had a bottle of Heinz 57 in the fridge and it's still good enough for me. Nowadays, with so many sauces made from chili peppers widely available, I like to specify the kind of chili sauce called for in a recipe to avoid potential confusion.

1. Fold a 2-foot (60-cm) piece of aluminum foil in half lengthwise. Place on bottom and up the sides of slow cooker stoneware.

2. In a large bowl, combine ingredients and mix well. Shape into loaf and place on foil stoneware in slow cooker. Tuck ends of foil under lid. Cover and cook on **Low** for 8 to 10 hours or on **High** for 4 to 5 hours, or until juices run clear when meat loaf is pierced with a fork or meat thermometer reads 170°F (75°C).

Hot Italian Meatball Sandwiches

Everyone loves these zesty, oversized sandwiches which make a great weeknight dinner or weekend lunch. If you're certain that everyone likes the same degree of hotness, add the roasted banana peppers to the sauce just before serving. To play it safe, serve the peeled, chopped peppers in a separate dish so that people can help themselves. • *SERVES 4 TO 6*

Meatballs

1 lb	lean ground beef	500 g
¼ cup	grated onion	50 mL
2	cloves garlic, minced	2
2 tbsp	finely chopped parsley	25 mL
½ tsp	ground nutmeg	2 mL
½ tsp	salt	2 mL
½ tsp	black pepper	2 mL
2 tbsp	freshly grated Parmesan cheese	25 mL
½ cup	bread crumbs	125 mL
1 tbsp	vegetable oil	15 mL

Tomato Sauce

1	onion, finely chopped	1
2	stalks celery, peeled and thinly sliced	2
2	cloves garlic, minced	2
2 tsp	dried oregano leaves	10 mL
½ tsp	salt	2 mL
½ tsp	black pepper	2 mL
6	whole cloves	6
1	can (28 oz/796 mL) tomatoes, drained and chopped (see Tip, page 32)	1
½ cup	dry red wine	125 mL
2 to 4	banana peppers, roasted (see page 70), peeled and cut into ½-inch (1-cm) slices (see Tip, right)	2 to 4
4 to 6	kaiser buns, halved	4 to 6
	Freshly grated Parmesan cheese	

Tip

Hot banana peppers, which are long, thin, yellow peppers ending in a sharp point, are available in most supermarkets or greengrocers. Although they are fiery and should, therefore, be used with discretion, they are far more subdued than their chili pepper relatives.

1. In a bowl, combine ingredients for meatballs, except for oil, and mix well. Form into 8 balls of uniform size.

2. In a skillet, heat oil over medium-high heat. Add meatballs, in batches, if necessary, and brown on all sides. Transfer to slow cooker stoneware. Drain off all but 1 tbsp (15 mL) fat from pan. If you used extra-lean meat, you may have to add oil to reach 1 tbsp (15 mL).

continued on page 106

3. To make Tomato Sauce: Reduce heat to medium. Add onions and celery to pan and cook, stirring, until softened. Add garlic, oregano, salt, pepper and cloves and cook, stirring, for 1 minute. Stir in tomatoes and wine, bring to a boil and cook, stirring until mixture is reduced by one third, depending upon the size of your pan, about 5 minutes. Pour over meatballs, cover and cook on **Low** for 6 to 8 hours or on **High** for 3 to 4 hours, until meatballs are no longer pink inside.

4. Place 1 to 2 meatballs on one half of kaiser bun, spoon additional sauce over all and top with the other half of the bun. Serve with a small bowl containing the roasted peppers and another containing grated Parmesan cheese. Allow people to garnish to taste. These sandwiches are best eaten with a knife and fork.

Brisket of Beef with Dilled Onion Gravy

Don't let the simplicity of this recipe fool you. This is one of those yummy comfort food dishes your family will remember and request time and again. I like to add sour cream to the gravy just before serving although this isn't essential. Serve with plenty of fluffy mashed potatoes and a green vegetable, such as fresh green beans. • *SERVES 6 TO 8*

1 tbsp	vegetable oil	15 mL
4 to 5 lbs	double beef brisket, trimmed	2 to 2.5 kg
4	medium onions, thinly sliced	4
6	cloves garlic, minced	6
1 tsp	salt	5 mL
1 tbsp	cracked black peppercorns	15 mL
1 cup	chopped dill, divided	250 mL
½ cup	tomato-based chili sauce (see Tip, page 103)	125 mL
1	can (10 oz/284 mL) condensed beef broth (undiluted)	1
	Sour cream, to taste (optional)	

Make ahead

Since brisket is easier to slice when cold and tastes better reheated in its sauce, I suggest cooking this a day ahead or overnight. Once cooked, refrigerate immediately. When meat is cool, slice thinly. Place in a Dutch oven, cover with sauce and reheat on stovetop over medium-low heat. When mixture is bubbling, stir in remaining dill and sour cream, if using. Serve immediately.

1. In a skillet, heat oil over medium-high heat. Add brisket and brown well on both sides. Transfer to slow cooker stoneware.

2. Reduce heat to medium. Add onions to pan and cook until soft. Add garlic, salt, pepper and half of dill and cook for 1 minute. Add chili sauce and broth and bring to a boil. Pour mixture over brisket. Cover and cook on **Low** for 12 hours, until beef is very tender.

3. Transfer brisket to a deep platter. Stir remaining dill and sour cream, if using, into gravy and pour over meat. When ready to serve, slice thinly across the grain and top with gravy.

Southwestern Brisket

I've never met anyone, except vegetarians, who didn't enjoy a properly cooked brisket. Juicy and full of flavor, brisket is tender and delicious and lends itself to a wide variety of sauces and seasonings. This version, which relies on New Mexico chilies for its rich, tangy taste, is mildly piquant and can be enjoyed by all family members. I like to serve this over piping hot mashed potatoes. • *SERVES 8*

2	dried New Mexico chili peppers (see Tip, page 48)	2
2 cups	boiling water	500 mL
1 tbsp	vegetable oil	15 mL
4 lb	double beef brisket, trimmed	2 kg
2	onions, thinly sliced	2
6	stalks celery, peeled and thinly sliced	6
6	cloves garlic, minced	6
1 tbsp	dry mustard	15 mL
1 tbsp	dried oregano leaves	15 mL
2 tsp	cumin seeds	10 mL
1 tbsp	cracked black peppercorns	15 mL
2 tsp	salt	10 mL
¼ cup	all-purpose flour	50 mL
2 cups	tomato sauce	500 mL
½ cup	condensed beef broth (undiluted)	125 mL
¼ cup	red wine vinegar	50 mL
½ cup	packed brown sugar	125 mL
4	bay leaves	4
2	green bell peppers, thinly sliced	2
½ cup	finely chopped parsley	125 mL

Make ahead

Brisket responds very well to moist slow cooking. For best results, cook overnight on **Low** heat for 12 hours. Once cooked, refrigerate immediately. When meat is cool, slice thinly. Place in a Dutch oven, cover with sauce and reheat on stovetop over medium-low heat, until hot and bubbling. Serve immediately.

Tip

If you prefer a spicier version, add 1 to 2 finely chopped jalapeño peppers, along with the garlic.

1. In a heatproof bowl, soak New Mexico chilies in boiling water for 30 minutes. Drain, discarding soaking liquid and stems. Pat dry, chop finely and set aside.

2. In a large skillet, heat oil over medium-high heat. Brown brisket on both sides and place in slow cooker stoneware.

3. Reduce heat to medium. Add onions, celery and reserved New Mexico chili peppers to pan. Cook, stirring, until vegetables are softened. Add garlic, mustard, oregano, cumin seeds, pepper and salt and cook, stirring, for 1 minute. Sprinkle with flour and cook, stirring, for 1 minute.

4. Add tomato sauce, beef broth and red wine vinegar to pan and cook, stirring, until thickened. Stir in brown sugar and bay leaves and pour mixture over brisket. Cover and cook on **Low** for 12 hours, until brisket is very tender.

5. Stir in green peppers. Cover and cook on **High** for an additional 30 minutes, until peppers are soft. Discard bay leaf. To serve, slice brisket thinly and place on a deep platter. Spoon sauce over and garnish liberally with parsley.

Shepherd's Pie with Creamy Corn Filling

Shepherd's Pie is home cooking at its most basic. This is a great dish for those evenings when everyone is coming and going at different times. Just leave the slow cooker on Low or Warm and let people help themselves. Serve with a big tossed salad. • SERVES 6

1 tbsp	vegetable oil	15 mL
1 lb	lean ground beef	500 g
2	onions, finely chopped	2
4	cloves garlic, minced	4
2 tsp	paprika	10 mL
1 tsp	salt	5 mL
½ tsp	cracked black peppercorns	2 mL
2 tbsp	all-purpose flour	25 mL
1 cup	condensed beef broth (undiluted)	250 mL
2 tbsp	tomato paste	25 mL
1	can (19 oz/540 mL) cream-style corn	1
4 cups	mashed potatoes, seasoned with 1 tbsp (15 mL) butter, ½ tsp (2 mL) salt and ¼ tsp (1 mL) black pepper (see Tip, right)	1 L
¼ cup	shredded Cheddar cheese	50 mL

1. In a skillet, heat oil over medium-high heat. Add beef and cook, breaking up with the back of a spoon, until meat is no longer pink. Using a slotted spoon, transfer to slow cooker stoneware. Drain off liquid.

2. Reduce heat to medium. Add onions to pan and cook until softened. Add garlic, paprika, salt and pepper and cook, stirring, for 1 minute. Sprinkle flour over mixture, stir and cook for 1 minute. Add beef broth and tomato paste, stir to combine and cook, stirring, until thickened.

3. Transfer mixture to slow cooker stoneware. Spread corn evenly over mixture and top with mashed potatoes. Sprinkle cheese on top, cover and cook on **Low** for 4 to 6 hours or on **High** for 3 to 4 hours, until hot and bubbly.

Make ahead

This dish can be partially prepared the night before it is cooked. Make mashed potatoes, cover and refrigerate. Complete Steps 1 and 2, chilling cooked meat and onion mixture separately. Refrigerate overnight. The next morning, continue cooking as directed in Step 3.

Tip

For perfect mashed potatoes, invest in a ricer, a handy gadget resembling a large garlic press. It eliminates those pesky lumps and is particularly useful for this recipe, since the long cooking time rules out adding milk to the potatoes to ease smoothness.

Ranch House Chicken Fried Steak

There's no chicken in it, so where did this classic cowboy dish get its name? Frankly, who cares? Making it in the slow cooker eliminates the traditional tasks of pounding the meat and watching the frying pan. It also produces melt-in-your-mouth results. The rich, spicy pan gravy served over mashed potatoes is a marriage made in heaven. To turn up the heat, increase the quantity of jalapeño pepper. • *SERVES 6*

1 tbsp	vegetable oil	15 mL
2 lbs	round steak or "simmering" steak (see Tip, page 114)	1 kg
2	onions, thinly sliced	2
3	cloves garlic, minced	3
1 to 2	jalapeño peppers, finely chopped	1 to 2
1 tsp	salt	5 mL
1 tsp	cracked black peppercorns	5 mL
1 tsp	paprika	5 mL
¼ tsp	cayenne pepper	2 mL
1 tsp	celery seeds	5 mL
¼ cup	all-purpose flour	50 mL
¾ cup	condensed chicken broth (undiluted)	175 mL
½ cup	whipping cream	125 mL

1. In a skillet, heat oil over medium-high heat. Brown steak, in pieces, if necessary, on both sides and transfer to slow cooker stoneware.

2. Reduce heat to medium-low. Add onions to skillet and cook until softened. Add garlic, jalapeño pepper, salt, pepper, paprika, cayenne pepper and celery seeds and cook for 1 more minute. Sprinkle flour over mixture and cook, stirring, for 1 minute. Add chicken broth and cook, stirring, until thickened. (Sauce will be very thick.)

3. Spoon sauce over meat in slow cooker, cover and cook on **Low** for 8 to 10 hours or on **High** for 4 to 5 hours, until meat is tender. Add cream and cook on **High** for 15 minutes. Serve with hot, fluffy mashed potatoes.

Make ahead

This dish can be partially prepared the night before it is cooked. Complete Step 2, heating 1 tbsp (15 mL) oil in pan before softening onions. Cover and refrigerate mixture overnight. The next morning, brown steak (Step 1), or skip this step and place meat directly in stoneware. Continue cooking as directed in Step 3. Alternately, cook steak overnight and refrigerate without adding the cream. When ready to serve, bring to a boil in a large skillet and simmer for 10 minutes, until meat is heated through and sauce is hot and bubbling. Stir in cream and serve.

Saucy Swiss Steak

Here's a dish that many people will remember from the 1950s. Back then it required a fair bit of muscle to pound the steak with a mallet. Today, you can avoid all that dreary work by using the slow cooker. This is so good, you'll want seconds. Serve with garlic mashed potatoes and a plain green vegetable. • *SERVES 6*

1 tbsp	vegetable oil	15 mL
2 lbs	round steak or "simmering" steak (see Tip, page 114)	1 kg
2	medium onions, finely chopped	2
¼ cup	thinly sliced carrots	50 mL
1	small carrot, thinly sliced, about ¼ cup (50 mL)	1
I	small stalk celery, thinly sliced, about ¼ cup (50 mL)	1
½ tsp	salt	2 mL
¼ tsp	black pepper	1 mL
2 tbsp	all-purpose flour	25 mL
1	can (28 oz/796 mL) plum tomatoes, drained and chopped, ½ cup (125 mL) juice reserved (see Tip, page 32)	1
1 tbsp	Worcestershire sauce	15 mL
1	bay leaf	1

1. In a skillet, heat oil over medium-high heat. Add steak, in pieces, if necessary, and brown on both sides. Transfer to slow cooker stoneware.

2. Reduce heat to medium-low. Add onion, carrots, celery, salt and pepper to pan. Cover and cook until vegetables are softened, about 8 minutes. Sprinkle flour over vegetables and cook for 1 minute, stirring. Add tomatoes, reserved juice and Worcestershire sauce. Bring to a boil, stirring until slightly thickened. Add bay leaf.

3. Pour tomato mixture over steak and cook on **Low** for 8 to 10 hours or on for **High** 4 to 5 hours, until meat is tender. Discard bay leaf.

Make ahead

This dish can be partially prepared the night before it is cooked. Complete Step 2, heating 1 tbsp (15 mL) oil in pan before softening onions, carrots and celery. Cover and refrigerate mixture overnight. The next morning, brown steak (Step 1), or skip this step and place steak directly in stoneware. Continue cooking as directed. Alternately, cook steak overnight and refrigerate. When ready to serve, bring to a boil in a large skillet and simmer for 10 minutes, until meat is heated through and sauce is hot and bubbling.

Steak with Black Bean Gravy

This hearty beef-and-bean combination makes a great stick-to-your-ribs dinner. All you need is a crisp green salad and a creative hand with toppings and garnishes to make a delicious meal. To stretch this further, serve with hot, fluffy rice. • *SERVES 4 TO 6*

3	slices bacon, chopped	3
2 lbs	round or "simmering" steak (see Tip, right)	1 kg
2	onions, finely chopped	2
3	cloves garlic, minced	3
1 tsp	dried oregano leaves	5 mL
1 tsp	cumin seeds	5 mL
1 tsp	salt	5 mL
1 tsp	cracked black peppercorns	5 mL
1	jalapeño pepper, finely chopped	1
1	can (19 oz/540 mL) black beans, rinsed and drained, or 2 cups (500 mL) cooked and drained black beans	1
½ cup	condensed beef broth (undiluted) or water	125 mL
	Zest and juice of 1 lime	

1. In a skillet over medium-high heat, cook bacon until browned. Remove with a slotted spoon and drain on paper towel. Drain off all but 2 tbsp (25 mL) fat in pan. Add steak, in pieces, if necessary, and brown on both sides. Transfer to slow cooker stoneware.

2. Reduce heat to medium. Add onion and cook, stirring, until softened. Add garlic, oregano, cumin seeds, salt, pepper and jalapeño pepper and cook for 1 minute. Add beans, broth or water, stir to combine and bring to a boil. Stir in reserved bacon and lime zest and juice.

3. Pour contents of pan over meat. Cover and cook on **Low** for 8 to 10 hours or on for **High** for 4 to 5 hours, until meat is tender. Serve piping hot, topped with any combination of finely chopped red or green onion, finely chopped tomato, finely chopped cilantro, shredded Monterey Jack or Cheddar cheese, sour cream and hot or mild salsa.

Make ahead

This dish can be partially prepared the night before it is cooked. Complete Step 2, heating 1 tbsp (15 mL) oil in pan before softening onions. Cover and refrigerate mixture overnight. The next morning, brown steak (Step 1), or if you're pressed for time, skip this step and place steak directly in stoneware. Continue cooking as directed in Step 3. Alternately, cook steak overnight and refrigerate. When ready to serve, bring to a boil in a large skillet and simmer for 10 minutes, until meat is heated through and beans are hot and bubbling.

Tip

While round steak is traditionally used for this dish, an equally successful version can be made with "simmering steak." This is cut from the blade or cross rib and is available at many supermarkets.

"Down Home" Smothered Steak

This traditional favorite from the Deep South is usually cooked on top of the stove where it requires a fair bit of watching. Not only does the slow cooker do away with that tedious work, it produces outstanding results. Serve the rich gravy over mashed potatoes with a side dish of yellow squash. • *SERVES 6*

1 tbsp	vegetable oil	15 mL
2 lbs	round or "simmering" steak (see Tip, page 114)	1 kg
1	onion, thinly sliced	1
2	stalks celery, peeled and thinly sliced	2
½ tsp	salt	2 mL
½ tsp	cracked black peppercorns	2 mL
¼ cup	all-purpose flour	50 mL
1½ cups	beef stock	375 mL
2	green bell peppers, cut into thin strips	2

1. In a skillet, heat oil over medium-high heat. Brown steak, in pieces, if necessary, on both sides. Transfer to slow cooker stoneware.

2. Reduce heat to medium-low. Add onions, celery, salt and pepper to pan. Cover and cook until vegetables are softened, about 8 minutes. Sprinkle flour over vegetables and cook for 1 minute, stirring. Add stock and cook until thickened, stirring to scrape up brown bits.

3. Pour over meat, cover and cook on **Low** for 8 to 10 hours or on **High** for 4 to 5 hours, until meat is tender.

4. Stir in green peppers. Cover and cook on **High** for 20 to 25 minutes, until peppers are tender. Serve piping hot.

Make ahead

This dish can be partially prepared the night before it is cooked. Complete Step 2, heating 1 tbsp (15 mL) oil in pan before softening onions and celery. Cover and refrigerate mixture overnight. The next morning, brown steak (Step 1), or if you're pressed for time, skip this step and add steak directly to stoneware. Continue cooking as directed in Steps 3 and 4. Alternately, cook steak overnight and refrigerate. When ready to serve, bring to a boil in a large skillet and simmer for 10 minutes, until meat is heated through and sauce is hot and bubbling.

Stuffed Cabbage with Mushrooms, Tomatoes and Red Peppers

I love to cook Savoy cabbage when it's in season, not only because it tastes so good, but also because its beautiful leaves, which resemble the petals of a huge flower, are so pretty. Easy to make, this recipe has great visual appeal, and if you have six to eight people to feed, it's easy to stretch simply by doubling the amount of stuffing. Leave the core of the cabbage in during cooking to anchor it for presentation and ease of serving. However, be sure to cut around the tough center when serving. • *SERVES 4*

• **LARGE (MINIMUM 5 QUART) OVAL SLOW COOKER**

1 cup	boiling water	250 mL
1	package (½ oz/14 g) dried porcini mushrooms	1
1	head Savoy cabbage, about 1½ lbs (750 g) (see Tip, right)	1
4	slices bacon or 2 oz (60 g) salt pork belly, chopped (see Tip, page 118)	4
1 lb	lean ground beef	500 g
4	cloves garlic, minced	4
1 tsp	dried thyme leaves	5 mL
1 tsp	cracked black peppercorns	5 mL
1 tsp	salt	5 mL
¼ cup	dry red wine	50 mL
2 tbsp	tomato paste	25 mL
¼ cup	condensed beef broth (undiluted)	50 mL
4	oil-packed sun-dried tomatoes, finely chopped, about ¼ cup (50 g) (see Tip, right)	4
2	large red bell peppers, cut into ¼-inch (0.5-cm) dice	2
¼ cup	finely chopped pitted black olives (optional)	50 mL

Tip

You can use regular cabbage for this recipe, but it won't be as easy to stuff as the leaves are more tightly packed.

Tip

If your sun-dried tomatoes aren't packed in oil, remember to rehydrate them by soaking in hot or boiling water before using.

1. In a heatproof bowl, soak mushrooms in boiling water for 30 minutes. Strain through a fine sieve, reserving liquid. Pat mushrooms dry, chop finely and set aside.

2. Remove outer layer of cabbage leaves, reserving two for later use. In a large deep pot of boiling water, cook cabbage for 5 minutes. Lift out, drain in a colander and set aside to cool.

continued on page 118

3. In a skillet, over medium-high heat, cook bacon or salt pork until crisp. Remove with a slotted spoon and drain on paper towel. Drain off all but 1 tbsp (15 mL) fat in pan. Add beef and cook, stirring, until lightly browned and no longer pink. Drain off liquid.

4. Add garlic, thyme, pepper, salt and mushrooms to pan. Cook, stirring, for 1 minute. Add wine and cook, stirring, until all the alcohol has evaporated. Add tomato paste, broth and reserved mushroom liquid and bring to a boil. Cook, stirring, until sauce is slightly reduced, about 3 minutes. Stir in sun-dried tomatoes, red peppers and bacon or salt pork.

5. On a large clean plate, place cabbage. Gently pull cabbage apart and spoon filling between leaves. (If not doubling quantity, you'll have too many leaves for filling, so only fill those toward the center of the cabbage.) Tie cabbage together with string and place in slow cooker. Place reserved cabbage leaves over top and pour any juices that may have collected on plate over all. Cover and cook on **Low** for 8 to 10 hours or on **High** for 4 to 5 hours. When ready to serve, use string as a handle and lift cabbage out of slow cooker and place on a large, deep platter. Untie string and discard. Sprinkle with chopped black olives, if using.

Tip

If using salt pork for this recipe, make sure you purchase cured pork belly, not "fatback," which comes from the back of the pig and is simply pork fat that has not been cured.

Hearty Short Ribs with Carrot-Studded Gravy

I think short ribs are one of the tastiest cuts of beef. The only trick to cooking them is to remove as much fat as possible before cooking. This traditional approach reminds me of the kind of short ribs my mother used to make — hearty with a rich, robust gravy. Serve with plenty of fluffy mashed potatoes. • *SERVES 6 TO 8*

• **PREHEATED BROILER**

4 lbs	beef short ribs (see Tip, right)	2 kg
1 tbsp	vegetable oil	15 mL
2	onions, finely chopped	2
4	cloves garlic, minced	4
1 tbsp	dried thyme leaves	15 mL
½ cup	finely chopped parsley	125 mL
1 tsp	salt	5 mL
1 tsp	cracked black peppercorns	5 mL
¼ cup	all-purpose flour	50 mL
½ cup	condensed beef broth (undiluted)	125 mL
½ cup	tomato-based chili sauce (see Tip, page 103)	125 mL
2 tbsp	cider vinegar	25 mL
2 tbsp	Worcestershire sauce	25 mL
2 tbsp	packed brown sugar	25 mL
1 tsp	dry mustard	5 mL
1	bag (1 lb/454 g) peeled baby carrots (see Tip, right)	1

Make ahead

This dish can be partially prepared the night before it is cooked. Complete Step 2. Cover and refrigerate mixture overnight. The next morning, brown ribs (Step 1), and continue cooking as directed.

Tip

Short ribs are a particularly delicious cut of beef, but they are high in fat. Broiling them before adding to the slow cooker is essential to reduce fat.

Tip

The peeled baby carrots are visually appealing and convenient, but regular carrots, peeled and diced, taste just as good.

1. Under preheated broiler, brown ribs, turning once, about 6 minutes per side. Transfer to a paper-towel-lined platter to drain.

2. In a skillet, heat oil over medium heat. Add onions and cook, stirring, until softened. Add garlic, thyme, parsley, salt and pepper and cook, stirring, for 1 minute. Sprinkle flour over mixture and cook, stirring, for 1 minute. Add beef broth, chili sauce, vinegar, Worcestershire sauce, brown sugar and mustard and bring to a boil. Stir in carrots.

3. Place short ribs in slow cooker. Pour sauce over and stir to combine. Cover and cook on **Low** for 10 to 12 hours or on **High** for 5 to 6 hours, until ribs are tender and falling off the bone.

Korean-Style Short Ribs

Thanks to Andrew Chase, a gifted chef, for the stovetop version of this recipe that appears in *The Asian Bistro Cookbook.* According to Andrew, who is a walking encyclopedia on Asian cuisine, Koreans love tasty, chewy cuts of meat and have devised a myriad of ways for tenderizing and flavoring them, building on basic ingredients such as garlic, ginger, chilies (in many different forms) and sesame oil. Although my experience with Korean cuisine is quite limited, I've enjoyed what I've sampled. I hope you will, too. This rendering has simplified the ingredients that Andrew uses, but the results are still sensational. • *SERVES 4 TO 6*

• **PREHEATED BROILER**

12	dried shiitake mushrooms (see Tip, page 121)	12
1 cup	boiling water	250 mL
3 lbs	beef short ribs	1.5 kg
1 tsp	freshly ground black pepper	5 mL
1 tbsp	vegetable oil	15 mL
2	onions, thinly sliced	2
2	carrots, peeled and thinly sliced	2
1 cup	daikon radish or white turnip, cut into ½-inch (1-cm) cubes (see Tip, right)	250 mL
1 tbsp	minced garlic	15 mL
1 tbsp	minced gingerroot	15 mL
3 tbsp	sake, dry sherry or vodka	45 mL
½ cup	condensed beef broth (undiluted)	125 mL
¼ cup	soya sauce	50 mL
3 tbsp	corn syrup	45 mL
1 cup	sliced bamboo shoots	250 mL
2	green onions, thinly sliced	2
1 to 2	serrano chilies, finely chopped (see Tip, page 138)	1 to 2
1 tsp	sesame oil	5 mL
	Hot cooked rice	

Make ahead

This dish can be partially prepared the night before it is cooked. Complete Steps 1 and 3. Cover and refrigerate mixture overnight. The next morning, brown ribs (Step 2), and continue cooking as directed.

Tip

If using daikon radish, add toward the end of the cooking time as, unlike turnip, it does not require much cooking.

1. In a heatproof bowl, soak mushrooms in boiling water for 30 minutes. Strain and reserve liquid. Discard stems and slice each mushroom in half. Pat dry with paper towels. Set aside.

2. Position broiler rack 6 inches (15 cm) from heat source. Sprinkle ribs with pepper and broil on both sides, until browned, about 5 minutes per side. Drain on paper towels, separate ribs, if in strips, and place in slow cooker.

3. In a skillet, heat oil over medium heat. Add onions, carrots and turnip, if using, and stir-fry, until vegetables are softened. Add garlic, gingerroot and mushrooms and cook, stirring, for 1 minute. Add sake, sherry or vodka and cook for 1 minute, until alcohol evaporates. Add beef stock, soya sauce, corn syrup and reserved mushroom liquid. Bring mixture to a boil.

4. Pour mixture over ribs. Cover and cook on **Low** for 8 to 10 hours or on **High** for 4 to 6 hours, until ribs are tender and falling off the bone. Add bamboo shoots and daikon radish, if using. Cover and cook on **High** for 25 minutes, until radish is tender. Just before serving, stir in green onions, chilies and sesame oil. Serve over hot cooked rice.

Tip

Although dried shiitake mushrooms and daikon radish are available in many supermarkets, I recommend buying the quantity of dried mushrooms required for this recipe in a store specializing in Asian foods, as they are likely to be quite expensive if purchased in the small packages sold in most supermarkets.

Osso Buco with Lemon Gremolata

This is probably my all-time favorite veal dish. I love the wine-flavored sauce and the succulent meat, enhanced with just a soupçon of gremolata, pungent with fresh garlic and lemon zest. But best of all, I adore eating the marrow from the bones, a rare and delicious treat. Pass coffee spoons to ensure that every mouthwatering morsel is extracted from the bone. • *SERVES 6 TO 8*

• **LARGE (MINIMUM 5 QUART) SLOW COOKER**

1	package (½ oz/14 g) dried porcini mushrooms	1
1 cup	boiling water	250 mL
¼ cup	all-purpose flour	50 mL
1 tsp	salt	5 mL
½ tsp	black pepper	2 mL
⅛ tsp	cayenne pepper	0.5 mL
6 to 8	sliced veal shanks	6 to 8
1 tbsp	olive oil	15 mL
1 tbsp	butter	15 mL
3	leeks, white part only, cleaned and thinly sliced (see Tip, page 212)	3
2	carrots, peeled and finely chopped	2
2	stalks celery, finely chopped	2
2	cloves garlic, finely chopped	2
1 tsp	dried thyme or 2 sprigs fresh thyme	5 mL
½ cup	dry white wine	125 mL

Lemon Gremolata

2	cloves garlic, minced	2
1 cup	finely chopped parsley	250 mL
	Zest of 1 lemon	
1 tbsp	extra-virgin olive oil	15 mL

Make ahead

This dish can be partially prepared before it is cooked. Complete Steps 1 and 4. Cover sauce and refrigerate overnight. The next morning, complete Steps 2, 3 and 5. When ready to serve, make Gremolata. Alternately, Osso Buco can be cooked overnight in slow cooker and refrigerated. When ready to serve, spoon off congealed fat, and transfer to a Dutch oven. Bring to a boil and simmer for 10 minutes, until meat is heated through and sauce is bubbling.

1. In a heatproof bowl, combine porcini mushrooms and boiling water. Let stand for 30 minutes. Drain through a fine sieve, reserving liquid. Pat mushrooms dry with paper towel and chop finely. Set aside.

2. In a bowl, mix together flour, salt, black pepper and cayenne. Lightly coat veal shanks with mixture, shaking off the excess. Set any flour mixture remaining aside.

continued on page 124

3. In a large skillet, heat olive oil and butter over medium heat. Add veal and cook until lightly browned on both sides. Transfer to slow cooker stoneware.

4. Add leeks, carrots and celery to pan and stir well. Reduce heat to **Low**, cover and cook until vegetables are softened, about 10 minutes. Increase heat to medium. Add garlic, thyme and mushrooms and cook, stirring, for 1 minute. Add reserved flour mixture, stir and cook for 1 minute. Add wine and reserved mushroom liquid and bring to a boil.

5. Pour mixture over veal, cover and cook on **Low** for 12 hours, until veal is very tender.

6. To make Lemon Gremolata: Combine ingredients in a small serving bowl and pass around the table, allowing guests to individually garnish.

Variation

Glazed Osso Buco: Preheat broiler. Transfer the cooked and, if necessary, reheated shanks to a baking/serving dish large enough to accommodate them in a single layer. Spoon approximately 1 tbsp (15 mL) puréed sauce over each shank and heat under broiler until the top looks glazed and shiny, about 5 minutes.

Tip

This Osso Buco is delicious served straight from the slow cooker, but if you have special guests you want to impress, I recommend glazing the meat, and puréeing and reducing the sauce to intensify flavor.

Tip

To purée and reduce sauce: Spoon into food processor and process until smooth. In a saucepan, over medium heat, simmer sauce while the Osso Buco is being glazed.

Blanquette of Veal Florentine with Porcini Mushroom Gravy

A *blanquette* is a French term for braised meat which is not browned before it is cooked. The technique is usually reserved for more delicate meats such as veal and poultry. Even though the meat isn't browned, you'll be amazed by the deep rich flavor of this sauce — the turnips and porcini mushrooms are a heavenly combination. Serve with mashed or parsleyed potatoes and a green vegetable. • *SERVES 6 TO 8*

1	package (½ oz/14 g) dried porcini mushrooms	1
1 cup	boiling water	250 mL
2 tbsp	butter	25 mL
6	leeks, white part only, cleaned and thinly sliced (see Tip, page 212)	6
1 tsp	dried thyme leaves	5 mL
1 tsp	salt	5 mL
½ tsp	black pepper	2 mL
¼ cup	all-purpose flour	50 mL
¼ cup	white wine	50 mL
¼ cup	condensed chicken broth (undiluted)	50 mL
2 lbs	stewing veal, cut into 1-inch (2.5-cm) cubes	1 kg
1 lb	fresh spinach leaves or 1 package (10 oz/300 g) spinach, washed, stems removed and coarsely chopped	500 g
2 tbsp	lemon juice	25 mL
	Parsley or chives	

Make ahead

This dish can be partially prepared the night before it is cooked. Complete Steps 1 and 2. Cover sauce and refrigerate overnight. The next morning, add to slow cooker stoneware along with veal and continue cooking as directed.

Tip

I like to keep a few packages of dried mushrooms on hand at all times as the mushrooms and their soaking liquid enhance many sauces.

1. In a heatproof bowl, soak mushrooms in boiling water for 30 minutes. Strain through a fine sieve, reserving liquid. Pat mushrooms dry and chop finely. Set aside.

2. In a skillet, melt butter over medium heat. Add leeks and cook until soft. Add mushrooms, thyme, salt and pepper and cook, stirring, for 1 minute. Sprinkle flour over mixture and cook, stirring, for 2 minutes. Add reserved mushroom liquid, wine and broth and cook, stirring, until mixture thickens.

3. Transfer mixture to slow cooker. Add veal and stir well. Cover and cook on **Low** for 8 to 10 hours or on **High** for 4 to 6 hours, until meat is tender. Stir in spinach and lemon juice. Cover and cook on **High** for 20 to 30 minutes, until spinach is cooked. Garnish with finely chopped parsley or chives.

Dilled Veal Stew

This is a streamlined and lower fat version of a Veal Blanquette I've been making for many years from *The Silver Palate Cookbook*. My husband likes to increase the quantity of nutmeg and cream, so feel free to do so, if that appeals to your taste buds. All variations are delicious. I like to serve this for Sunday dinner, over hot buttered noodles. • *SERVES 6 TO 8*

2 tbsp	all-purpose flour	25 mL
1 tbsp	paprika	15 mL
¼ tsp	ground nutmeg	1 mL
1 tsp	salt	5 mL
½ tsp	black pepper	2 mL
3 tbsp	butter, divided	45 mL
2 lbs	stewing veal, cut into 1-inch (2.5-cm) cubes	1 kg
2	onions, thinly sliced	2
2	large carrots, peeled, cut in quarters lengthwise and very thinly sliced	2
4	stalks celery, peeled and thinly sliced	4
1	can (10 oz/284 mL) condensed chicken broth (undiluted)	1
½ cup	dry vermouth or white wine	125 mL
½ cup	whipping cream	125 mL
½ cup	finely chopped dill	125 mL
	Hot buttered noodles (optional)	

Make ahead

This dish can be partially prepared the night before it is cooked. Complete Step 3. Cover and refrigerate sauce. The next morning, continue cooking as directed, beginning at Step 1.

1. In a bowl, combine flour, paprika, nutmeg, salt and pepper. Set aside.

2. In a skillet, over medium heat, melt 2 tbsp (25 mL) butter. Add veal and cook, stirring, for 3 to 4 minutes without browning. Sprinkle flour mixture over meat, stir to combine and transfer to slow cooker stoneware.

3. Add remaining butter to pan. Add onions, carrots and celery and cook, stirring, until vegetables are softened, about 5 minutes. Add chicken broth, dry vermouth or wine and bring to a boil.

4. Pour mixture over veal, cover and cook on **Low** for 8 to 10 hours or on **High** for 4 to 5 hours, until stew is hot and bubbling. Stir in cream and dill and serve.

Bullshot Veal Stew with a Twist

I call this Bullshot Veal Stew because it reminds me of a bullshot, the cocktail made with vodka, lemon juice, Worcestershire sauce and beef bouillon. Don't be put off by this relationship or the simplicity of the recipe. This is a very tasty stew that is a snap to make and which all family members will enjoy. It's delicious over mashed potatoes, buttered noodles or fluffy white rice. • *SERVES 6 TO 8*

2 tbsp	butter	25 mL
1	bunch green onions, white part only, cut into 1-inch (2.5-cm) lengths	1
1 tsp	celery seeds	5 mL
1 tsp	dried thyme leaves	5 mL
1 tsp	salt	5 mL
½ tsp	black pepper	2 mL
2 tbsp	all-purpose flour	25 mL
¼ cup	vodka	50 mL
¼ cup	condensed beef broth (undiluted)	50 mL
1½ cups	vegetable or tomato juice	375 mL
1 tbsp	Worcestershire sauce	15 mL
2 lbs	stewing veal, cut into 1-inch (2.5-cm) cubes	1 kg
1	twist of lemon peel	1
	Mashed potatoes, hot buttered noodles or cooked rice (optional)	

Make ahead

This dish can be partially prepared the night before it is cooked. Complete Step 1. Cover sauce and refrigerate overnight. The next morning, continue cooking as directed.

1. In a skillet, over medium heat, melt butter. Add onions and cook until softened. Add celery seeds, thyme, salt and pepper and cook, stirring, for 1 minute. Sprinkle flour over mixture and cook, stirring, for 1 minute. Add vodka and cook until alcohol evaporates. Add beef broth, juice and Worcestershire sauce and bring to a boil. Cook, stirring, until mixture thickens.

2. Place veal in slow cooker stoneware. Add lemon twist, pour sauce over veal, cover and cook on **Low** for 8 to 10 hours or on **High** for 4 to 5 hours, until veal is tender.

Pork and Lamb

Pork Roast with Chili-Orange Sauce

There's a lot more to Mexican cuisine than tacos and burritos — as demonstrated by the delicious sweet and spicy flavors of this pork roast. The combination of fruit and chili peppers derives from a simple country dish, but the results should inspire you to learn more about the cuisine of our neighbors to the south. Serve over fluffy white rice. • *SERVES 8*

4	slices bacon, finely chopped	4
1	boneless pork shoulder butt roast, trimmed of excess fat, about 3 lbs (1.5 kg)	1
2	large onions, thinly sliced	2
3	cloves garlic, minced	3
2	jalapeño peppers, finely chopped	2
1½ tbsp	chili powder	20 mL
1 tsp	salt	5 mL
1 tsp	cracked black peppercorns	5 mL
¼ cup	all-purpose flour	50 mL
1 tbsp	orange zest	15 mL
1½ cups	orange juice	375 mL
2	bananas, thinly sliced	2
	Hot cooked rice	

1. In a skillet, over medium-high heat, cook bacon until crisp. Remove with a slotted spoon to paper towel and drain thoroughly.

2. In same pan, brown roast on all sides. Transfer to slow cooker stoneware.

3. Remove all but 1 tbsp (15 mL) fat from pan. Reduce heat to medium. Add onions and cook, stirring, until softened. Add garlic, jalapeño peppers, chili powder, salt and pepper and cook, stirring, for 1 minute. Sprinkle flour over mixture and cook, stirring, for 1 minute. Add orange zest, orange juice and bananas and cook, stirring to scrape up any brown bits and mashing bananas into sauce. Stir in bacon pieces.

4. Pour mixture over pork. Cover and cook on **Low** for 8 to 10 hours or on **High** for 4 to 5 hours, until meat is very tender.

Make ahead

This dish can be partially prepared the night before it is cooked. Complete Steps 1 and 3. Cover and refrigerate mixture overnight. The next morning, heat 1 tbsp (15 mL) oil in skillet and brown roast (Step 2), or skip this step if you're pressed for time and place roast directly in stoneware. Continue cooking as directed. Alternately, cook roast overnight. Cover and refrigerate. When ready to serve, spoon off congealed fat, remove meat from sauce and slice. Place sliced meat in a Dutch oven, cover with sauce and bring to a boil. Simmer, covered, for 10 minutes and serve.

Caribbean Pork Roast with Rum

I love how complex flavors meld in this sauce. It's sweet, yet spicy, with more than a hint of citrus. If you like heat, use a whole chili, and if citrus appeals to you, double the quantity of lime zest and juice. For dinner with a Caribbean theme, serve with baked squash or sweet potato purée and your favorite beans 'n' rice. • *SERVES 4 TO 6*

- PREHEATED BROILER
- BROILER PAN OR BAKING SHEET WITH SIDES

1	boneless pork shoulder butt roast, trimmed of excess fat, about 2 to 3 lbs (1 to 1.5 kg)	1
6	cloves garlic, cut into thin slivers	6
1	piece of gingerroot, about 2 inches (5 cm), cut in two lengthwise and then into thin slivers	1
20	whole cloves	20
2 tbsp	packed brown sugar	25 mL
1 tsp	dry mustard	5 mL
½	chili pepper (serrano or Scotch bonnet), finely chopped (see page 14)	½
1 tsp	salt	5 mL
1 tsp	cracked black peppercorns	5 mL
½ cup	dark rum	125 mL
	Zest and juice of 1 lime	
1 tbsp	cornstarch, dissolved in 1 tbsp (15 mL) cold water	15 mL

1. On all sides of the meat, make a series of small slits. Insert garlic and ginger slivers and whole cloves. Pat roast dry with paper towel.

2. In a small bowl, combine brown sugar and mustard. Rub mixture all over roast and place under broiler. Broil, turning to ensure that roast is browned on all sides, about 15 minutes. Transfer to slow cooker stoneware.

3. In a small bowl, combine chili pepper, salt, pepper, rum and zest and lime juice. Pour over roast and cook on **Low** for 10 to 12 hours or on **High** for 5 to 6 hours, until pork is tender.

4. Remove roast from slow cooker and keep warm. Skim off accumulated fat and pour cooking juices into a medium saucepan. Bring to a boil over medium-high heat. Add cornstarch mixture and stir constantly until thickened. Serve in a sauceboat alongside sliced pork.

Make ahead

If you're pressed for time on the day you plan to serve this dish, I recommend cooking the roast overnight. The next morning, cover and refrigerate. When you're ready to serve, spoon off the congealed fat, remove roast from liquid and slice meat. Place meat in an ovenproof serving dish, cover with aluminum foil and place in a warm oven at 325°F (163°C) for 15 to 20 minutes, until meat is heated through. Meanwhile, complete Step 4. Pour sauce over meat and serve.

Tip

One of the best ways of removing fat from cooking liquid is to pour juices into a heatproof glass measure and place in freezer until the fat solidifies on top. Then spoon it off and make sauce. If you cook this dish overnight and refrigerate until you're ready to serve, the fat will congeal when the dish has chilled.

Creamy Ragout of Pork with Wine-Soaked Prunes

This simple dish owes its origins to French-country cooking, but it is elegant enough to grace the most sophisticated table. The creamy sauce, enhanced with red currant jelly, complements the pork and the prunes. For an even fruitier version, add 1 tsp (5 mL) orange zest just before serving. I like to serve this with crispy roast potatoes. • *SERVES 6*

1½ cups	pitted prunes, coarsely chopped	375 mL
¾ cup	dry white wine	175 mL
2 lbs	stewing pork, cut into 1-inch (2.5-cm) cubes	1 kg
¼ cup	all-purpose flour	50 mL
1 tbsp	olive oil	15 mL
2	sprigs fresh thyme or 1 tsp (5 mL) dried thyme leaves	2
¼ cup	finely chopped parsley	50 mL
1 tsp	salt	5 mL
½ tsp	black pepper	2 mL
½ cup	condensed beef broth (undiluted)	125 mL
1 tbsp	red currant jelly	15 mL
½ cup	whipping cream	125 mL
1 tsp	orange zest (optional)	5 mL

Make ahead

To facilitate preparation, soak prunes in wine overnight.

1. In a small bowl, combine prunes and wine. Cover and set aside for 1 hour at room temperature or refrigerate overnight. When you are ready to begin cooking, strain, reserving wine. Place prunes in slow cooker.

2. On a dinner plate, roll pork pieces in flour, ensuring that all sides are lightly coated. Discard excess flour. In a skillet, heat oil over medium-high heat. Brown pork, in batches, adding more oil, if necessary. Transfer to slow cooker stoneware.

3. Add thyme, parsley, salt and pepper to pan and cook, stirring, for 1 minute. Add beef broth and reserved wine and cook until thickened. Pour mixture over pork and prunes and stir to combine. Cover and cook on **Low** for 8 to 10 hours or on **High** for 4 to 5 hours, until pork is tender.

4. With a slotted spoon, transfer pork and prunes to a heatproof platter and keep warm. Pour cooking liquid from slow cooker into a small saucepan and bring to a boil over medium-high heat, cooking until sauce is slightly reduced, about 5 minutes. Add red currant jelly and stir until dissolved. Add cream and orange zest, if using, and stir. Pour over pork and serve.

Pork Stew with Sage-and-Onion Dumplings

If you hanker for an old-fashioned stew, but are suffering from "beef fatigue," try this delicious combination of pork and seasoned vegetables, simmered in red wine and topped with savory dumplings. Sage and onion are a marriage made in heaven (my family won't allow me to stuff turkey with anything other than traditional sage and onion stuffing), and the almost minty astringency of the sage perfectly complements the pork in this recipe. • *SERVES 8*

1 cup	dry red wine	250 mL
4	cloves garlic, minced	4
1 tsp	dried thyme leaves	5 mL
½ tsp	cracked black peppercorns	2 mL
2 lbs	boneless pork shoulder, cut into 2-inch (5-cm) cubes	1 kg
1 tbsp	vegetable oil	15 mL
2	onions, finely chopped	2
3	carrots, peeled and cut into ½-inch (1-cm) cubes	3
4	stalks celery, peeled and cut into ½-inch (1-cm) cubes	4
2 tbsp	all-purpose flour	25 mL
1 tbsp	tomato paste	15 mL
½ cup	condensed chicken broth (undiluted)	125 mL
1 tsp	salt	5 mL
1	bay leaf	1
2 cups	frozen peas, thawed	500 mL

Dumplings

1½ cups	all-purpose flour	375 mL
1 tbsp	baking powder	15 mL
1 tsp	salt	5 mL
½ cup	milk	125 mL
1	egg	1
6	green onions, white part only	6
½ tsp	dried sage or 6 fresh sage leaves	2 mL

Make ahead

This dish can be partially prepared the night before it is cooked. Marinate pork overnight in refrigerator (Step 1).

1. In a bowl, combine red wine, garlic, thyme, pepper and pork. Marinate for 1 hour at room temperature or 4 hours, or more, in refrigerator. Strain, reserving marinade and pat pork dry with paper towel.

2. In a skillet, heat oil over medium-high heat. Brown pork, in batches, and, using a slotted spoon, transfer to slow cooker stoneware.

3. Reduce heat to medium-low. Add onions, carrots and celery to pan. Cover and cook for 8 to 10 minutes, until vegetables are soft. Sprinkle with flour, stir well and cook for 1 minute. Add tomato paste, chicken broth, salt and reserved marinade and cook until thickened. Add bay leaf and pour mixture over pork. Cover and cook on **Low** for 8 to 10 hours or on **High** for 4 to 5 hours, until pork is tender. Add peas to stew and stir well. Discard bay leaf.

4. To make Dumplings: In a bowl, combine flour, baking powder and salt. In a food processor or blender, process milk, egg, green onions and sage until smooth. Stir milk mixture into flour until moistened (lumps are fine). Increase slow cooker to **High**. Drop dumpling dough, by spoonfuls, onto hot pork mixture. Cover and cook on **High** for 30 to 40 minutes or until toothpick inserted in center of dumplings comes out clean.

Tip

To ensure that dumplings are fluffy, drop the batter directly onto pieces of meat. If the batter is submerged in the liquid, the dumplings will be soggy. Turning the slow cooker heat to **High** before adding the batter will also help to ensure fluffiness as the dumplings will start to cook immediately if the stew is already bubbling.

Portuguese Pork with Clams

Although it may seem to be an unusual combination, Pork with Clams is Portugal's national dish and I've been serving it to surprised and delighted guests for many years. For a particularly impressive presentation, transfer the stew to a large, rustic serving dish and top with hot steamed clams still in their shell. • *SERVES 6 TO 8*

4	slices bacon, finely chopped	4
2 lbs	pork shoulder, trimmed of excess fat and cut into 2-inch (5-cm) cubes	1 kg
¼ cup	all-purpose flour	50 mL
1 tbsp	vegetable oil (optional)	15 mL
3	onions, thinly sliced	3
4	cloves garlic, minced	4
1 tbsp	paprika	15 mL
1 tsp	dried thyme leaves	5 mL
Pinch	cayenne pepper	Pinch
½ tsp	salt, or more to taste	2 mL
½ tsp	black pepper	2 mL
1 cup	white wine	250 mL
1	can (28 oz/796 mL) tomatoes, including juice, coarsely chopped (see Tip, page 32)	1
1	bay leaf	1
12	steamed clams in shells (see Tip, right) or 1 can (5 oz/142 g) baby clams, drained and rinsed	12
	Finely chopped parsley	
	Hot cooked rice	

1. In a skillet, over medium-high heat, cook bacon until crisp. Remove with a slotted spoon to paper towel and drain thoroughly.

2. Dredge pork in flour, shaking off excess. Add to pan, in batches, and brown. Transfer to slow cooker stoneware.

3. Reduce heat to medium and add oil to pan, if necessary. Add onions and cook until softened. Add garlic, paprika, thyme, cayenne, salt and pepper and cook for 1 minute. Add wine, tomatoes and bay leaf and bring to a boil. Cook, stirring, for 4 or 5 minutes, until liquid is reduced by about a third.

4. Pour mixture over pork and add bacon. Cover and cook on **Low** for 8 to 10 hours or on **High** for 4 to 6 hours, until meat is very tender. Discard bay leaf. Top stew with steamed clams and their liquid and serve. Or stir in canned baby clams, if using, and cook on **High** for 10 minutes, until heated through. Garnish with parsley. Serve over rice.

Make ahead

This dish can be partially prepared the night before it is cooked. Complete Step 3, heating 1 tbsp (15 mL) oil in pan before softening onions. Cover and refrigerate mixture overnight. The next morning, complete Steps 1 and 2, and continue cooking as directed in Step 4. Alternately, cook stew overnight. When you're ready to serve, bring to a boil in a Dutch oven and simmer for 10 minutes, until bubbling. Add canned clams and cook until heated through or top with steamed clams.

Tip

To steam clams: Scrub clams thoroughly and soak in several changes of cold salted water. Spoon 1 cup (250 mL) liquid from cooked stew into a heavy pot, add ½ cup (125 mL) dry white wine and bring to boil. Add clams, cover and cook over medium heat, shaking the pot occasionally, until all the clams open. Discard any that don't open.

Pork Colombo

This rich, flavorful curry is a Caribbean specialty. It has a uniquely spicy taste and fluffy white rice is all it needs to make a delicious meal. • *SERVES 6 TO 8*

1 tbsp	vegetable oil	15 mL
2 lbs	pork shoulder, trimmed of excess fat and cut into 1-inch (2.5-cm) cubes	1 kg
2	onions, finely chopped	2
6	cloves garlic, minced	6
1 tbsp	minced gingerroot	15 mL
1 tsp	cumin seeds	5 mL
1 tsp	ground allspice	5 mL
1 tsp	ground cinnamon	5 mL
1 tsp	salt	5 mL
1 tsp	cracked black peppercorns	5 mL
1	serrano chili or ½ Scotch bonnet pepper, finely chopped (see Tip, right)	1
½ cup	condensed chicken broth (undiluted)	125 mL
4 cups	cubed, peeled yellow-fleshed squash, such as as acorn or butternut	1 L
1 tsp	lime zest	5 mL
2 tbsp	lime juice	25 mL
	Hot cooked rice	
	Finely chopped cilantro (optional)	

1. In a skillet, heat oil over medium-high. Add pork, in batches, and brown. Transfer to slow cooker stoneware. Drain off all but 1 tbsp (15 mL) fat in pan.

2. Reduce heat to medium. Add onions to pan and cook until softened. Add garlic, gingerroot, cumin seeds, allspice, cinnamon, salt, pepper and chili pepper and cook, stirring, for 1 minute. Stir in chicken broth and bring to a boil.

3. Add squash to slow cooker stoneware. Pour contents of pan into slow cooker and stir to combine. Cover and cook on **Low** for 8 to 10 hours or on **High** for 4 to 5 hours, until pork is tender.

4. Stir in lime zest and juice and serve immediately over hot fluffy rice. Garnish with cilantro, if using.

Variation

Pork and Black Beans Colombo: If you want to stretch the quantity of this recipe, after cooking is completed, add 1 can (19 oz/ 540 mL) black beans, drained and rinsed, or 2 cups (500 mL) dried black beans, cooked and drained. Cover and cook on **High** for an additional 20 minutes, until beans are heated through.

Make ahead

This dish can be partially prepared the night before it is cooked. Complete Step 2, heating 1 tbsp (15 mL) oil in pan before softening onions. Cover and refrigerate mixture overnight. Peel and cut squash, cover and refrigerate overnight. The next morning, brown pork (Step 1), or if you're pressed for time, omit browning and place pork directly in stoneware. Continue cooking as directed in Steps 3 and 4. Alternately, this dish may be cooked overnight and refrigerated. When you're ready to serve, bring to a boil in a Dutch oven and simmer for 10 minutes, until mixture is hot and bubbling. Then complete Step 4.

Tip

Look for serrano chilies in Asian grocery stores or well-stocked supermarkets. They are long and thin, usually green, but sometimes red, and about the size of a baby finger. (The green variety has been described as a "skinny jalapeño.")

Pork Vindaloo

This flavorful pork, marinated and cooked in vinegar and spices, is excellent as part of a buffet or as one dish in an Indian meal. It reheats well and leftovers make an excellent sandwich on French bread. • *SERVES 6 TO 8*

1 tbsp	cumin seeds	15 mL
2 tsp	coriander seeds	10 mL
1 tbsp	clarified butter or ghee (see Tip, right)	15 mL
1	onion, finely chopped	1
8	cloves garlic, minced	8
1 tbsp	minced gingerroot	15 mL
1	piece cinnamon stick, about 2 inches (5 cm)	1
6	whole cloves	6
½ tsp	salt	2 mL
2 tsp	mustard seeds	10 mL
¼ tsp	cayenne pepper	1 mL
2 lbs	stewing pork, cut into 1-inch (2.5-cm) cubes	1 kg
4	bay leaves	4
½ cup	red wine vinegar	125 mL

1. In a skillet, over medium heat, cook cumin and coriander seeds, stirring constantly, until they release their aroma and just begin to turn golden. Remove pan from heat and transfer seeds to a mortar or a cutting board. Using a pestle or a rolling pin, crush seeds coarsely. Set aside.

2. In a skillet, heat butter or ghee over medium heat. Add onion, garlic and gingerroot and cook for 1 minute. Add cumin and coriander seeds, cinnamon, cloves, salt, mustard seeds and cayenne and cook for 1 more minute. Remove from heat. Let cool.

3. Place pork in a mixing bowl. Add bay leaves and contents of pan. Add vinegar and stir to combine. Cover and marinate overnight in refrigerator. The next day, transfer to slow cooker stoneware, cover and cook on **Low** for 8 to 10 hours or on **High** for 4 to 5 hours, until pork is tender. Discard bay leaves, cinnamon stick and whole cloves.

Make ahead

This dish must be assembled the night before it is cooked as it needs to be marinated overnight. Follow preparation directions and refrigerate overnight. The next day, transfer to stoneware and cook as directed.

Tip

Ghee is a type of clarified butter, highly valued in Indian cooking as it can be heated to a very high temperature. It is available in grocery stores specializing in Indian ingredients and will keep, refrigerated, for as long as a year.

Leek and Sausage Shepherd's Pie

For many years, I have been making a crust-topped version of this delicious pie, based on a recipe by the late Craig Claiborne, who was a food writer for *The New York Times*. Although it's a wonderful dish, making pie crust adds work to its preparation. This slow cooker version, with a mashed potato topping, is so easy you can enjoy it every day. For a less rich dish, increase chicken stock to 1½ cups (375 mL) and reduce whipping cream to ½ cup (125 mL). • *SERVES 4 TO 6*

1 lb	pork breakfast sausages	500 g
1 tbsp	butter	15 mL
6	large leeks, white part only, cleaned and cut into 2-inch (5-cm) lengths (see Tip, page 212)	6
2	cloves garlic, minced	2
¼ tsp	ground nutmeg	1 mL
Pinch	cayenne pepper	Pinch
½ tsp	salt	2 mL
½ tsp	black pepper	2 mL
¼ cup	all-purpose flour	50 mL
1 cup	chicken stock	250 mL
1 cup	whipping cream	250 mL
¼ cup	freshly grated or bottled horseradish	50 mL
4 cups	mashed potatoes, seasoned with 1 tbsp (15 mL) butter, ½ tsp salt (2 mL) and ¼ tsp (1 mL) pepper	1 L

Make ahead

This dish can be partially prepared the night before it is cooked. Complete Steps 1 and 2, chilling cooked sausage and leek mixture separately. Cover and refrigerate overnight. The mashed potatoes can also be made ahead and refrigerated. The next morning, assemble the dish and continue cooking as directed.

Tip

Do not cook this for a longer time on **Low**, as the cream may curdle.

1. Prick sausages all over with a fork and in a skillet, over medium-high heat, brown well on all sides. Reduce heat to medium and cook, stirring, until sausages are cooked through. Drain on paper towels. When cool, cut into 1-inch (2.5-cm) lengths. Set aside.

2. Drain off all but 1 tbsp (15 mL) fat and return pan to element. Reduce heat to medium and add butter. When melted, add leeks and cook until they begin to soften. Add garlic, nutmeg, cayenne, salt and pepper and cook, stirring, for 1 minute. Add flour and cook for 1 minute. Add chicken stock and cream and cook until mixture thickens. Stir in horseradish.

3. Arrange sausage on bottom of slow cooker. Pour leek mixture over and top with mashed potatoes. Cover and cook on **High** for 3 to 4 hours, until bubbling and heated through.

Sausage Pie with Polenta Crust

This delicious one-dish dinner couldn't be easier. I love the flavor and texture of the cornmeal with the sausage and tomatoes. Serve with a crisp green salad for a complete and nutritious meal. And, if you're feeling festive, open a bottle of Chianti. • *SERVES 6 TO 8*

2 lbs	Italian sausage, hot or mild, removed from casing	1 kg
4	stalks celery, peeled and thinly sliced	4
1 tsp	dried oregano leaves	5 mL
1	can (28 oz/796 mL) tomatoes, including juice, coarsely chopped (see Tip, page 32)	1

Polenta Crust

3 cups	chicken stock or water	750 mL
1 tbsp	butter	15 mL
1 tsp	salt	5 mL
½ tsp	black pepper	2 mL
1 cup	cornmeal (see Tip, right)	250 mL
½ cup	freshly grated Parmesan cheese	125 mL
¼ cup	finely chopped Italian parsley	50 mL

1. In a skillet, over medium-high heat, cook sausages, breaking up meat with a spoon, until meat is no longer pink. Using a slotted spoon, transfer to slow cooker stoneware. Drain off liquid.

2. Reduce heat to medium. Add celery to pan and cook until soft. Add oregano and cook, stirring, for 1 minute. Add tomatoes and bring to a boil. Transfer mixture to slow cooker stoneware.

3. To make Polenta Crust: In a large heavy-bottomed saucepan, bring chicken stock or water to a boil. Stir in butter, salt and pepper. Reduce heat to **Low**. Gradually add cornmeal in a thin stream, stirring constantly until all cornmeal is absorbed. Cook for 2 or 3 minutes, stirring every minute or so, until mixture begins to solidify. Stir in Parmesan and parsley and remove from heat.

4. Spoon polenta over sausage mixture and, using a spatula, smooth it out to make an even crust. Cover and cook on **Low** for 6 to 8 hours or on **High** for 3 to 4 hours, until hot and bubbling.

Make ahead

This dish can be partially prepared the night before it is cooked. Complete Steps 1 and 2, chilling cooked sausage and tomato mixtures separately. Refrigerate overnight. The next morning, combine in stoneware and continue cooking as directed.

Tip

If you want your polenta to cook quickly, use a fine grind of cornmeal. The coarser the cornmeal, the longer it takes to cook.

Old South Pulled Pork on a Bun

I was thrilled when I tried this recipe on a neighbor who grew up in the South and his face broke out in a big grin. He immediately identified it as "pulled pork," a beloved slow-cooked barbecue specialty from North Carolina. The term "pulled" is another word for shredded, which is desirable in this recipe as the rough texture of the meat holds on to the sauce better than a sliced version. This is a great dish for weekends in the country, Friday night dinners or evenings when you have a house full of teenaged boys who can't get enough of the rich, smoky sauce. • *SERVES 6 TO 8*

1 tbsp	vegetable oil	15 mL
2	onions, finely chopped	2
6	cloves garlic, minced	6
1 tbsp	chili powder	15 mL
1 tsp	cracked black peppercorns	5 mL
1 cup	tomato-based chili sauce (see Tip, page 103)	250 mL
¼ cup	packed brown sugar	50 mL
¼ cup	cider vinegar	50 mL
1 tbsp	Worcestershire sauce	15 mL
1 tsp	liquid smoke	5 mL
1	boneless pork shoulder, trimmed of excess fat, about 3 lbs (1.5 kg)	
	Kaiser or onion buns, halved and warmed	

Make ahead

This dish can be partially prepared the night before it is cooked. Complete Step 1. Cover and refrigerate sauce overnight. The next morning, continue cooking as directed.

1. In a skillet, heat oil over medium heat. Add onions and cook until soft. Add garlic, chili powder and pepper and cook, stirring, for 1 minute. Add chili sauce, brown sugar, vinegar, Worcestershire sauce and liquid smoke. Stir to combine and bring to a boil.

2. Place pork in slow cooker stoneware and pour sauce over. Cover and cook on **Low** for 10 to 12 hours or on **High** for 6 hours, until pork is falling apart.

3. Transfer pork to a cutting board and pull the meat apart in shreds, using two forks. Return to sauce and keep warm. When ready to serve, spoon shredded pork and sauce over warm buns.

Spicy Pork Chops Florentine with Chickpeas

This simple combination of pork, spinach and chickpeas, flavored with garlic, cumin and hot pepper, seems deliciously Mediterranean. Vary the recipe by substituting 2 cups (500 mL) of cooked brown or green lentils for the chickpeas. Serve with country-style Italian bread and a green salad for a complete and nutritious meal. • *SERVES 6*

1 tbsp	vegetable oil	15 mL
6	pork chops, 1 inch (2.5 cm) thick	6
1	head garlic, peeled and minced	1
¼ tsp	cayenne pepper	1 mL
1 tsp	cumin seeds	5 mL
1 tsp	salt	5 mL
½ tsp	cracked black peppercorns	2 mL
1 tbsp	Dijon mustard	15 mL
¼ cup	lemon juice	50 mL
1	can (19 oz/540 mL) chickpeas, rinsed and drained, or 2 cups (500 mL) cooked and drained chickpeas	1
1 lb	fresh spinach leaves or 1 package (10 oz/300 g) spinach, washed, stems removed and chopped	500 g

Make ahead

This dish can be partially prepared the night before it is cooked. Complete Step 2, heating 1 tbsp (15 mL) oil in pan before sautéing garlic. Cover and refrigerate mixture overnight. The next morning, brown pork (Step 1), or if you're pressed for time, omit browning and place pork directly in stoneware. Continue cooking as directed in Step 3.

1. In a skillet, heat oil over medium-high heat. Brown pork on both sides, in batches, and transfer to slow cooker stoneware.

2. Reduce heat to medium. Add garlic, cayenne, cumin seeds, salt and pepper to pan and cook for 1 minute. Remove from heat and immediately add mustard, lemon juice and chickpeas. Stir to combine.

3. Pour mixture over pork. Cover and cook on **Low** for 5 hours or on **High** for 2½ hours. Increase heat to **High**. Add spinach, stirring to combine with chickpea mixture as best you can. Cover and cook on **High** for 20 minutes, until spinach is cooked and just a hint of pink remains in pork. Transfer to a warm platter and serve immediately.

Savory Pork Chops with Sauerkraut

Even if you don't like sauerkraut, I can't believe you won't like this dish. Sauerkraut has earned its negative reputation because most prepared versions are extremely vinegary. However, good sauerkraut, which you can make at home or often purchase at a farmers' market, is slightly creamy and tastes only mildly of vinegar. It's delicious and you'll be surprised at how mouth-watering this combination is. • *SERVES 6*

1 tbsp	vegetable oil	15 mL
6	thick-cut pork chops	6
1 tbsp	all-purpose flour	15 mL
1 tsp	salt	5 mL
½ tsp	cracked black peppercorns	2 mL
Pinch	cayenne pepper	Pinch
1 tsp	dry mustard	5 mL
2 cups	sauerkraut (see Tip, right)	500 mL
1	Granny Smith apple, peeled, cored and grated	1
½ cup	condensed chicken broth (undiluted), apple juice or apple cider	125 mL

Tip

For this dish, store-bought sauerkraut is acceptable, but rinse it thoroughly under cold water before adding to the recipe to reduce the vinegary taste.

1. In a skillet, heat oil over medium-high heat. Add pork chops, in batches, and brown on both sides. Transfer to slow cooker stoneware. Sprinkle with flour, salt, pepper, cayenne and dry mustard.

2. In a bowl, combine sauerkraut and grated apple. Spread over top of pork. Add chicken stock. Cover and cook on **Low** for 5 hours or on **High** for 2½ hours, until just a hint of pink remains in pork.

Pork Chops with Onions in Creamy Mustard Sauce

I learned about cooking pork chops with mustard more than twenty years ago from a friend who had just returned from a year in France, and ever since I've been making variations of this tasty combination. At home and in their ubiquitous bistros, the French, who know a thing or two about delicious food, eat pan-fried renditions of this dish. For the slow cooker version, use thick-cut loin or shoulder chops and serve with plenty of mashed potatoes to soak up the sauce. • *SERVES 4 TO 6*

1 tbsp	vegetable oil	15 mL
4 to 6	pork chops, 1 inch (2.5 cm) thick	4 to 6
2	onions, thinly sliced	2
4	cloves garlic, minced	4
1 tsp	dry mustard	5 mL
½ tsp	salt	2 mL
1 tsp	cracked black peppercorns	5 mL
Pinch	cayenne pepper (optional)	Pinch
2 tbsp	all-purpose flour	25 mL
1 tbsp	cider vinegar	15 mL
½ cup	white wine or condensed chicken stock (undiluted)	125 mL
2 tbsp	Dijon mustard	25 mL
½ cup	whipping cream	125 mL

Make ahead

This dish can be partially prepared the night before it is cooked. Complete Step 2, heating 1 tbsp (15 mL) oil in pan before softening onions. Cover and refrigerate mixture overnight. The next morning, brown pork chops (Step 1), or if you're pressed for time, omit browning and place pork directly in stoneware. Continue cooking as directed in Step 3.

1. In a skillet, heat oil over medium-high heat. Brown pork chops on both sides and transfer to slow cooker stoneware.

2. Reduce heat to medium. Add onions to pan and cook, stirring, until softened. Add garlic, dry mustard, salt, pepper and cayenne, if using, and cook for 1 minute. Add flour and cook, stirring, for 1 minute. Add vinegar and wine or stock and cook until thickened.

3. Pour mixture over meat and cook on **Low** for 4 to 5 hours or on **High** for 2 to 2½ hours, until pork is tender and just a hint of pink remains. Remove pork chops from slow cooker and place on a deep platter. Stir Dijon mustard and whipping cream into juices in slow cooker. Pour over pork and serve immediately.

Country-Style Ribs 'n' Beans

Cut from the loin rather than the rib, country-style pork ribs are meatier than spareribs. I think the combination of flavors in the sauce blends particularly well with pinto beans, but cranberry or red kidney beans make an acceptable substitute. You can jack up the heat by increasing the quantity of jalapeño peppers. I like to serve this at a Friday night pot luck, with lots of hot garlic bread, a big tossed salad and plenty of robust red wine. • *SERVES 6*

1 tbsp	vegetable oil	15 mL
3 lbs	country-style pork ribs, cut into individual ribs	1.5 kg
2	onions, finely chopped	2
4	stalks celery, peeled and diced	4
4	cloves garlic, finely chopped	4
1 to 2	jalapeño peppers, finely chopped	1 to 2
1 tbsp	chili powder	15 mL
2 tsp	cumin seeds	10 mL
1 tsp	salt	5 mL
1 tsp	cracked black peppercorns	5 mL
1	can (28 oz/796 mL) tomatoes, including juice (see Tip, page 32)	1
1	can (10 oz/284 mL) condensed chicken broth (undiluted)	1
1 cup	dry red wine	250 mL
1 cup	dried pinto beans, cooked and drained (see Preparing Dried Beans, page 17), or 1 can (19 oz/540 mL) pinto beans, drained and rinsed	250 mL
2	green bell peppers, cut into thin slivers	2

Make ahead

This dish can be partially prepared the night before it is cooked. Complete Step 2, heating 1 tbsp (15 mL) oil in pan before softening onions and celery. Cover and refrigerate mixture overnight. The next morning, brown ribs (Step 1), and continue cooking as directed. Alternately, cook overnight, cover and refrigerate. When you're ready to serve, bring ribs and beans to a boil in a Dutch oven and simmer for 10 minutes, until sauce is bubbling and meat is heated through.

1. In a skillet, heat oil over medium-high heat. Add ribs, in batches, and brown on all sides. Transfer to slow cooker stoneware and drain off all but 1 tbsp (15 mL) fat from pan.

2. Reduce heat to medium. Add onion and celery to pan and cook until soft. Add garlic, jalapeño peppers, chili powder, cumin seeds, salt and pepper and cook, stirring, for 1 minute. Stir in tomatoes, chicken broth and wine. Bring to a boil and cook, stirring, until liquid is reduced by one third, about 5 minutes, depending upon size of pan.

3. Pour mixture into slow cooker stoneware, add beans, cover and cook on **Low** for 6 to 8 hours or on **High** for 3 to 4 hours, until pork is tender.

4. Add bell peppers. Cover and cook on **High** for an additional 30 minutes.

Hearty Ribs with Rigatoni

This is another dish that I like to serve on Friday night, when the busy week is over and we enjoy being able to relax with friends. With a basket of hot garlic bread, a big salad, plenty of robust red wine and lively conversation, it's a great way to wind down. While the cream is not essential, it's a nice enrichment for the sauce. • *SERVES 6*

1 tbsp	vegetable oil	15 mL
3 lbs	country-style pork spareribs, cut into individual ribs	1.5 kg
2	onions, finely chopped	2
1	head garlic, peeled and finely chopped	1
1 tbsp	cracked black peppercorns	15 mL
1 tsp	salt	5 mL
4	sprigs fresh thyme or 1 tsp (5 mL) dried thyme leaves	4
½ tsp	ground nutmeg	2 mL
¼ tsp	cayenne pepper	1 mL
10	whole cloves	10
1	can (28 oz/796 mL) tomatoes, including juice, coarsely chopped (see Tip, page 32)	1
1 tbsp	tomato paste	15 mL
1 cup	dry red wine	250 mL
½ cup	whipping cream (optional)	125 mL
1 lb	rigatoni, cooked and drained	500 g
⅓ cup	finely chopped parsley	75 mL
	Freshly grated Parmesan cheese	

Make ahead

This dish can be partially prepared the night before it is cooked. Complete Step 2, heating 1 tbsp (15 mL) oil in pan before softening onions. Cover and refrigerate mixture overnight. The next morning, brown ribs (Step 1), and continue with Steps 3 and 4. Alternately, cook overnight, cover and refrigerate. When you're ready to serve, cook pasta, bring ribs and sauce to a boil in a Dutch oven and simmer for 10 minutes, until sauce is bubbling and meat is heated through. Then complete Step 4.

1. In a skillet, heat oil over medium-high heat. Add ribs, in batches, and brown on both sides. Transfer to slow cooker stoneware. Drain off all but 1 tbsp (15 mL) fat.

2. Reduce heat to medium. Add onions to pan and cook, stirring, until softened. Add garlic, pepper, salt, thyme, nutmeg, cayenne and cloves and cook, stirring, for 1 minute. Add tomatoes, tomato paste and wine. Bring to a boil and cook, stirring, until liquid is reduced by one third, about 5 minutes, depending upon the size of your pan.

3. Pour mixture into slow cooker stoneware and stir well. Cover and cook on **Low** for 8 hours or on **High** for 4 hours, until pork is tender.

4. Discard whole cloves. Add cream, if using, and stir to combine. Place cooked pasta in a large, deep platter and spoon ribs and sauce over all. Garnish liberally with parsley and pass the Parmesan in a small bowl.

Orange-Flavored Moroccan Lamb with Prunes

This variation on a lamb tagine, flavored with fruit and spices, is remarkably easy. The prunes thicken the sauce, which eliminates the need for flour, and you'll love the smell of cinnamon and nutmeg wafting through the house as the lamb slowly cooks. For a genuine Moroccan touch, serve over hot couscous. • *SERVES 6*

1 tbsp	vegetable oil	15 mL
2 lbs	boneless lamb shoulder, trimmed and cut into 1-inch (2.5-cm) cubes	1 kg
2	onions, thinly sliced	2
2	cloves garlic, minced	2
2	cinnamon sticks, broken into 4 pieces	2
¼ tsp	ground nutmeg	1 mL
½ tsp	salt	2 mL
½ tsp	black pepper	2 mL
½ cup	white wine	125 mL
¼ cup	condensed beef broth (undiluted)	50 mL
1 cup	pitted dried prunes, coarsely chopped	250 mL
	Zest and juice of 1 orange	
½ cup	whole blanched almonds, toasted	125 mL
2 tbsp	toasted sesame seeds	25 mL
	Couscous or hot cooked rice	

Make ahead

This dish can be partially prepared the night before it is cooked. Complete Step 2, heating 1 tbsp (15 mL) oil in pan before softening onions. Cover and refrigerate mixture overnight. The next morning, brown lamb (Step 1), or if you're pressed for time, omit browning and place lamb directly in stoneware. Continue cooking as directed.

1. In a skillet, heat oil over medium-high heat. Brown lamb, in batches, and, using a slotted spoon, transfer to slow cooker stoneware.

2. Reduce heat to medium. Add onions to pan and cook, stirring, until softened. Add garlic, cinnamon, nutmeg, salt and pepper and cook, stirring, for 1 minute. Add wine, beef broth, prunes and zest and juice of orange. Bring to a boil, stirring, and cook for 2 or 3 minutes, to reduce sauce slightly.

3. Pour mixture over lamb in stoneware. Cover and cook on **Low** for 8 to 10 hours or on **High** for 4 to 6 hours, until mixture is bubbling. Discard cinnamon sticks. Garnish with almonds and sesame seeds and serve over couscous or hot rice.

Lamb Keema

Since cows are sacred in many parts of India, cooks there have developed many marvelous recipes for preparing lamb. None are easier than those made with ground meat slowly simmered in spices. Serve over plain white rice and accompany with a salad of sliced cucumbers, tossed in sour cream, and an Indian bread such as naan, if available. • *SERVES 6 TO 8*

1 tbsp	vegetable oil	15 mL
2 lbs	ground lamb	1 kg
2	onions, finely chopped	2
6	cloves garlic, minced	6
2 tbsp	gingerroot, minced	25 mL
1 to 2	serrano chilies, finely chopped (see Tip, page 138)	1 to 2
1	piece cinnamon stick, about 2 inches (5 cm)	1
2 tsp	ground coriander	10 mL
1 tsp	cumin seeds	5 mL
1 tsp	turmeric	5 mL
1 tsp	salt	5 mL
½ tsp	cracked black peppercorns	2 mL
Pinch	ground cloves	Pinch
1	bay leaf	1
1	can (28 oz/796 mL) tomatoes, drained and coarsely chopped (see Tip, page 32)	1
1 tbsp	lemon juice	15 mL
1 cup	frozen peas, thawed	250 mL
½ cup	plain yogurt (optional)	125 mL
	Hot cooked rice	

Make ahead

This dish can be partially prepared the night before it is cooked. Complete Steps 1 and 2, chilling cooked meat and onion mixtures separately. Cover and refrigerate overnight. The next morning, combine in stoneware, and continue cooking as directed.

1. In a skillet, heat oil over medium-high heat. Add meat and cook, breaking up with a spoon, until no longer pink, about 5 minutes. Using a slotted spoon, transfer to slow cooker stoneware. Drain off liquid.

2. Reduce heat to medium. Add onions and cook, stirring, until softened. Add garlic, gingerroot, chili pepper, cinnamon, coriander, cumin seeds, turmeric, salt, pepper and cloves and cook, stirring, for 1 minute. Add bay leaf, tomatoes and lemon juice and bring to a boil.

3. Pour mixture over meat. Cover and cook on **Low** for 6 to 10 hours or on **High** for 3 to 4 hours, until hot and bubbling. Add peas. Cover and cook on **High** for 15 to 20 minutes. Discard bay leaf. Just before serving, stir in yogurt, if using. Serve immediately.

Variation

Beef Keema: Substitute 2 lbs (1 kg) lean ground beef for the lamb.

Lamb Korma with Spinach

A korma is an Indian dish of meat or vegetables braised in a minimal amount of liquid. This version, although very simple, is delicious and benefits from the addition of spinach and yogurt to enrich the sauce. Serve with fluffy white rice, preferably basmati, a steamed vegetable and Indian bread. • *SERVES 6 TO 8*

1 tbsp	vegetable oil	15 mL
2 lbs	boneless lamb shoulder roast, trimmed and cut into 1-inch (2.5-cm) cubes	1 kg
2	onions, finely chopped	2
4	cloves garlic, minced	4
2 tbsp	minced gingerroot	25 mL
4	cardamom pods, split	4
1 tbsp	turmeric	15 mL
1 tbsp	mustard seeds	15 mL
1 tsp	salt	5 mL
½ tsp	cracked black peppercorns	2 mL
1 to 2	serrano chilies, finely chopped (see Tip, page 138)	1 to 2
¼ cup	water	50 mL
1 lb	fresh spinach leaves or 1 package (10 oz/300 g) spinach, washed, dried, stems removed and finely chopped	500 g
½ cup	yogurt	125 mL
	Hot cooked rice	

1. In a skillet, heat oil over medium-high heat. Add lamb, in batches, and brown. Using a slotted spoon, transfer to slow cooker stoneware.

2. Reduce heat to medium. Add onions and cook, stirring, until softened. Add garlic, gingerroot, cardamom pods, turmeric, mustard seeds, salt, pepper and chili peppers. Cook, stirring, for 1 minute. Add water and stir.

3. Transfer mixture to slow cooker stoneware and stir to combine thoroughly with lamb. Cover and cook on **Low** for 8 to 10 hours, until lamb is tender.

4. Add spinach and stir well, pushing leaves down into the hot stew. Cover and cook on **High** for 20 minutes, or until spinach is soft. Stir in yogurt and serve over hot cooked rice.

Variation

Beef Korma with Spinach: Substitute 2 lbs (1 kg) stewing beef for the lamb.

Make ahead

This dish can be partially prepared the night before it is cooked. Complete Step 2, heating 1 tbsp (15 mL) oil in pan before softening onions. Cover and refrigerate mixture overnight. The next morning, brown lamb (Step 1), or omit browning and place lamb directly in stoneware. Continue cooking as directed. Alternately, the Korma may be cooked overnight (Steps 1 through 3) and refrigerated. When ready to serve, bring to a boil in a Dutch oven and simmer for 10 minutes, until mixture is hot and bubbling and meat is heated through. Add spinach and cook. Stir in yogurt and serve (Step 4).

Tip

Use your lettuce spinner to dry the whole leaves of spinach, then chop them finely for this recipe.

Poultry

Chicken Enchiladas

If you have a yen for rustic Mexican food, there's nothing like an enchilada to satisfy your craving. This zesty flavored combination of textures and flavors is hearty and delicious. All you need is a tossed green salad and cold beer for a perfect meal. • *SERVES 6*

• **LARGE (MINIMUM 5 QUART) OVAL SLOW COOKER**

1 tbsp	vegetable oil	15 mL
2	onions, thinly sliced	2
3	cloves garlic, minced	3
2 to 3	jalapeño peppers, thinly sliced	2 to 3
1 tsp	salt	5 mL
1 tsp	cracked black peppercorns	5 mL
1	can (28 oz/795 mL) tomatoes, including juice, chopped (see Tip, page 32)	1
1½ cups	tomato juice	375 mL
12	flour tortillas	12
1	Shredded Chicken (see recipe, page 159)	1
½ cup	finely chopped green onion	125 mL
3 cups	Monterey Jack cheese, shredded	750 mL
	Finely chopped cilantro	
	Shredded lettuce	
	Hot or mild salsa	
	Sour cream	

Make ahead

Prepare Shredded Chicken (see recipe, page 159) a day ahead or cook overnight in the slow cooker so it's ready to use for this recipe. (Works best if your slow cooker switches to **Warm** after 6 hours.) Enchiladas can be prepared the night before they are cooked. Follow preparation directions (Steps 1 through 3), and refrigerate overnight. The next day, continue cooking as directed in Step 4.

1. In a skillet, heat oil over medium heat. Add onions and cook until softened. Add garlic, jalapeño peppers, salt and pepper and cook, stirring, for 1 minute. Add tomatoes and cook for 5 minutes, until sauce thickens slightly.

2. Meanwhile, pour tomato juice into a large bowl. One at a time, dip tortillas in juice, turning to ensure all parts are moistened. Lay tortilla on a plate, spread with about ⅓ cup (75 mL) shredded chicken, sprinkle with approximately 1 tsp (5 mL) green onion and 2 tbsp (25 mL) shredded cheese. Fold ends over and roll up. Repeat with remaining tortillas. (When you're finished, you should have about 1 cup of cheese left over.) Discard remaining tomato juice.

3. Lay filled tortillas, seam-side down, in slow cooker stoneware. Pour sauce over tortillas and sprinkle with remaining cheese and green onions.

4. Cover and cook on **Low** for 7 to 8 hours or on **High** for 3 to 4 hours, until hot and bubbling. Garnish with cilantro, lettuce, salsa and sour cream.

Easy Chicken Tacos

This is a great way to provide your family with a hot meal on those nights when everybody is on a different schedule. Make Shredded Chicken the night before (see recipe, page 159). Assemble the filling, cook in the slow cooker and leave tortillas and garnishes out so people can help themselves. • *SERVES 4 TO 6*

2 cups	refried beans, canned or homemade	500 mL
4	jalapeño peppers, sliced	4
2 cups	Monterey Jack cheese, shredded	500 mL
1	Shredded Chicken (see recipe, page 159)	1
8 to 12	tortillas, flour or corn	8 to 12
	Shredded lettuce	
	Chopped green or red onion	
	Hot or mild salsa	
	Sour cream	

Make ahead

If chicken is already cooked, the filling can be assembled the night before. Combine beans, peppers, cheese and shredded chicken, cover and refrigerate overnight. The next day, continue cooking as directed in Step 1.

1. In slow cooker stoneware, combine beans, peppers, cheese and shredded chicken. Cook on **Low** for 6 to 8 hours or on **High** for 3 to 4 hours, until hot and bubbly. Leave on **Low** or **Warm**, if you have the setting, so people can help themselves to the filling.

2. To make tacos, spoon filling onto tortillas. Top with lettuce, onion, salsa and sour cream. Roll up and enjoy.

Shredded Chicken

Shredded chicken is the basis for many dishes. Not only is it extremely easy to make in the slow cooker, the results are excellent. Since the cooking broth will be discarded, there's no need to worry about extra fat, so leave the skin on to ensure that chicken is as moist as possible. • *MAKES 4 TO 6 CUPS*

3 to 4 lbs	chicken pieces, skin on	1.5 to 2 kg
1	onion, peeled and quartered	1
1 tsp	dried oregano leaves	5 mL
1 tsp	salt	5 mL
1 tsp	cracked black peppercorns	5 mL
1	bay leaf	1

Make ahead

When using shredded chicken in a recipe, prepare a day ahead or cook overnight in the slow cooker. (Works best if your slow cooker switches to **Warm** after 6 hours.)

1. Place all ingredients in slow cooker stoneware, laying dark meat (legs and thighs) on bottom and white meat (breasts) on top. Add water to cover. Cover and cook on **Low** for 6 hours, until chicken is cooked through. Allow to cool in liquid. Remove skin and bones from chicken and shred by pulling the meat off the bones and apart with your fingers. Cover and refrigerate for use the next day in tacos or enchiladas.

Mexican-Style Chicken with Cilantro and Lemon

With a sauce of pumpkin seeds, cumin seeds, oregano and cilantro, this dish reminds me of warm evening dinners in the courtyard of a charming Mexican hacienda. Mexicans have been thickening sauces with pumpkin seeds long before the Spanish arrived and, today, every cook has their own recipes for *mole*, one of the world's great culinary concoctions. Serve this with rice and fresh corn on the cob. • *SERVES 4 TO 6*

¼ cup	raw pumpkin seeds	50 mL
2 tsp	cumin seeds	10 mL
1 tbsp	vegetable oil	15 mL
3 lbs	chicken pieces, skin on breasts, removed from legs and thighs	1.5 kg
2	onions, sliced	2
4	cloves garlic, minced	4
2 tbsp	tomato paste	25 mL
1 tsp	salt	5 mL
1 tsp	crushed black peppercorns	5 mL
1 tsp	dried oregano leaves	5 mL
1 to 2	serrano chilies, chopped (see Tip, page 138)	1 to 2
¼ tsp	ground cinnamon	1 mL
2 cups	cilantro leaves (see Tip, right)	500 mL
1 tbsp	lemon zest	15 mL
2 tbsp	lemon juice	25 mL
½ cup	condensed chicken broth (undiluted)	125 mL
	Finely chopped cilantro and green onion	
	Lemon zest	

1. In a skillet, over medium-high heat, toast pumpkin and cumin seeds, until pumpkin seeds are popping and cumin has released its flavor. Transfer to a small bowl and set aside.

2. In the same skillet, heat oil over medium-high heat. Add chicken and brown in batches. Using a slotted spoon, transfer to slow cooker stoneware. Reduce heat to medium.

3. Add onions to pan and cook, stirring, until softened. Add garlic, tomato paste, salt, pepper, oregano, chili pepper, cinnamon and cilantro and cook, stirring, for 1 minute. Transfer contents of pan to a food processor. Add lemon zest and juice, chicken broth, pumpkin and cumin seeds and process until smooth.

4. Pour sauce over chicken and cook on **Low** for 5 to 6 hours, until juices run clear when chicken is pierced with a fork. When ready to serve, garnish with cilantro, green onion and lemon zest.

Make ahead

This dish can be partially prepared the night before it is cooked. Complete Step 1 and set toasted seeds aside. Proceed to Step 3, heating 1 tbsp (15 mL) oil in pan before softening onions. Cover and refrigerate puréed sauce. The next morning, brown chicken (Step 2), or if you're pressed for time, omit browning and place chicken directly in stoneware. Continue cooking as directed in Step 4.

Tip

If you don't have enough cilantro leaves to make 2 cups (500 mL), use some of the stems in the sauce.

Tip

Buy seeds and nuts at a health or bulk food store with high turnover, as they are likely to be much fresher than those in packages.

Easy Chicken Paprikash

This simple dish reminds me of my student days when, feeling very sophisticated, we often dined out at an inexpensive Hungarian restaurant, close to the campus. Chicken Paprikash with dumplings was the house specialty and it has remained a sentimental favorite ever since. For convenience, I've simplified the sauce and dispensed with the dumplings. I like to serve this with hot buttered noodles and a salad, instead. • *SERVES 6*

1 tbsp	vegetable oil	15 mL
3 lbs	chicken pieces, skin on breasts, removed from legs and thighs	1.5 kg
2	medium onions, finely chopped	2
1	clove garlic, minced	1
1 tbsp	sweet paprika	15 mL
½ tsp	salt	2 mL
½ tsp	cracked black peppercorns	2 mL
2 tbsp	all-purpose flour	25 mL
¼ cup	condensed chicken broth (undiluted)	50 mL
1	can (10 oz/284 mL) condensed tomato soup	1
½ cup	sour cream	125 mL
½ cup	half-and-half cream	125 mL
¼ cup	finely chopped dill	50 mL
	Hot buttered noodles	

Make ahead

This dish can be partially prepared the night before it is cooked. Complete Step 2, heating 1 tbsp (15 mL) oil in pan before softening onions. Cover and refrigerate mixture overnight. The next morning, brown chicken (Step 1), or if you're pressed for time, omit this step and place chicken directly in stoneware. Continue cooking as directed in Step 3.

1. In a skillet, heat oil over medium-high heat. Add chicken, in batches, and brown on all sides. Transfer to slow cooker stoneware.

2. Reduce heat to medium. Add onions and cook until soft. Add garlic, paprika, salt, pepper and cook, stirring, for 1 minute. Sprinkle flour over mixture, stir well and cook for 1 minute. Add chicken broth and cook for 1 minute, until almost all evaporates. Remove pan from heat, stir soup into mixture.

3. Pour mixture over chicken. Cover and cook on **Low** for 6 hours or on **High** for 3 hours, until juices run clear when chicken is pierced with a fork.

4. In a bowl, mix together sour cream and cream. Add to chicken along with dill. Stir well and serve over hot buttered noodles.

Cheesy Chicken-Noodle Casserole

You'll need a large oval slow cooker for this quintessential comfort-food dish. All you need to add is a big salad for a great family meal. • *SERVES 6 TO 8*

- **LARGE (MINIMUM 5 QUART) OVAL SLOW COOKER**
- **LIGHTLY GREASED SLOW COOKER STONEWARE**

1 tbsp	vegetable oil	15 mL
1 lb	ground chicken	500 g
2	onions, finely chopped	2
4	stalks celery, peeled and thinly sliced	4
2	cloves garlic, minced	2
1 tbsp	sweet paprika	15 mL
1 tsp	dry mustard	5 mL
1 tsp	poultry seasoning	5 mL
1/2 tsp	each salt and black pepper	2 mL
1	can (10 oz/284 mL) condensed cream of mushroom soup	1
1/2 cup	condensed chicken broth (undiluted)	125 mL
1	jar (4 1/2 oz/128 mL) pimento, drained and finely chopped	1
8 oz	cream cheese, cut into 2-inch (5-cm) cubes and softened	250 g
1	package (12 oz/375 g) egg noodles, cooked and drained	1
Topping		
1 cup	bread crumbs	250 mL
1 cup	shredded Cheddar cheese	250 mL
2 tbsp	melted butter	25 mL

Make ahead

This dish can be partially prepared the night before it is cooked. Complete Steps 1 and 2, chilling cooked meat and sauce separately. Refrigerate overnight. Shred cheese, cover and refrigerate. The next morning, cook noodles and continue as directed in Steps 3, 4 and 5.

1. In a skillet, heat oil over medium-high heat. Add chicken and cook, breaking up with a spoon, until meat is no longer pink. Drain off liquid and set chicken aside.

2. Reduce heat to medium. Add onions and celery and cook until softened. Add garlic, paprika, mustard, poultry seasoning, salt and pepper and cook, stirring, for 1 minute. Blend in soup and chicken broth. Add pimento and cream cheese, stirring, until cheese is melted. Stir in reserved chicken.

3. To assemble casserole: Spoon 1 cup (250 mL) chicken mixture in bottom of prepared stoneware. Add a layer of noodles. Repeat until all ingredients are used up, finishing with a layer of sauce.

4. To make Topping: In a bowl, toss bread crumbs with butter. Add cheese and spread over casserole.

5. Cover and cook on **Low** for 8 hours or on **High** for 4 hours, until hot and bubbling.

Homestyle Chicken with Gingersnap Gravy

Although it may seem like an unusual idea, using gingersnaps to thicken gravy is a technique that has been around for a long time. Often, *sauerbraten*, a flavorful pot roast of German origin, is finished with a gingersnap gravy. The idea for this recipe comes from a different part of the world — the "low country" around Charleston, South Carolina, one of my favorite cities. If you prefer a spicier version, add a finely chopped jalapeño pepper (or two!) along with the garlic. • *SERVES 4 TO 6*

3½ lbs	chicken pieces, skin on breasts, removed from legs and thighs	1.75 kg
2	onions, finely chopped	2
3	stalks celery, peeled and thinly sliced	3
2	cloves garlic, minced	2
1	jalapeño pepper (optional)	1
1 tbsp	minced gingerroot	15 mL
1 tsp	salt	5 mL
1 tsp	cracked black peppercorns	5 mL
1 tsp	chili powder	5 mL
½ tsp	ground nutmeg	2 mL
¼ cup	all-purpose flour	50 mL
1 cup	condensed chicken broth (undiluted)	250 mL
½ cup	yogurt	125 mL
¼ cup	gingersnap crumbs (see Tip, right)	50 mL
	Mashed potatoes or hot cooked rice (optional)	

1. In a skillet, heat oil over medium-high heat. Add chicken and brown on all sides, in batches, if necessary. Using a slotted spoon, transfer to slow cooker stoneware.

2. Reduce heat to medium. Add onions and celery to pan and cook, stirring, until softened. Add garlic, jalapeño, if using, gingerroot, salt, pepper, chili powder and nutmeg and cook, stirring, for 1 minute. Sprinkle flour over mixture and cook, stirring, for 1 minute. Add broth and cook until thickened.

3. Pour mixture over chicken, cover and cook on **Low** for 5 to 6 hours, until juices run clear when chicken is pierced with a fork. Add yogurt and gingersnap crumbs. Cover and cook on **High** for 20 minutes, until hot and bubbling. Serve over mashed potatoes or rice.

Make ahead

This dish can be partially prepared the night before it is cooked. Complete Step 2, heating 1 tbsp (15 mL) oil in pan before softening onions and celery. Cover and refrigerate mixture overnight. The next morning, brown chicken (Step 1), or omit browning and place chicken directly in stoneware. Continue with Step 3.

Tip

In this recipe, the quality of the gravy depends on the "snap" in your gingersnaps. Buy high-quality gingersnaps from a premium bakery or make your own. Taste the gravy and if the gingersnap flavor is not pronounced enough, mix together 1 tsp (5 mL) ground ginger and 1 tbsp (15 mL) brown sugar. Stir into gravy in 1-tsp (5-mL) increments, until desired flavor is achieved.

Piquant Chicken Wings with Goat Cheese

This simple, yet satisfying dish is sure to become a family favorite. If you prefer a spicer version, add finely chopped chili pepper, to taste, just before serving. Serve over hot pasta and accompany with a green salad for a complete meal. • *SERVES 6*

• PREHEATED BROILER

1 tbsp	sweet paprika	15 mL
1 tbsp	cracked black peppercorns	15 mL
2 tsp	garlic powder	10 mL
2 tsp	onion powder	10 mL
2 tsp	dried oregano leaves	10 mL
¼ tsp	cayenne (optional)	1 mL
3 lbs	chicken wings, tips removed, about 16 wings	1.5 kg
3 cups	good quality tomato sauce	750 mL
¼ cup	crumbled fresh goat cheese	50 mL
	Finely chopped chili pepper (optional)	

1. In a small bowl, combine paprika, pepper, garlic powder, onion powder, oregano and cayenne, if using. Mix well.

2. Position a broiler rack 6 inches (15 cm) from heat source. Place chicken wings on broiler pan or a baking sheet and sprinkle with spice mixture on both sides. Broil, turning once, for 15 minutes, or until browned. Transfer to slow cooker stoneware.

3. Add tomato sauce to stoneware and stir well. Cover and cook on **Low** for 5 to 6 hours or on **High** for 2½ to 3 hours. Using tongs, transfer wings to a large, deep platter. Add goat cheese and chili pepper, if using, to sauce and stir until cheese dissolves. Pour over wings and serve.

French-Country Chicken with Olives

I love the bold flavors of this hearty country-style dish. Served with a big bowl of fluffy mashed potatoes, there's nothing more satisfying on a chilly day. Accompany with crusty bread, a green salad and a robust red wine. • *SERVES 6*

4	slices bacon or 2 oz (56 g) salt pork belly, cut in ¼-inch (0.5-cm) cubes	4
3 to 4 lbs	chicken pieces, skin on breasts, removed from legs and thighs	1.5 to 2 kg
2	medium onions, finely chopped	2
4	cloves garlic, minced	4
1 tsp	dried Italian herb seasoning	5 mL
1 tsp	salt	5 mL
1 tsp	cracked black peppercorns	5 mL
¼ cup	all-purpose flour	50 mL
½ cup	dry white wine	125 mL
1 cup	good quality tomato sauce	250 mL
½ cup	condensed chicken broth (undiluted)	125 mL
1	bay leaf	1
½ cup	black olives, pitted and thinly sliced (see Tip, right)	125 mL
½ cup	green olives, pitted and thinly sliced Finely chopped Italian parsley	125 mL

1. In a skillet, over medium-high heat, cook bacon or salt pork until crisp. Drain on paper towels. If using bacon, when cool enough to handle, crumble and set aside.

2. Drain all but 2 tbsp (25 mL) fat from the pan. Add chicken pieces, in batches, and brown. Transfer to slow cooker stoneware.

3. Reduce heat to medium. Add onions and cook until soft. Add garlic, Italian seasoning, salt, pepper and cook, stirring, for 1 minute. Add flour and cook, stirring, for 1 minute. Add wine and stir well. Add tomato sauce and chicken broth and bring to a boil, stirring until mixture thickens. Add bay leaf and bacon or salt pork and stir to combine.

4. Pour sauce over chicken, cover and cook on **Low** for 5 to 6 hours or on **High** for 2½ to 3 hours, until juices run clear when chicken is pierced with a fork. Add olives, cover and cook on **High** for 15 minutes, until heated through. Discard bay leaf. Serve piping hot, garnished with parsley.

Make ahead

This dish can be partially prepared the night before it is cooked. Complete Steps 1 and 3 in method. Cover and refrigerate mixture overnight. The next morning, heat 1 tbsp (15 mL) oil in pan and brown chicken (Step 2), or if you're pressed for time, omit browning and place chicken directly in stoneware. Continue cooking as directed in Step 4.

Tip

Although there may be a few exceptions, as a general rule of thumb, the best olives do not come in cans or jars. This is particularly true of black olives as most of the canned varieties are processed by the "California" method, which artificially "ripens" them in an alkaline solution, rendering them particularly tasteless. I always buy olives in bulk, from a trusted purveyor, and I make a point of tasting first.

Tuscan Chicken with Sage

This simple, yet delicious, chicken gets its distinctive slightly peppery flavor from the addition of fresh sage, which has a pleasantly pungent flavor. In many ways, its an Italian variation of *coq au vin*. Serve with a basic risotto, a robust green vegetable, such as broccoli or rapini, and hot crusty bread to soak up the sauce. • *SERVES 4 TO 6*

½ cup	all-purpose flour	125 mL
3 lbs	chicken pieces, skin on breasts, removed from legs and thighs	1.5 kg
2 tbsp	olive oil	25 mL
2	onions, finely chopped	2
2	cloves garlic, minced	2
1 tsp	salt	5 mL
½ tsp	cracked black peppercorns	2 mL
½ cup	fresh sage leaves or 1 tsp (5 mL) dried sage (see Tip, right)	125 mL
2 cups	dry robust red wine, such as Chianti	500 mL

1. On a plate, coat chicken on all sides with flour, shaking off the excess. Discard excess flour.

2. In a skillet, heat oil over medium-high heat. Add chicken, in batches, and brown on all sides. Transfer to slow cooker stoneware.

3. Reduce heat to medium. Add onions to pan, adding 1 tbsp (15 mL) additional oil, if needed. Cook, stirring, until softened. Add garlic, salt, pepper and sage and cook, stirring, for 1 minute. Pour in wine, bring to boil and cook, stirring, for 5 minutes, until sauce is reduced by one third.

4. Pour mixture over chicken, cover and cook on **Low** for 5 to 6 hours or on **High** for 2½ to 3 hours, until juices run clear when chicken is pierced with a fork. Serve immediately.

Make ahead

This dish can be partially prepared the night before it is cooked. Complete Step 3, heating 1 tbsp (15 mL) oil in pan before softening onions. Cover and refrigerate mixture overnight. The next morning brown chicken (Steps 1 and 2), and continue cooking as directed in Step 4.

Tip

For optimum results, make an effort to find fresh sage, which is often available in the produce section of well-stocked supermarkets or specialty stores. If you can't locate it, dried sage produces an acceptable substitute in this recipe.

Italian-Style Braised Chicken

The Italians have many recipes for braised chicken. This version, which uses a whole chicken, is particularly delicious and light. I like to serve it with roasted potatoes, brushed with extra-virgin olive oil infused with rosemary. • *SERVES 4 TO 6*

• **LARGE (MINIMUM 5 QUART) OVAL SLOW COOKER**

1	roasting chicken, about 3 to 6 lbs (1.5 to 3 kg)	1
2	red bell peppers, roasted, peeled and cut into strips (see Tip, page 70)	2
2	lemon slices, about ½ inch (1 cm) thick	2
2 tbsp	olive oil	25 mL
2 cups	leeks, white with some green part, but discard tough outer leaves, cleaned and thinly sliced (see Tip, page 212)	500 mL
4	cloves garlic, minced	4
½ cup	chopped parsley	125 mL
1 tsp	dried thyme leaves or 2 sprigs fresh thyme	5 mL
1 tsp	salt	5 mL
½ tsp	black pepper	2 mL
2	bay leaves	2
½ cup	dry vermouth or dry white wine	125 mL
1	can (28 oz/796 mL) tomatoes, drained and coarsely chopped (see Tip, page 32)	1
½ cup	prosciutto or Black Forest ham, finely chopped	125 mL
2	zucchini, cut into ¼-inch (0.5-cm) slices, sweated and drained (see Tip, right)	2

1. Rinse chicken inside and out and pat dry. Place lemon slices inside cavity and truss chicken loosely (see Tip, page 174).

2. In a large skillet, heat oil over medium-high heat. Brown chicken on all sides, using two wooden spoons to turn so skin isn't punctured. Transfer to stoneware and drain off all but 1 tbsp (15 mL) fat.

3. Reduce heat to medium. Add leeks to pan and cook until soft. Add garlic, red peppers, parsley, thyme, salt, pepper and bay leaves and cook for 1 minute. Add vermouth or white wine and tomatoes and bring to a boil. Cook until liquid is reduced by about one third.

4. Pour sauce over chicken. Cover and cook on **Low** for 7 to 9 hours or on **High** for 3½ to 4½ hours, until juices run clear when thigh is pierced with a fork or meat thermometer reads 170°F (77°C). Discard bay leaves. Add ham and zucchini. Cover and cook on **High** for 30 minutes, until zucchini is tender. To serve, place carved chicken on a platter and cover with sauce.

Make ahead

This dish can be partially prepared the night before it is cooked. Complete Step 3, heating 1 tbsp (15 mL) oil in pan before softening leeks. Cover and refrigerate sauce. The next morning, continue cooking as directed in Steps 1, 2 and 4.

Tip

Because of its high water content, zucchini should be "sweated" before adding to the slow cooker. Arrange the sliced zucchini in a colander, sprinkle with 1 tsp (5 mL) salt and leave for 20 to 30 minutes. Rinse well under cold running water before adding to the recipe.

Chicken with White Beans and Chorizo

Both the Spanish and the Portuguese claim the spicy chorizo sausage for their own and this dish owes something to both cultures. It's a complete meal in itself — just add salad. I like to serve this with hot cornbread and Piri Piri sauce, which we pass at the table. Piri Piri, a bottled hot sauce, popular in Portugal, is made from hot peppers grown in Africa. While it has a unique flavor, if you can't find it, any bottled hot sauce, such as Tabasco or Louisiana Hot Sauce, will do. • *SERVES 6 TO 8*

1 tbsp	vegetable oil	15 mL
8 oz	hard chorizo sausage, cut into ¼-inch (0.5-cm) slices or removed from casing and chopped, depending on your preference (see Tip, right)	250 g
3 lbs	chicken pieces, skin on breasts, removed from legs and thighs	1.5 kg
¼ cup	brandy (optional)	50 mL
2	onions, diced	2
4	cloves garlic, finely chopped	4
1 tbsp	paprika	15 mL
1 tsp	dried thyme leaves	5 mL
1 tsp	salt	5 mL
1 tsp	cracked black peppercorns	5 mL
¼ tsp	cayenne pepper (optional)	1 mL
½ cup	dry sherry	125 mL
1	can (28 oz/796 mL) tomatoes, including juice, coarsely chopped (see Tip, page 171)	1
1 tsp	granulated sugar	5 mL
1	can (19 oz/540 mL) white beans, rinsed and drained, or 2 cups (500 mL) dried white beans, cooked and drained	1
1 cup	large green pimento-stuffed olives, thinly sliced	250 mL

Make ahead

This dish can be partially prepared the night before it is cooked. Complete Step 2, heating 1 tbsp (15 mL) oil in pan before softening onions. Cover and refrigerate mixture overnight. The next morning, brown sausage and chicken (Step 1), or if you're pressed for time, omit Step 1, placing sausage and chicken directly in stoneware and omitting brandy from recipe. Continue cooking as directed in Step 3.

Tip

If you can't find hard chorizo sausage, substitute an equal quantity of pepperoni or kielbasa.

1. In a skillet, heat oil over medium-high heat. Lightly brown sausage and, with a slotted spoon, transfer to slow cooker stoneware. Add chicken, in batches, and brown, transferring to slow cooker stoneware as completed. If using brandy, return chicken pieces to pan and turn element off. Pour brandy over chicken and ignite. When flames have subsided, transfer chicken to slow cooker stoneware with a slotted spoon. Drain off all but 2 tbsp (25 mL) fat from pan.

2. Reduce heat to medium. Add onions to pan and cook, stirring, until softened. Add garlic, paprika, thyme, salt, pepper and cayenne, if using, and cook, stirring, for 1 minute or until onion is softened. Add sherry and cook, stirring, for 1 minute, until alcohol evaporates. Add tomatoes and sugar and bring to a boil. Cook, stirring, until liquid is reduced by one third, about 5 minutes. Add beans and stir.

3. Pour mixture over chicken and sausage. Cover and cook on **Low** for 6 hours or on **High** for 3 hours, until juices run clear when chicken is pierced with a fork. Add olives and cook on **High** for 15 minutes, until heated through.

Tip

I use imported Italian canned tomatoes, which are thicker than their North American counterparts, for this recipe. If you're using domestic canned tomatoes, I recommend adding 1 tbsp (15 mL) tomato paste, along with the tomatoes.

Indonesian Chicken

Although this chicken dish is remarkably easy, its slightly sweet, yet spicy coconut-milk sauce gives it an exotic flavor. For a more fiery version, increase the quantity of *sambal oelek*. Serve over fluffy white rice. • *SERVES 4 TO 6*

1 tbsp	vegetable oil	15 mL
3 lbs	chicken pieces, skin on breasts, removed from legs and thigh	1.5 kg
2	onions, sliced	2
4	cloves garlic, minced	4
1 tbsp	minced gingerroot	15 mL
1 tsp	ground coriander	5 mL
1 tsp	turmeric	5 mL
8	almonds, blanched and peeled	8
1	can (14 oz/398 mL) coconut milk	1
1	stalk lemongrass, bruised and cut into 2-inch (5-cm) pieces, or 1 tbsp (15 mL) lemon zest (see Tip, right)	1
1½ tsp	soya sauce, preferably dark	7 mL
1 tsp	brown sugar	5 mL
1 tbsp	sambal oelek (see page 16)	15 mL
	Hot cooked rice	

1. In a skillet, heat oil over medium-high heat. Add chicken and cook, turning, until brown. Transfer to slow cooker stoneware. Drain off all but 1 tbsp (15 mL) fat in the pan.

2. Reduce heat to medium. Add onions to pan and cook, stirring, until softened. Add garlic, ginger, coriander, turmeric and almonds and cook, stirring, for 1 minute. Add coconut milk and stir. Transfer contents of pan to food processor and process until smooth.

3. Pour mixture over chicken and add lemongrass or lemon zest. Cover and cook on **Low** for 6 hours or on **High** for 3 hours, until juices run clear when chicken is pierced with a fork.

4. Discard lemongrass. Stir in soya sauce, brown sugar and sambal oelek and serve over fluffy white rice.

Make ahead

This dish can be partially prepared the night before it is cooked. Complete Step 2, heating 1 tbsp (15 mL) oil in pan before softening onions. Cover and refrigerate puréed mixture overnight. The next morning, brown chicken (Step 1), or if you're pressed for time, omit browning and place chicken directly in stoneware. Continue cooking as directed in Step 3.

Tip

Lemongrass, which has a unique woody-lemony flavor, is available in Asian markets and many supermarkets. Before adding lemongrass to a recipe, "smash" it with the flat side of a chef's knife, so it can release its flavor when it cooks.

Spicy Chinese Chicken

I've been making variations of this basic recipe for more than twenty years and I still love it. This one is particularly good, as the vinegar, brown sugar and chili pepper add a nice complexity to the basic sauce. • SERVES 6

¾ cup	condensed chicken broth (undiluted)	175 mL
3 tbsp	rice vinegar	45 mL
2 tsp	packed brown sugar	10 mL
¼ cup	soya sauce, preferably dark (see Tip, right)	50 mL
4	green onions, including stems, cut into 2-inch (5-cm) pieces	4
4	cloves garlic, minced	4
1 tbsp	minced gingerroot	15 mL
1	serrano chili or 2 Thai chilies, finely chopped (see Tip, page 138)	1
1 tsp	cracked black peppercorns	5 mL
3 lbs	skinless chicken pieces	1.5 kg
3 tbsp	cornstarch	45 mL
	Hot cooked rice	

Make ahead

This dish can be assembled the night before it is cooked and, in fact, improves in flavor for marinating in the sauce overnight. Complete Step 1. Pour sauce over chicken and refrigerate overnight. The next day, transfer mixture to stoneware in slow cooker and continue cooking as directed in Step 2.

1. In a bowl, combine chicken broth, rice vinegar, brown sugar and soya sauce, stirring well to ensure sugar is dissolved. Add green onions, garlic, gingerroot, chili peppers and pepper.

2. Place chicken in slow cooker stoneware. Pour sauce over chicken. Cover and cook on **Low** for 5 to 6 hours or on **High** for 2½ to 3 hours, until juices run clear when chicken is pierced with a fork.

3. With a slotted spoon, transfer chicken to a platter and cover with foil to keep warm. Strain liquid into a saucepan. Whisk in 3 tbsp (45 mL) cornstarch dissolved in 2 tbsp (25 mL) cold water. Bring to a boil. Reduce heat to simmer and stir for about 3 minutes or until thickened and glossy. Pour over chicken. Serve with hot fluffy rice.

Tip

Dark soya sauce, which is aged for a longer period of time than the lighter version, is thicker and more flavorful and works better in braising-type recipes such as this one. It is available in Asian grocery stores and many supermarkets with an Asian section. If you can't find it, use the same quantity of light soya sauce mixed with 1 tbsp (15 mL) molasses.

Roast Chicken in Tarragon-Cream Sauce

Chicken and tarragon have a natural affinity and the French have many variations of this tasty dish that, for many years, has been a favorite in our house. For the slow cooker version, I've flavored the chicken with lemon and shallots in addition to tarragon. Although it's a bit cumbersome, I like to brown the chicken first, not only for eye appeal but because it releases some flavorful fat in which to soften the shallots and enrich the cooking liquid. While not absolutely necessary, the addition of brandy enhances the rich cream sauce that makes a superb accompaniment to simple boiled potatoes with parsley, mashed potatoes or plain steamed rice. • *SERVES 4 TO 6*

• LARGE (MINIMUM 5 QUART) OVAL SLOW COOKER

1	roasting chicken, about 3 to 6 lbs (1.5 to 3 kg)	1
2	slices lemon, about ½ inch (1 cm) thick	2
1 tsp	dried tarragon or 2 sprigs fresh tarragon	5 mL
1 tbsp	vegetable oil	15 mL
2 tbsp	brandy (optional)	25 mL
3 tbsp	finely chopped shallots	45 mL
1 tsp	salt	5 mL
¼ tsp	black pepper	1 mL
½ cup	dry white wine	125 mL
½ cup	condensed chicken broth (undiluted)	125 mL

Tarragon-Cream Sauce

	Cooking liquid from chicken	
¼ cup	chopped fresh tarragon or 2 tbsp (25 mL) dried tarragon	50 mL
½ cup	whipping cream	125 mL
	Salt and black pepper, to taste	

Tip

I suggest trussing the chicken loosely for ease of browning and lifting. However, it is important to keep the string loose or the inner part of the thigh, which is less exposed to heat, will not cook properly.

1. Rinse chicken inside and out and pat dry. Place lemon slices inside cavity along with tarragon and truss chicken loosely (see Tip, right).

2. In a skillet, heat oil over medium-high heat. Brown chicken on all sides, using two wooden spoons to turn the bird so you don't puncture the skin, finishing with the breast-side up. Turn off heat and pour brandy, if using, over chicken. Ignite and, when flames subside, transfer chicken to slow cooker stoneware.

continued on page 176

3. Drain off all but 1 tbsp (15 mL) fat in pan. Over medium heat, cook shallots until soft. Season with salt and pepper. Add wine and chicken broth and bring to a boil. Cook until sauce is reduced by about one third, about 5 minutes. Pour over chicken, cover and cook on **Low** for 7 to 9 hours or on **High** for 3½ to 4½ hours, until juices run clear when pierced with a fork or a meat thermometer inserted in the thickest part of the thigh reads 170°F (77°C).

4. Carefully lift chicken from liquid, transfer to a large heatproof platter and keep warm while you make the sauce.

5. To make Tarragon-Cream Sauce: Pour cooking liquid into a 4-cup (1-L) heatproof measure and place in the freezer for a few minutes until the fat rises to the surface. Skim off as much fat as possible. Transfer remaining liquid to a saucepan and, over high heat, boil rapidly until sauce is reduced by half. Stir in tarragon and cream and season to taste with salt and pepper. Serve in a sauceboat alongside carved chicken.

Mellow Chicken Curry

By Indian standards, this is a simple chicken curry, but the results are delicious nonetheless. In Indian cooking it is customary for chicken to be cut up into fairly small pieces. Legs are separated into drumsticks and thighs and whole breasts are cut into four parts, which makes for a more elegant presentation. • *SERVES 4 TO 6*

1 tbsp	vegetable oil	15 mL
3½ lbs	chicken pieces (see Tip, right)	1.75 kg
3	onions, thinly sliced	3
4	cloves garlic, minced	4
1 tbsp	minced gingerroot	15 mL
1 tsp	ground coriander	5 mL
1 tsp	turmeric	5 mL
3	black or green cardamom pods	3
¼ tsp	ground cinnamon	1 mL
2 tsp	cumin seeds	10 mL
1 to 2	serrano chilies, finely chopped (see Tip, page 138)	1 to 2
1 tsp	salt	5 mL
½ tsp	black pepper	2 mL
1 tbsp	lemon juice	15 mL
1	can (28 oz/796 mL) tomatoes, drained and chopped (see Tip, page 32)	1
1	bay leaf	1
1 cup	yogurt	250 mL
	Hot cooked rice	

1. In a large skillet, heat oil over medium-high heat. Add chicken, in batches, brown on all sides and transfer to slow cooker.

2. Reduce heat to medium. Add onions and cook, stirring, until softened. Add garlic, gingerroot, coriander, turmeric, cardamom, cinnamon, cumin seeds, chili pepper, salt and black pepper and cook, stirring, for 1 minute. Add lemon juice, tomatoes and bay leaf and stir to combine.

3. Pour sauce over chicken, cover and cook on **Low** for 5 to 6 hours or on **High** for 2½ to 3 hours, until juices run clear when pierced with a fork. When ready to serve, stir in yogurt. Discard cardamom pods and bay leaf. Serve over hot cooked rice.

Make ahead

This dish can be partially prepared the night before it is cooked. Complete Step 2, heating 1 tbsp (15 mL) oil in pan before softening onions. Cover and refrigerate mixture overnight. The next morning, brown chicken (Step 1), or if you're pressed for time, omit browning and place meat directly in stoneware. Continue cooking as directed in Step 3.

Tip

Indian cooks usually remove the skin from chicken before cooking, but since the breast, in particular, tends to become dry in the slow cooker, you'll get better results if you leave the skin on the white meat and remove it from the dark. Placing the dark meat on the bottom and the white on the top will also help to maintain moisture.

Turkey Breast Madras

As well as a province in India, Madras is also a curry powder. It's available in Oriental grocery stores and I like to use it because it is a well-balanced mix of sweet and piquant spices. The addition of cream and flour to an Indian-style dish makes this something of an East-West fusion recipe. The mildly flavored sauce is delicious over fluffy white rice. Accompany with a green vegetable or salad. • *SERVES 6*

1 tbsp	vegetable oil	15 mL
1	turkey breast, skin on, about 2 to 3 lbs (1 to 1.5 kg)	1
2	onions, finely chopped	2
3	stalks celery, peeled and thinly sliced	3
2	carrots, cut into ½-inch (1-cm) cubes	2
1 tbsp	curry powder, preferably Madras	15 mL
1 tsp	salt	5 mL
1 tsp	cracked black peppercorns	5 mL
2 tbsp	all-purpose flour	25 mL
1 tbsp	tomato paste	15 mL
½ cup	condensed chicken broth (undiluted)	125 mL
½ cup	whipping cream	125 mL
	Hot cooked rice	

Make ahead

This dish can be partially prepared the night before it is cooked. Complete Step 2, heating 1 tbsp (15 mL) oil in pan before softening onions, celery and carrots. Cover and refrigerate mixture overnight. The next morning, brown turkey breast (Step 1), or if you're pressed for time, remove skin from turkey breast, omit browning and place directly in stoneware. Continue cooking as directed in Steps 3 and 4.

1. In a skillet, heat oil over medium-high heat. Add turkey breast and brown on all sides. Transfer to slow cooker stoneware.

2. Reduce heat to medium. Add onions, celery and carrots to pan. Cook, stirring, until vegetables are softened. Add curry powder, salt and pepper and cook, stirring, for 1 minute. Sprinkle flour over mixture and cook, stirring, for 1 minute. Stir in tomato paste and chicken broth and cook until thickened.

3. Spoon sauce over turkey breast. Cover and cook on **Low** for 6 to 8 hours, until turkey is tender and no longer pink inside or meat thermometer reads 170°F (77°C).

4. Transfer turkey to a warm platter. Stir cream into sauce and spoon over turkey or serve alongside in a sauceboat. Serve over hot cooked rice.

Turkey Wings with Corn and Red Pepper Gravy

In my opinion, the wings are the best part of any turkey or chicken because they have the most flavor, so whenever we have a roasted bird, I put my dibs in for at least one. This "down home" dish is a weeknight favorite at our house, served over plain rice or polenta. For company, serve it with beans and rice and collard greens. If you prefer a spicier version, add a jalapeño pepper, finely chopped, along with the red pepper and corn. • *SERVES 4 TO 6*

1 tbsp	vegetable oil	15 mL
8	turkey wings, cut in two, at the joint (see Tip, right)	8
2	onions, finely chopped	2
4	stalks celery, peeled and thinly sliced	4
1 tsp	poultry seasoning	5 mL
2	sprigs fresh thyme or 1 tsp (5 mL) dried thyme leaves	2
1 tsp	salt	5 mL
1 tsp	cracked black peppercorns	5 mL
¼ cup	all-purpose flour	50 mL
1 cup	condensed chicken broth (undiluted)	250 mL
1	red bell pepper, finely chopped	1
1 cup	corn niblets, thawed if frozen	250 mL

Make ahead

This dish can be partially prepared the night before it is cooked. Complete Step 2, heating 1 tbsp (15 mL) oil in pan before softening onions and celery. Cover and refrigerate mixture overnight. The next morning, brown turkey wings (Step 1), and continue cooking as directed in Step 3.

Tip

For best results, buy fresh, not previously frozen, turkey wings that are air-chilled and/or free range.

1. In a skillet, heat oil over medium-high heat. Add turkey, in batches, and brown on all sides. Transfer to slow cooker stoneware.

2. Reduce heat to medium. Add onion and celery to pan and cook, stirring, until softened. Add poultry seasoning, thyme, salt, pepper and cook, stirring, for 1 minute. Sprinkle flour over mixture and cook, stirring, for 1 minute. Add broth and cook until thickened.

3. Pour onion mixture over turkey, cover and cook on **Low** for 8 hours or on **High** for 4 hours, until juices run clear when turkey is pierced with a fork. Add red pepper and corn. Cover and cook on **High** for 20 to 25 minutes before serving.

Turkey Mole

In Mexico, no special occasion is complete without turkey cooked in *mole poblano*. Since the authentic version is quite a production, I'm grateful that turkey breast, which is much easier to cook than a whole bird, is now available in most supermarkets. Although this *mole* has been greatly simplified from traditional recipes, I think it is very good. Serve with hot tortillas, fluffy white rice and creamed corn. • *SERVES 6*

2	dried ancho chilies (see Tip, right)	2
2 cups	boiling water	500 mL
1 tbsp	vegetable oil	15 mL
1	turkey breast, skin on, about 2 to 3 lbs (1 to 1.5 kg)	1
2	onions, sliced	2
3	cloves garlic, sliced	3
1 to 2	serrano chilies, chopped (see Tip, page 138)	1 to 2
4	whole cloves	4
1 tbsp	chili powder	15 mL
¼ tsp	ground cinnamon	1 mL
1 tsp	salt	5 mL
1 tsp	cracked black peppercorns	5 mL
1	can (28 oz/796 mL) tomatillos, drained (see Tip, right)	1
½ cup	whole blanched almonds	125 mL
1 oz	unsweetened chocolate, broken in pieces	25 g
¼ cup	finely chopped cilantro	50 mL
3 tbsp	diced mild green chilies (optional)	45 mL

1. In a heatproof bowl, soak dried chilies in boiling water for 30 minutes, making sure that all parts of the pepper are submerged. Drain and discard water. Coarsely chop chili and set aside.

2. In a skillet, heat oil over medium-high heat. Add turkey breast and brown on both sides. Transfer to slow cooker stoneware.

3. Reduce heat to medium. Add onions to pan and cook, stirring, until softened. Add ancho chilies, garlic, serrano chilies, cloves, chili powder, cinnamon, salt and pepper and cook, stirring, for 1 minute. Transfer mixture to a food processor. Add tomatillos, almonds and chocolate and process until smooth.

4. Pour sauce over turkey, cover and cook on **Low** for 8 hours or on **High** for 4 hours, until juices run clear when turkey is pierced with a fork or meat thermometer reads 170°F (77°C). When ready to serve, sprinkle with cilantro and diced green chilies, if using.

Make ahead

This dish can be partially prepared the night before it is cooked. Complete Steps 1 and 3, heating 1 tbsp (15 mL) oil in pan before softening onions. Cover and refrigerate puréed sauce. The next morning, brown turkey (Step 2), or remove skin from turkey, omit browning and place directly in stoneware. Continue with Step 4.

Tip

Ancho and other dried Mexican chilies are usually available in supermarkets and specialty food stores, in cellophane packages, near the fresh produce.

Tip

Tomatillos are small green tomatoes with a distinctive mildly acidic flavor that are often used in Mexican cooking. They are available in the Mexican food section of supermarkets.

Southwestern Turkey Pot Pie with Cornbread Cheddar Crust

Turkey or chicken pot pie has always been one of my favorite dishes. I love the combination of meat, vegetables and creamy sauce in a tasty crust. This version, with jalapeño peppers and portobello mushrooms, puts a contemporary spin on the dish, but it's every bit as delicious as those I remember from my childhood. • *SERVES 6 TO 8*

• **LARGE (MINIMUM 5 QUART) OVAL SLOW COOKER**

1 tbsp	vegetable oil	15 mL
2 lbs	skinless, boneless turkey, cut into ½-inch (1-cm) cubes	1 kg
1	large portobello mushroom, stem removed, cut into quarters and thinly sliced	1
2	medium onions, finely chopped	2
4	large carrots, peeled and cut into ¼-inch (0.5-cm) dice	4
4	stalks celery, peeled and cut into ¼-inch (0.5-cm) dice	4
2	jalapeño peppers, finely chopped	2
2 tsp	cumin seeds	10 mL
1 tsp	salt	5 mL
1 tsp	cracked black peppercorns	5 mL
2 tbsp	all-purpose flour	25 mL
1	can (10 oz/284 mL) condensed chicken broth (undiluted)	1

Cornbread Cheddar Crust

3 cups	chicken stock	750 mL
1 tsp	salt	5 mL
¼ tsp	black pepper	1 mL
1 cup	cornmeal	250 mL
3 tbsp	butter	45 mL
1 cup	finely grated Cheddar cheese	250 mL
2	green onions, finely chopped	2

Make ahead

This dish can be partially prepared the night before it is cooked. Complete Step 2, heating 1 tbsp (15 mL) oil in pan before sautéing mushrooms. Return sautéed mushrooms to thickened mixture, cover and refrigerate overnight. The next morning, brown turkey (Step 1), or if you're pressed for time, omit browning and place turkey directly in stoneware. Continue cooking as directed in Steps 3 and 4.

1. In a skillet, heat oil over medium-high heat. Add turkey pieces, in batches, and brown. Using a slotted spoon, transfer to slow cooker stoneware.

2. Add mushrooms to pan and sauté until they begin to lose their liquid. Using a slotted spoon, transfer to slow cooker stoneware. Reduce heat to medium-low and add onions, carrots and celery to pan. Stir well, cover and cook until vegetables are soft, about 10 minutes. Increase heat to medium. Add jalapeño pepper, cumin seeds, salt and black pepper and cook, stirring, for 1 minute. Add flour and cook, stirring, for 1 minute. Add broth and cook, stirring, until thickened.

3. Pour mixture over turkey and mushrooms and stir to combine thoroughly. Cover and cook on **Low** for 7 to 9 hours or on **High** for 4 to 5 hours, until turkey is no longer pink inside.

4. To make Cornbread Cheddar Crust: In a large saucepan, over medium heat, bring chicken broth to a boil. Season with salt and pepper, then add cornmeal slowly in a steady stream, stirring constantly until thick. Stir in butter, half the cheese and green onions. Spoon over turkey mixture, top with remaining cheese, cover and cook on **High** for 45 minutes.

Fish, Seafood and Vegetarian Favorites

Jambalaya

Like its Spanish relative, *paella*, Jambalaya is an ever-changing mixture depending upon the cook's whim and the available ingredients. This recipe uses Italian sausage, instead of the more traditional ham or andouille and produces a medium-spicy result. For more heat, add chopped banana or serrano chili pepper along with the shrimp — not jalapeño peppers, as their Tex-Mex overtones won't work well in this Creole dish. • *SERVES 6 TO 8*

1 tbsp	vegetable oil	15 mL
1 lb	hot Italian sausage, casings removed	500 g
½ lb	skinless, boneless chicken breasts, cut into 1-inch (2.5-cm) cubes	250 g
2	onions, finely chopped	2
2	stalks celery, cut into ¼-inch (0.5-cm) dice	2
4	cloves garlic, finely chopped	4
1 tsp	salt	5 mL
½ tsp	black pepper	2 mL
1 tsp	dried thyme leaves	5 mL
1 tsp	dried oregano leaves	5 mL
1	bay leaf	1
2 cups	chicken stock	500 mL
1	can (28 oz/796 mL) tomatoes, including juice, chopped (see Tip, page 32)	1
2 tbsp	Worcestershire sauce	25 mL
2 cups	long-grain rice, preferably converted	500 mL
1 lb	medium shrimp, cooked, peeled and deveined (see Tip, page 189)	500 g
1	hot banana pepper or serrano chili, finely chopped (optional)	

1. In a skillet, heat oil over medium-high heat. Add sausage and cook, breaking up with a spoon, until no longer pink. Transfer to slow cooker stoneware with a slotted spoon. In same pan, lightly brown chicken and transfer to stoneware with a slotted spoon.

2. Drain off all but 1 tbsp (15 mL) fat in pan. Reduce heat to medium. Add onions and celery and cook, stirring, until softened. Add garlic, salt, pepper, thyme and oregano and cook, stirring, for 1 minute.

3. Add bay leaf, chicken stock, tomatoes and Worcestershire sauce and bring to a boil. Transfer to slow cooker. Add rice and stir. Cover and cook on **Low** for 6 to 8 hours or on **High** for 3 to 4 hours. Add shrimp and hot pepper, if using. Cover and cook on **High** for 15 to 20 minutes or until shrimp are heated through. Discard bay leaf and serve.

Make ahead

This dish can be partially prepared the night before it is cooked. Complete Step 2, heating 1 tbsp (15 mL) oil in pan before softening onions and celery. Cover and refrigerate mixture overnight. The next morning, brown sausage and chicken (Step 1), and continue cooking as directed. Cook, peel and devein shrimp and refrigerate overnight.

Tip

For a more authentic Jambalaya, substitute thinly sliced andouille, a Louisiana smoked sausage, for the hot Italian sausage. Since andouille is quite strongly flavored, I suggest using only ½ lb (250 g). Add, along with the chicken, without browning.

Crab Timbale with Spinach Sauce

This is a versatile dish — delicious as a starter to an elegant meal, for lunch, a light dinner or as part of a buffet table. For a light family dinner, make a big salad and try the timbale without the Spinach Sauce — it's great on its own with a few drops of hot pepper sauce and makes a nice alternative to scrambled eggs or an omelet. • *SERVES 4 TO 6*

• **LIGHTLY GREASED 4-CUP (1-L) BAKING DISH**

Crab Timbale

2 cups	table cream	500 mL
2	whole eggs, plus 2 yolks	2
1 tsp	each paprika and salt	5 mL
¼ tsp	cayenne pepper	1 mL
¼ tsp	white pepper	1 mL
2	cans (6 oz/170 g) crabmeat, drained	2

Spinach Sauce

1 lb	fresh spinach leaves or 1 package (10 oz/300 g) spinach, washed, stems removed and coarsely chopped	500 g
¼ cup	chicken or vegetable stock or water	50 mL
Pinch	dried tarragon	Pinch
1 tsp	Dijon mustard	5 mL
¼ cup	freshly grated Parmesan cheese	50 mL
¼ tsp	salt	1 mL
Pinch	black pepper	Pinch

Make ahead

Both the timbale and the sauce can be made ahead and refrigerated until you're ready to serve. They reheat very well in the microwave.

Tip

Timbales are usually baked in individual ramekins, but unfortunately no slow cooker can physically accommodate the required pottery to serve even four people. However, I bake this in a 7-inch (17.5-cm) square ovenproof dish which works well. You can also use a round bowl or soufflé dish, but be aware that cooking times will change depending upon how the mixture is distributed in the dish.

1. In a bowl, whisk cream with eggs until well integrated. Whisk in paprika, salt, cayenne and white pepper. Stir in crab. Transfer to prepared dish. Cover with aluminum foil and tie with string. Place in slow cooker stoneware and pour in enough boiling water to reach 1 inch (2.5 cm) up the sides of dish. Cover and cook on **High** for 3 hours or until a knife inserted in timbale comes out clean.

2. To make Spinach Sauce: In a large heavy pot, with a tight-fitting lid, combine wet spinach with stock or water. Cover. Bring to a boil and cook until wilted.

3. Transfer spinach and cooking liquid to a blender or food processor. Add tarragon, mustard, Parmesan, salt and pepper and process until smooth.

4. When ready to serve, remove aluminum foil from baking dish. Run a sharp knife around the outside of the dish and invert onto a serving plate. Spoon Spinach Sauce over timbale and serve immediately.

Shrimp Creole

This classic Louisiana dish needs only fluffy white rice, a green salad and hot crusty bread to make a delicious meal. For a special treat, add crisp white wine. • *SERVES 4 TO 6*

1 tbsp	vegetable oil	15 mL
1	medium onion, finely chopped	1
4	stalks celery, peeled and cut into ¼-inch (0.5-cm) dice	4
2	cloves garlic, minced	2
1 tsp	dried oregano leaves	5 mL
½ tsp	dried thyme leaves	2 mL
½ tsp	salt	2 mL
½ tsp	cracked black peppercorns	2 mL
½ to 1	serrano chili, finely chopped (see Tip, page 138)	½ to 1
1	can (28 oz/796 mL) tomatoes, drained and chopped (see Tip, page 32)	1
½ cup	fish stock, clam juice or white wine	125 mL
1 tbsp	Worcestershire sauce	15 mL
¼ cup	finely chopped parsley	50 mL
	Zest of 1 lemon	
1	green bell pepper, thinly sliced	1
1 lb	medium shrimp, cooked, peeled and deveined (see Tip, right)	500 g
	Hot cooked rice	

1. In a skillet, heat oil over medium heat. Add onions and celery and cook, stirring, until softened. Add garlic, oregano, thyme, salt, pepper and chili pepper and cook, stirring, for 1 minute. Add tomatoes, stock or wine and Worcestershire sauce and bring to a boil.

2. Transfer mixture to slow cooker stoneware, cover and cook on **Low** for 6 to 8 hours or on **High** for 3 to 4 hours, until hot and bubbling. Add parsley, lemon zest, green pepper and shrimp and stir thoroughly. Cover and cook on **High** for 20 minutes or until peppers are soft and shrimp are heated through.

Make ahead

This dish can be partially prepared the night before it is cooked. Complete Step 1. Cover and refrigerate mixture overnight. Chop parsley, zest lemon and slice green pepper. Cover and refrigerate. Cook shrimp. Peel and devein and refrigerate. The next day, continue cooking as directed in Step 2.

Tip

To cook shrimp, immerse shrimp, in shells, in a large pot of boiling salted water. Cook over **High** heat, until the shells turn pink, about 2 to 3 minutes. Allow to cool, then peel and devein.

Snapper Vera Cruz

This traditional Mexican recipe has many variations. Most often, filleted fish is fried and covered with a sauce that is cooked separately. For this slow cooker version, I've sliced the fish very thinly and poached it in the sauce during the last 20 minutes of cooking. For an authentic Mexican touch, serve with hot tortillas to soak up the sauce. Feel free to use any firm white fish instead of snapper. • *SERVES 4 TO 6*

1 tbsp	vegetable oil	15 mL
1	medium onion, finely chopped	1
2	cloves garlic, minced	2
½ tsp	dried oregano leaves	2 mL
¼ tsp	ground cinnamon	1 mL
⅛ tsp	ground cloves	0.5 mL
1 to 2	jalapeño peppers, finely chopped	1 to 2
1	can (28 oz/796 mL) tomatoes, drained and chopped (see Tip, page 32)	1
½ cup	fish stock or clam juice	125 mL
1 lb	snapper fillets, cut in half lengthwise and sliced as thinly as possible on the horizontal	500 g
2 tbsp	lemon juice	25 mL
1 tbsp	drained capers	15 mL
10	olives, pitted and thinly sliced	10
	Hot tortillas (optional)	

Make ahead

This dish can be partially prepared the night before it is cooked. Complete Step 1. Cover and refrigerate mixture overnight. The next day, continue cooking as directed in Step 2.

1. In a skillet, heat oil over medium heat. Add onions and cook, stirring, until softened. Add garlic, oregano, cinnamon, cloves and jalapeño peppers and cook, stirring, for 1 minute. Add tomatoes and stock or clam juice and bring to a boil.

2. Transfer mixture to slow cooker stoneware. Cover and cook on **Low** for 6 to 8 hours or on **High** for 3 to 4 hours, until hot and bubbling. Stir in fish and lemon juice. Cover and cook on **High** for 20 minutes or until fish is cooked through. Stir in capers and pour mixture onto a deep platter. Garnish with olives and serve.

Tuna and Beans with Aioli

The French are very fond of enriching fish or seafood stews with flavorful concoctions such as *pistou* or anchovy mayonnaise. This is another variation on that theme which, when made with canned tuna, makes a nice weeknight meal. If you have access to a good fish market, you can easily move the dish upmarket by using fresh tuna. All it needs is crusty country-style rolls, such as *calabrese*, a green salad and cold white wine. • *SERVES 6*

1 tbsp	vegetable oil	15 mL
2	leeks, white part only, cleaned, cut in half lengthwise and thinly sliced (see Tip, page 212)	2
4	stalks celery, peeled and thinly sliced	4
1	serrano chili, finely chopped	1
2 tsp	dried thyme leaves	10 mL
1 tsp	cracked black peppercorns	5 mL
½ tsp	salt	2 mL
1	can (28 oz/796 mL) tomatoes, including juice, coarsely chopped (see Tip, page 32)	1
1	bottle (8 oz/240 mL) clam juice or 1 cup (250 mL) fish stock	1
1 cup	dry white wine	250 mL
1	can (19 oz/540 mL) white kidney beans, drained and rinsed, or 2 cups (500 mL) cooked and drained beans	1
2	cans (6.5 oz/184 g) tuna, drained and chopped, or 1-lb (500-g) piece of fresh tuna, seared and thinly sliced (see Tip, right)	1

Easy Aioli

3 to 4	cloves garlic, minced	3 to 4
1 cup	good quality prepared mayonnaise Chopped parsley or chives	250 mL

1. In a skillet, heat oil over medium heat. Add leeks and celery and cook, stirring, until vegetables are softened. Add chili pepper, thyme, pepper and salt and cook, stirring, for 1 minute. Add tomatoes, clam juice or fish stock and white wine and bring to a boil. Cook, stirring, until liquid is reduced by one-third, about 5 minutes.

2. Transfer contents of pan to slow cooker stoneware. Add beans and stir to combine. Cover and cook on **Low** for 8 hours or on **High** for 4 hours, until hot and bubbling. Stir in canned tuna, if using. Cover and cook on **High** for 20 minutes or until tuna is heated through. (If using fresh tuna, see Tip, right.)

3. To make Easy Aioli: In a bowl, beat ingredients until well combined. Ladle stew into bowls and top with aioli.

Make ahead

This dish can be partially prepared the night before it is cooked. Complete Step 1. Cover and refrigerate mixture overnight. The next day, continue cooking as directed in Step 2. Aioli can be made ahead and refrigerated.

Tip

If using fresh tuna for this recipe, sear it before serving over the stew. To sear tuna: In a skillet, heat 1 tbsp (15 mL) vegetable oil over high heat, until smoking. Add whole piece of tuna and sear, about 30 seconds per side (tuna will be quite rare). Transfer to a cutting board and slice, crosswise, into thin slices. Ladle stew into bowls and arrange strips of tuna in a spoke pattern on top. Top with a dollop of aioli.

Eggplant and Tomato Gratin

This dish reminds me of *Ratatouille*, the French vegetable stew. Excellent as a rich vegetable accompaniment to roasted poultry or meat, this sumptuous combination also makes a great lunch or light supper dish served with a green salad. • *SERVES 6*

3	medium eggplants, peeled, cut into 2-inch (5-cm) cubes and drained of excess moisture (see Tip, page 22)	3
1	package (½ oz/14 g) dried porcini or chanterelle mushrooms	1
1 cup	boiling water	250 mL
1 tbsp	vegetable oil (approximate)	15 mL
4	cloves garlic, minced	4
1 tsp	dried oregano leaves	5 mL
1 tsp	cracked black peppercorns	5 mL
4 cups	good quality tomato sauce	1 L
½ cup	freshly grated Parmesan cheese	125 mL
1 cup	grated mozzarella cheese	250 mL
1 cup	bread crumbs	250 mL

Make ahead

This dish can be partially prepared the night before it is cooked. Complete Steps 1 through 4 in method, refrigerating eggplant and bread crumb mixtures separately and refrigerate overnight. The next day, assemble in stoneware and continue cooking as directed in Step 4.

Tip

I have not included a quantity of salt in this recipe as there may be residual salt on the sweated eggplant, which will affect the seasoning. Taste the mixture when it is combined in the slow cooker and salt accordingly.

1. In a heatproof bowl, soak mushrooms in boiling water for 30 minutes. Strain through a fine sieve, reserving liquid. Dry mushrooms on paper towel and chop finely. Set aside.

2. In a skillet, heat oil over medium heat. Add sweated eggplant, in batches, and cook, until browned, adding more oil, if needed. Transfer to slow cooker stoneware.

3. Add reserved mushrooms, garlic, oregano and pepper to pan and cook, stirring, for 1 minute. Add reserved mushroom liquid along with tomato sauce and bring to a boil. Pour over eggplant and stir to combine.

4. In a bowl, combine Parmesan, mozzarella and bread crumbs. Mix well and spoon over eggplant mixture. Cover and cook on **Low** for 8 to 10 hours or on **High** for 4 to 6 hours, until bubbling.

Pipérade

There are many different ways of serving this luscious combination of sweet peppers, onions and tomatoes from the Basque region of France. It can be made in a strictly vegetarian version or with the addition of ham or eggs. In Italy, they call it *Peperonata* and often serve it cold, as an accompaniment to meat. I like to add chopped, cooked ham after the Pipérade is cooked and serve it over a plain omelet (about 2 cups (500 mL) Pipérade is enough for two 3-egg omelets). • *MAKES ABOUT 6 CUPS*

1 tbsp	olive oil	15 mL
2	large onions, finely chopped	2
3	cloves garlic, minced	3
1 tsp	salt	5 mL
½ tsp	freshly ground black pepper	2 mL
12	plum tomatoes, peeled and chopped	12
3 cups	thinly sliced red bell peppers, about 3 large peppers	750 mL
4 oz	cooked ham, finely chopped (optional)	125 g

Make ahead
Pipérade can be assembled the night before it is cooked but without adding the ham. Follow preparation directions in Step 1 and refrigerate overnight. The next day, continue cooking as directed in Step 2.

1. In a skillet, heat oil over medium heat. Add onions and cook, stirring, until softened. Add garlic, salt and pepper and cook, stirring, for 1 minute. Add tomatoes and cook, stirring, breaking up tomatoes with the back of a spoon, until most of the liquid has evaporated, about 5 minutes. Stir in peppers.

2. Transfer mixture to slow cooker stoneware. Cover and cook on **Low** for 6 hours or on **High** for 3 hours. Add ham, if using, and stir to combine. Cover and cook on **High** for 15 minutes or until ham is heated through.

Variation

Scrambled Eggs and Pipérade: Another way of serving Pipérade is to ladle 2 cups (500 mL) of the cooked sauce into a saucepan and add beaten eggs (about 4 eggs for 2 cups (500 mL) Pipérade). Cook over low heat, stirring constantly until eggs achieve the consistency of scrambled eggs. Or you can serve Pipérade like a vegetable stew with a hot country-style loaf of bread. I also freeze this in 2-cup (500-mL) batches. Defrost, bring to a simmer on top of the stove, then add the chopped ham or eggs, if desired.

Creamy Leek, Potato and Mushroom Stew with Blue Cheese

If you have vegetarians in the family, try this robust stew. It is as rich and satisfying as any containing meat and makes a delicious dinner with a salad and crusty bread. • SERVES 6

1	package (½ oz/14 g) dried porcini mushrooms	1
1 cup	boiling water	250 mL
1 tbsp	vegetable oil	15 mL
2	large leeks, white part only, cleaned and thinly sliced (see Tip, page 212)	2
4	stalks celery, peeled and thinly sliced	4
2	cloves garlic, minced	2
1 tsp	dried thyme leaves	5 mL
1 tsp	cracked black peppercorns	5 mL
1 tsp	salt	5 mL
1 lb	portobello or cremini mushrooms (see Tip, right)	500 g
1	can (28 oz/796 mL) tomatoes, including juice, coarsely chopped (see Tip, page 32)	1
1 cup	condensed chicken broth or vegetable stock (undiluted)	250 mL
2 to 3	potatoes, peeled and cut into ½-inch (1-cm) cubes	2 to 3
½ cup	whipping cream	125 mL
3 oz	good quality blue cheese, such as Maytag or Gorgonzola, crumbled (see Tip, right)	90 g

Make ahead

This dish can be partially prepared the night before it is cooked. Complete Steps 1 through 3. Cover and refrigerate. The next morning continue with Step 4.

Tip

If you're using portobello mushrooms, discard the stem, cut them into quarters and thinly slice. If you're using cremini mushrooms, trim off the tough end of the stem and cut them into quarters.

Tip

Use only good quality blue cheese such as Maytag or Italian Gorgonzola for this recipe as blue cheese of lesser quality tends to be very harsh.

1. In a heatproof measuring cup or bowl, combine dried mushrooms and boiling water. Let stand for 30 minutes and strain, reserving liquid. Pat mushrooms dry, chop finely and set aside.

2. In a skillet, heat oil over medium heat. Add leeks and celery and cook, stirring, until softened. Add garlic, thyme, pepper, salt and dried mushrooms and cook, stirring, for 1 minute. Add fresh mushrooms and cook, stirring, until they are well integrated into mixture. Add tomatoes, chicken broth or vegetable stock and reserved mushroom liquid and bring to a boil.

3. Place potatoes in stoneware. Add contents of pan and stir.

4. Cover and cook on **Low** for 8 to 10 hours or on **High** for 4 to 5 hours, until potatoes are tender. Stir in cream and cheese. Cover and cook on **High** for 15 minutes or until cheese is melted into sauce and mixture is hot and bubbling.

Vegetable Curry with Pepper and Cilantro Tadka

This delicious vegetable curry is a favorite weekday main course. *Tadka*, a fried garnish often used in Indian cooking, is traditionally a mixture of spices cooked in ghee, a type of clarified butter. It is usually served over a large bowl of dal made from dried beans or lentils. I like the spicy finish the tadka adds to this mellow stew, but I like to pass it in a small bowl, allowing people to season to taste. • *SERVES 6*

1 tbsp	vegetable oil	15 mL
2	large leeks, white part only, cleaned and thinly sliced, or red onions, thinly sliced (see Tip, page 212)	2
6	stalks celery, peeled and thinly sliced	6
6	carrots, thinly sliced	6
4	cloves garlic, minced	4
1 tbsp	minced gingerroot	15 mL
1	chili pepper, finely chopped	1
1 tbsp	curry powder	15 mL
1	can (28 oz/796 mL) tomatoes, including juice, coarsely chopped (see Tip, page 32)	1
6	small turnips, peeled and cut into ½-inch (1-cm) cubes	6
2	potatoes, peeled and shredded	2
2 cups	lentils, washed and picked over	500 mL
4 cups	chicken or vegetable stock or water	1 L
2 cups	green beans, cut into 1-inch (2.5-cm) pieces, or green peas, thawed if frozen	500 mL

Pepper and Cilantro Tadka

2 tbsp	ghee, clarified butter or vegetable oil	25 mL
1 tsp	cumin seeds	5 mL
2	green onions, white part only, finely chopped	2
½	chili pepper, finely chopped	½
1	red bell pepper, finely chopped	1
¼ cup	finely chopped cilantro	50 mL
1 tbsp	lemon juice	15 mL

Make ahead

This dish can be partially prepared the night before it is cooked. Complete Steps 1 though 3 and refrigerate overnight. The next morning, continue cooking as directed in Steps 4 and 5.

1. In a skillet, heat oil over medium heat. Add leeks or onions, celery and carrots and stir to combine. Reduce heat to low, cover and cook until vegetables are soft, about 10 minutes.

2. Increase heat to medium. Add garlic, gingerroot, chili pepper and curry powder and cook, stirring, for 1 minute. Stir in tomatoes and bring to a boil.

continued on page 198

3. Place turnips, potatoes and lentils in slow cooker stoneware. Pour contents of pan over mixture and stir well. Add stock or water barely to cover, about 4 cups (1 L).

4. Cover and cook on **Low** for 8 to 10 hours or on **High** for 4 to 5 hours, until vegetables are tender. Add green beans or peas. Cover and cook on **High** until tender, about 15 to 30 minutes.

5. To make Pepper and Cilantro Tadka: In a skillet, over medium heat, heat ghee, clarified butter or oil. Add cumin seeds and cook until flavor is released. Add green onions, chili pepper, red pepper and cook, stirring, for 1 minute. Remove from heat. Stir in cilantro and lemon juice. Spoon into a small bowl and serve as a garnish for curry.

Cheesy Rice and Mushroom Casserole with Spinach

The vegetarians in your family will love this delicious one-pot dinner. Add a green salad, if you prefer, but all this really needs is hot crusty rolls, making it an ideal meal for those evenings when everyone is coming and going at different times, as it can be kept warm in the slow cooker. • *SERVES 6*

2 tbsp	vegetable oil, divided	25 mL
2	large portobello mushrooms, stems removed, cut in half and thinly sliced	2
2	onions, finely chopped	2
4	stalks celery, peeled and thinly sliced	4
2	cloves garlic, minced	2
1 tbsp	minced gingerroot	15 mL
1 tbsp	cumin seeds	15 mL
1 tsp	salt	5 mL
1 tsp	black pepper	5 mL
¼ cup	oil-packed sun-dried tomatoes, finely chopped	50 mL
1	can (28 oz/796 mL) tomatoes, including juice, coarsely chopped (see Tip, page 32)	1
3 cups	vegetable stock	750 mL
2 cups	long-grain brown rice	500 mL
1 lb	fresh spinach or 1 package (10 oz/300 g) spinach, washed, stems removed and coarsely chopped	500 g
2 cups	shredded Cheddar cheese	500 mL

Make ahead

This dish can be partially prepared the night before it is cooked. Complete Steps 1 and 2. Cover and refrigerate overnight. The next day, continue cooking as directed in Step 3.

1. In a skillet, heat 1 tbsp (15 mL) oil over medium-high heat. Add mushrooms and cook, stirring, until they begin to soften. Remove with a slotted spoon and transfer to slow cooker stoneware.

2. Add remaining oil to pan and reduce heat to medium. Add onion and celery and cook, stirring, until softened. Add garlic, gingerroot, cumin seeds, salt and pepper and cook, stirring, for 1 minute. Add sun-dried tomatoes, tomatoes and vegetable stock and bring to a boil. Pour mixture over mushrooms.

3. Add rice and stir to combine. Cover and cook on **Low** for 7 to 8 hours, until rice is tender. Stir in spinach and sprinkle cheese over top of mixture. Cover and cook on **High** for 20 to 25 minutes, until spinach is cooked and cheese is melted. Serve piping hot.

Vegetable Cobbler

This one-dish meal reminds me of a vegetarian version of chicken pot pie, one of my all-time favorites. If you wish to serve a salad, sliced tomatoes tossed in oil and vinegar make a nice accompaniment. • *SERVES 6 TO 8*

1	package (½ oz/14 g) dried porcini mushrooms	1
1 cup	boiling water	250 mL
2 tbsp	butter	25 mL
2	onions, thinly sliced	2
4	stalks celery, peeled and thinly sliced	4
3	cloves garlic, minced	3
2 tsp	dried thyme leaves	10 mL
1 tsp	salt	5 mL
1 tsp	cracked black peppercorns	5 mL
2 tbsp	all-purpose flour	25 mL
1	can (10 oz/284 mL) condensed cream of mushroom soup (see Tip, right)	1
3 cups	carrots, peeled and thinly sliced	750 mL
2 cups	white turnip, peeled and cut into ½-inch (1-cm) cubes	500 mL
3	medium potatoes, peeled and thinly sliced	3
½ cup	whipping cream	125 mL
1 cup	frozen peas, thawed	250 mL
½ cup	finely chopped dill	125 mL

Topping

1½ cups	all-purpose flour	375 mL
1 tbsp	baking powder	15 mL
1 tsp	salt	5 mL
6	green onions, white part only, finely chopped	6
1	egg, beaten	1
½ cup	milk	125 mL

Make ahead

This dish can be partially prepared the night before it is cooked. Complete Steps 1 through 3 and refrigerate overnight. The next morning, continue cooking as directed in Steps 4 and 5.

Tip

Unlike milk or cream, condensed cream soup won't curdle if it is cooked for a long period of time. As a result, it's useful in slow cooker dishes based on a cream sauce.

1. In a heatproof bowl, soak mushrooms in boiling water for 30 minutes. Drain, reserving liquid. Pat mushrooms dry with paper towel and chop finely. Set aside.

2. In a skillet, melt butter over medium heat. Add onion and celery and cook, stirring, until softened. Add garlic, thyme, salt, pepper and mushrooms and cook, stirring, for 1 minute. Sprinkle flour over mixture and cook, stirring, for 1 minute. Add reserved mushroom liquid and stir until thick. Stir in mushroom soup until mixture is smooth (it will be very thick). Remove from heat.

3. In slow cooker stoneware, combine carrots, turnip and potatoes. Pour contents of pan over mixture and stir to combine.

4. Cover and cook on **Low** for 8 to 10 hours or on **High** for 4 to 5 hours, until vegetables are tender. Stir in cream, peas and dill. Taste for seasoning and adjust.

5. To make Topping: In a bowl, combine flour, baking powder and salt. Stir in green onions. Mix in egg and milk to make a lumpy dough. Spread batter over vegetable mixture as best you can to resemble a crust. Cover and cook on **High** for 30 to 40 minutes or until a toothpick inserted in center of batter comes out clean.

Vegetables

Cumin Beets

I love the simple, but unusual and effective combination of flavors in this dish, which is inspired by Indian cuisine. It's my favorite way of cooking small summer beets, fresh from the garden, because I don't have to heat up my kitchen with a pot of simmering water on the stovetop. Cooked this way, beets are a delicious accompaniment for meat or chicken cooked on the barbecue and a welcome addition to warm-weather dinners outdoors. If you prefer a spicy dish, add hot pepper sauce, to taste, after the beets have finished cooking. • *SERVES 4 TO 6*

1 tbsp	vegetable oil	15 mL
1	onion, finely chopped	1
3	cloves garlic, minced	3
1 tsp	cumin seeds	5 mL
1 tsp	salt	5 mL
½ tsp	black pepper	2 mL
2	medium tomatoes, peeled and coarsely chopped	2
1 cup	water	250 mL
1 lb	beets, peeled and used whole, if small, or sliced thinly (see Tip, right)	500 g

Make ahead

This dish can be assembled the night before it is cooked. Complete Step 1, add beets to mixture and refrigerate overnight. The next day, continue cooking as directed in Step 2.

Tip

Peeling the beets before they are cooked ensures that all the delicious cooking juices end up on your plate.

1. In a skillet, heat oil over medium-high heat. Add onion and cook, stirring, until softened. Stir in garlic, cumin, salt and pepper and cook for 1 minute. Add tomatoes and water and bring to a boil.

2. Place beets in slow cooker stoneware and pour tomato mixture over them. Cover and cook on **Low** for 8 to 10 hours or on **High** for 4 to 5 hours, until beets are tender.

Braised Beets with Sour Cream and Horseradish

This recipe is so good I don't need an excuse to make it, but it is delicious with roast meats, particularly roast beef. • *SERVES 6 TO 8*

6	medium beets, peeled and quartered (see Tip, page 204)	6
2 tbsp	granulated sugar	25 mL
¼ tsp	salt	1 mL
¼ tsp	black pepper	1 mL
1 tbsp	red wine vinegar	15 mL
2 tbsp	water	25 mL
¼ cup	sour cream	50 mL
1 tbsp	prepared horseradish	15 mL
	Finely chopped parsley or dill	

Make ahead

This dish can be partially prepared the night before it is cooked. Complete Step 1 and refrigerate overnight. The next day, continue cooking as directed in Steps 2 and 3.

1. In slow cooker stoneware, combine beets, sugar, salt, pepper, vinegar and water. Stir well.

2. Cover and cook on **Low** for 8 to 10 hours or on **High** for 4 to 5 hours, until beets are tender.

3. In a small bowl, combine sour cream and horseradish. Toss with beets. Transfer mixture to a serving dish and garnish with parsley or dill.

Variation

Braised Beets with Creamy Horseradish: Substitute ¼ cup (50 mL) whipping cream for the sour cream and add 2 tsp (10 mL) sherry wine vinegar along with the horseradish. Garnish with parsley rather than dill.

New Potato Curry

This is an excellent way to cook new potatoes, as they cook slowly, almost in their own juices, in a curry-flavored sauce. This dish goes well with grilled meat, poultry or fish. If you're cooking for vegetarians, serve it as a main course along with a bowl of dal and a green vegetable. It also makes a delicious summer meal, accompanied by a garden salad. • *SERVES 4 TO 6*

2 tbsp	clarified butter or vegetable oil	25 mL
1 lb	small new potatoes, about 10 new potatoes (see Tip, right)	500 g
2	onions, finely chopped	2
1	clove garlic, minced	1
1 tsp	curry powder, preferably Madras (see Curry Powder, page 15)	5 mL
½ tsp	salt	2 mL
½ tsp	cracked black peppercorns	2 mL
½ cup	water or vegetable or chicken stock	125 mL
2 tbsp	lemon juice	25 mL
¼ cup	finely chopped cilantro	50 mL

1. In a skillet, heat butter or oil over medium-high heat. Add potatoes and cook just until they begin to brown. Transfer to slow cooker stoneware.

2. Reduce heat to medium. Add onions and cook, stirring, until softened. Add garlic, curry powder, salt and pepper. Stir and cook for 1 minute. Add water or stock, bring to a boil and pour over potatoes.

3. Cover and cook on **Low** for 8 to 10 hours or on **High** for 4 to 5 hours, until potatoes are tender. Stir in lemon juice and garnish with cilantro.

Make ahead

This dish can be partially prepared the night before it is cooked. Complete Steps 1 and 2 and refrigerate overnight. The next day, continue cooking as directed in Step 3.

Tip

Leave the skins on potatoes, scrub thoroughly and dry on paper towels. Cut in half any that are larger than 1 inch (2.5 cm) in diameter.

No flavor ✓

Bakers' Potatoes

In France, before people had ovens, they often dropped the Sunday roast off at the local baker, surrounded by sliced onions and potatoes. Their midday meal cooked while they attended church and they retrieved it on the way home. The slow cooker version of *Potatoes Boulangère*, as the dish is known, is every bit as easy as the tasty original. • *SERVES 6 TO 8*

• LIGHTLY GREASED SLOW COOKER STONEWARE

2 tbsp	butter	25 mL
2	onions, thinly sliced	2
½ tsp	dried thyme leaves	2 mL
1 tsp	salt	5 mL
½ tsp	black pepper	2 mL
6	potatoes, thinly sliced	6
1 to 2 cups	chicken or beef stock	250 to 500 mL

Make ahead

This dish can be partially prepared the night before it is cooked. Complete Steps 1 and 2 and refrigerate overnight. The next day, continue cooking as directed in Step 3.

1. In a skillet, melt butter over medium heat. Add onions and cook, stirring, until softened. Add thyme, salt and pepper and cook for 1 minute. Remove from heat.

2. Place a thin layer of onions on the bottom of greased slow cooker stoneware. Add a layer of potatoes. Repeat until all potatoes and onions are used up, finishing with a layer of potatoes. Add chicken or beef stock to cover.

3. Cover and cook on **Low** for 8 to 10 hours or on **High** for 4 to 5 hours, until potatoes are tender.

Variation

Bakers' Potatoes Gratin: When the potatoes are cooked, transfer the contents of the slow cooker to a baking dish. Sprinkle 1 cup (250 mL) shredded Swiss or Gruyère cheese over top and brown under a preheated broiler.

Braised Carrots with Capers

This dish is simplicity itself and yet the results are startlingly fresh. Serve with grilled or roasted meats or fish or as an accompaniment to a vegetarian main course. • *SERVES 4 TO 6*

2 tbsp	extra-virgin olive oil	25 mL
12	large carrots, peeled and thinly sliced	12
12	cloves garlic, thinly sliced	12
½ tsp	salt	2 mL
½ tsp	black pepper	2 mL
½ cup	drained capers	125 mL

Make ahead

This dish can be partially prepared the night before it is cooked. Complete Step 1 and refrigerate overnight. The next day, continue cooking as directed in Step 2.

1. In slow cooker stoneware, combine oil, carrots, garlic, salt and pepper. Toss to combine.

2. Cover and cook on **Low** for 6 to 8 hours or on **High** for 3 to 4 hours, until carrots are tender. Add capers and toss to combine. Serve immediately.

Variation

Braised Carrots with Black Olives: Substitute ½ cup (125 mL) chopped black olives, preferably kalamata, a particularly pungent Greek variety, for the capers.

Turnip and Carrot Purée with Cumin

At our house, the Christmas turkey just wouldn't be the same without turnip and carrot purée. The cumin adds a slightly exotic note to our very traditional feast. • *SERVES 8*

4 cups	peeled turnip, cut into ½-inch (1-cm) cubes	1 L
2 cups	thinly sliced carrots	500 mL
1 tsp	toasted cumin seeds (see Tip, right)	5 mL
2 tbsp	butter	25 mL
1 tsp	granulated sugar	5 mL
½ tsp	salt	2 mL
¼ tsp	black pepper	1 mL
¼ cup	water or vegetable stock	50 mL

1. Combine ingredients in slow cooker stoneware. Cover and cook on **Low** for 8 to 10 hours or on **High** for 4 to 5 hours, until vegetables are tender.

2. Using a potato masher or a food processor or blender, mash or purée mixture until smooth. Serve immediately.

Variation

Turnip Purée with Cumin: Use 6 cups (1.5 L) cubed turnip, instead of the turnip-carrot combination.

Make ahead

Peel and cut turnips and carrots. Cover and refrigerate overnight.

Tip

To toast cumin seeds, place the required quantity in a dry skillet and heat over medium heat, stirring until the seeds release their aroma and just begin to brown. Immediately remove from heat and transfer to a small bowl to cool.

Casserole of Turnip and Leeks with Blue Cheese

The bold flavorings in this dish make it an ideal accompaniment to roast beef or lamb. I use condensed cream soup because, unlike milk, it holds up well during the long cooking time. Since canned soup is fairly salty, I have not added salt to the recipe. However, you should taste the mixture after it is puréed and season to taste. • *SERVES 8*

1 tbsp	butter	15 mL
3	large leeks, white part only, cleaned and thinly sliced (see Tip, page 212)	3
½ tsp	black pepper	2 mL
1	can (10 oz/284 mL) condensed cream of celery soup	1
½ cup	water	125 mL
2 lbs	turnips, peeled and cut into ½-inch (1-cm) cubes	1 kg
¼ cup	whipping cream	50 mL
3 tbsp	blue cheese, crumbled	45 mL
	Salt to taste	

Make ahead

This dish can be assembled the night before it is cooked. Complete Steps 1 and 2 and refrigerate overnight. The next day, continue cooking as directed in Step 3 and 4.

1. In a skillet, melt butter over medium heat. Add leeks and cook, stirring, until softened. Add pepper and celery soup and stir well. Add water and stir to combine thoroughly.

2. Place turnips in slow cooker stoneware and pour contents of pan over them. Stir to combine.

3. Cover and cook on **Low** for 8 to 10 hours or on **High** for 4 to 5 hours, until turnips are tender. Stir in cream and cheese. Cover and cook on **High** for 15 minutes until cheese is melted.

4. Transfer mixture to food processor, in batches, and process until smooth. Season to taste with salt. Serve immediately.

Leeks à la Greque

Cooked this way, leeks are delicious hot or cold. They can be served as a vegetable or as part of an antipasto buffet. • *SERVES 4 TO 6*

6	large leeks, white and light green part only, split lengthwise, cleaned and cut in half on the horizontal (see Tip, right)	6
¼ cup	olive oil	50 mL
2 tbsp	coriander seeds	25 mL
1 tsp	black peppercorns	5 mL
½ tsp	coarse sea salt	2 mL
¾ cup	dry white wine	175 mL
2	bay leaves	2

1. Place leeks in slow cooker stoneware.

2. In a saucepan, combine olive oil, coriander seeds, pepper, salt, white wine and bay leaves and bring to a boil. Pour mixture over leeks, cover and cook on **Low** for 6 to 8 hours or on **High** for 3 to 4 hours, until leeks are soft.

3. Using a slotted spoon, transfer leeks to a serving dish. Pour cooking liquid into a saucepan and, over high heat, bring to a boil. Boil rapidly for 5 minutes until sauce has reduced by half. Strain over leeks. Serve immediately or cover and chill thoroughly.

Make ahead

This dish can be made ahead and served chilled.

Tip

To clean leeks, fill sink full of lukewarm water. Split leeks in half lengthwise and submerge in water, swishing them around to remove all traces of dirt. Transfer to a colander and rinse under cold water.

Peppery Red Onions

I love making this nippy treat in the autumn when the farmers' markets are brimming over with freshly harvested red onions. They are a tasty low-fat alternative to creamed onions and an unusual accompaniment to roasted poultry, meat or grains. • *SERVES 4 TO 6*

4	large red onions, quartered	4
1 tbsp	extra-virgin olive oil	15 mL
1 tsp	dried oregano leaves	5 mL
¼ cup	water or chicken or vegetable stock	50 mL
	Salt and pepper, to taste	
	Hot pepper sauce, to taste (see Tip, right)	

Tip

Use your favorite hot sauce, such as Tabasco, Louisiana Hot Sauce, Piri Piri, or try other more exotic brands to vary the flavors in this recipe.

1. In slow cooker stoneware, combine all ingredients except hot sauce. Stir thoroughly, cover and cook on **Low** for 8 hours or on **High** for 4 hours, until onions are tender.

2. Toss well with hot sauce and serve.

Creamed Onions

Since long, slow cooking is the essence of getting the best out of onions, they have a natural affinity for the slow cooker. This simple, but elegant dish is a favorite with all members of my family from my teenaged daughter to my mother-in-law. It's a great accompaniment to grilled meats, meat loaf, roast turkey or chicken. Whether you add cheese is simply a matter of taste. My family likes it equally well, with or without. • *SERVES 6*

2 tbsp	butter	25 mL
1 tbsp	olive oil	15 mL
4 to 5	medium onions, quartered, about 2 lbs (1 kg)	4 to 5
2 tbsp	finely chopped parsley	25 mL
2	sprigs fresh thyme or 1 tsp (5 mL) dried thyme leaves	2
½ tsp	salt	2 mL
½ tsp	black pepper	2 mL
½ cup	chicken or beef stock	125 mL
½ cup	whipping cream	125 mL
¼ cup	freshly grated Parmesan cheese (optional)	50 mL

Make ahead

This dish can be partially prepared the night before it is cooked. Complete Step 1 and refrigerate overnight. The next day, continue cooking as directed in Step 2.

1. In a large skillet, melt butter and oil over medium heat. Add onions and cook, stirring, until they begin to brown. Add parsley, thyme, salt and pepper and cook for 1 to 2 minutes. Add stock and bring to a boil.

2. Transfer contents of pan to slow cooker stoneware and cook on **Low** for 8 to 10 hours or on **High** for 4 to 5 hours, until onions are tender. Stir in cream and cheese, if using. Cover and cook on **High** for an additional 15 minutes.

Sweet Potato and Onion Purée

This rich vegetable dish is perfect with the Thanksgiving turkey. Once it's in the slow cooker, you can forget about it until you're ready to carve the bird, which enables you to attend to the many other details associated with preparing a festive dinner. • *SERVES 6 TO 8*

2	onions, sliced	2
3	large sweet potatoes, peeled and cut into ½-inch (1-cm) cubes	3
¼ cup	chopped parsley leaves	50 mL
1 tsp	cracked black peppercorns	5 mL
1	can (10 oz/284 mL) condensed cream of mushroom and garlic soup	1
½ cup	water	125 mL
½ cup	whipping cream	125 mL
½ cup	shredded Swiss cheese	125 mL
	Salt, to taste	

Make ahead

This dish can be assembled the night before it is cooked. Complete Steps 1 and 2 and refrigerate overnight. The next day, continue cooking as directed in Steps 3 and 4.

1. In slow cooker stoneware, combine onions, sweet potatoes, parsley and pepper.

2. In a small bowl, combine soup and water, whisking until smooth. Pour over sweet-potato mixture and stir to combine.

3. Cover and cook on **Low** for 8 to 10 hours or on **High** for 4 to 5 hours, until sweet potatoes are tender. Stir in cream and cheese. Cover and cook on **High** for 20 minutes, until cheese is melted.

4. Transfer mixture to food processor, in batches, and process until smooth. Season to taste with salt. Serve immediately.

Spinach Soufflé with Horseradish Cream

This isn't really a soufflé — it's a custard — but its light texture reminds me of those airy delights. I like to serve this on special occasions as it makes a particularly elegant vegetable course. With the horseradish cream, it's an especially good accompaniment for roast beef, although it's also delicious with lamb, veal or poultry. • *SERVES 4 TO 6*

• **LIGHTLY GREASED 4-CUP (1-L) BAKING DISH**

1 lb	fresh spinach leaves or 1 package (10 oz/300 g) spinach, washed, stems removed and coarsely chopped	500 g
1 tbsp	butter	15 mL
¼ cup	finely chopped onion	50 mL
1	clove garlic, minced	1
½ tsp	salt	2 mL
¼ tsp	black pepper	1 mL
1 tsp	Dijon mustard	5 mL
¾ cup	half-and-half cream	175 mL
½ cup	shredded mozzarella cheese	125 mL
2	eggs, beaten	2

Horseradish Cream

¼ cup	whipping cream	50 mL
2 tbsp	prepared horseradish	10 mL

Tip

I make this in a 7-inch (17.5-cm) square dish. If you vary the dimensions of the dish, the cooking times will also vary. The custard will cook more quickly in a dish with larger dimensions.

1. In a large pot of boiling salted water, cook spinach until just wilted. Place in a colander to thoroughly drain, chop coarsely, then transfer to a mixing bowl and set aside.

2. In a skillet, melt butter over medium heat. Add onion and cook, stirring, until softened. Add garlic, salt and pepper and cook, stirring, for 1 minute. Add mustard and cream and stir to combine. Add cheese and cook, stirring, until melted.

3. In a bowl, mix together cheese mixture and spinach. Fold eggs into mixture and turn into prepared baking dish. Cover with aluminum foil and tie securely with string. Place in slow cooker stoneware and pour in enough boiling water to reach 1 inch (2.5 cm) up the sides of dish. Cover and cook on **High** for 2½ to 3 hours, until set.

4. To make Horseradish Cream: Whip cream until thick and blend in horseradish. Serve each serving of spinach soufflé with a dollop of horseradish cream.

Desserts

Thai-Style Coconut Flan

Coconut milk is a staple of Thai cuisine where it's used in a wide range of dishes, from simple soups and traditional seafood curries to more complicated desserts. On one memorable family vacation, in Phuket, Thailand, we were served a dessert to die for — deep-fried rice wrappers filled with a reduction of sweetened coconut milk and finely chopped fruits. Although this flan is very different in style, I think it's delicious and exotic enough to capture some of the magic of that evening. Since it's very rich, a small serving will satisfy. Thanks to Andrew Chase, a gifted and creative chef, for the idea of flavoring caramel with ginger and citrus juice. • *SERVES 8*

- 4-CUP (1-L) LIGHTLY GREASED MOLD OR SOUFFLÉ DISH
- LARGE (MINIMUM 5 QUART) OVAL SLOW COOKER

Caramel

½ cup	granulated sugar	125 mL
2 tbsp	water	25 mL
1 tbsp	grated gingerroot	15 mL
2 tbsp	lime or lemon juice	25 mL

Flan

1	can (14 oz/398 mL) coconut milk	1
¼ cup	granulated sugar	50 mL
2	green or white cardamom pods, crushed	2
2	slices gingerroot, cut ¼ inch (0.5 cm) wide	2
1	can (10½ oz/300 mL) sweetened condensed milk	1
¼ tsp	vanilla	1 mL
4	eggs, at room temperature	4
½ cup	unsweetened grated coconut, toasted (see Tip, page 221)	125 mL

1. In a heavy-bottomed saucepan, over medium heat, cook sugar and water until mixture becomes a deep shade of nutmeg. Add ginger and stir until bubbles subside, then quickly stir in lime or lemon juice. For instructions on how to make caramel in the microwave, see Tip, right. Pour into prepared dish and, working quickly, tip mixture around dish until sides are well coated. Set aside.

2. To make Flan: In a clean saucepan, bring coconut milk, sugar, cardamom and gingerroot to a boil. Over medium heat, cook, stirring, until sugar is completely dissolved. Add condensed milk and vanilla. Stir to combine thoroughly and set aside.

Make ahead

Flan should be made the night before it is served or very early in the day so it can be thoroughly chilled when served.

Tip

In my opinion, it's much easier to make caramel in a microwave oven than on top of the stove. In a microwaveable bowl, stir the sugar and water together. Cover tightly with plastic wrap and cook for 5 minutes on **High** power. Using oven mitts and standing well back, lift plastic to ensure that caramel is a rich nutty brown. If not, cover, return to microwave and cook in 30-second increments, until desired result is achieved. Immediately sprinkle ginger evenly over caramel and stir in lime or lemon juice. Proceed with recipe.

3. In a large bowl, beat eggs. Stir in coconut milk mixture and strain into caramel-coated dish.

4. Cover with aluminum foil and secure with string or an elastic band. Place dish in stoneware and add enough boiling water to reach 1 inch (2.5 cm) up the sides of dish. Cover and cook on **High** for 2 to 2½ hours or until knife inserted in custard comes out clean. Remove and refrigerate for 3 to 4 hours or overnight.

5. When ready to serve, remove aluminum foil and sprinkle toasted coconut over top of flan. Run a sharp knife around the edge of flan and invert onto a serving plate. Serve with fresh fruit, in season, if desired.

Tip

The shape of your baking dish can affect the cooking time. I make this in a 7-inch (17.5-cm) square baking dish, which takes 2½ hours in my slow cooker. Using a round dish, 6 inches (15 cm) in diameter, the flan may take as long as 4 hours to achieve the desired firmness.

Tip

To toast coconut, spread on a baking sheet and place in a preheated 350°F (180°C) oven for 7 to 8 minutes, stirring once or twice.

Delectable Apple-Cranberry Coconut Crisp

I love to make this delicious dessert in the fall when apples and cranberries are in season. This version is a little tart, which suits my taste, but if you have a sweet tooth, add more sugar to the cranberry mixture. • *SERVES 6 TO 8*

• **LIGHTLY GREASED SLOW COOKER STONEWARE**

4 cups	sliced, peeled apples	1 L
2 cups	cranberries, thawed if frozen	500 mL
½ cup	granulated sugar	125 mL
1 tbsp	cornstarch	15 mL
½ tsp	ground cinnamon	2 mL
2 tbsp	lemon juice or port wine	25 mL
Coconut Topping		
½ cup	packed brown sugar	125 mL
½ cup	rolled oats	125 mL
¼ cup	flaked sweetened coconut	50 mL
¼ cup	butter	50 mL

1. In a bowl, combine apples, cranberries, sugar, cornstarch, cinnamon and lemon juice or port. Mix well and transfer to prepared stoneware.

2. To make Coconut Topping: In a separate bowl, combine brown sugar, rolled oats, coconut and butter. Using two forks or your fingers, combine until crumbly. Spread over apple mixture.

3. Place two clean tea towels, each folded in half (so you will have four layers) over top of stoneware. Cover and cook on **High** for 3 to 4 hours, until crisp is hot and bubbly. Serve with whipped cream or ice cream, if desired.

Variation

Apple-Coconut Crisp: Use 6 cups (1.5 L) of sliced apples, reduce sugar to ¼ cup (50 mL) and use lemon juice rather than port wine.

Peach-Blueberry Cobbler

Peaches and blueberries are a wonderful combination and this simple old-fashioned cobbler is a great way to use these luscious fruits when they are in season. It is delicious just with sweetened whipped cream or vanilla ice cream. • *SERVES 4 TO 6*

• **LIGHTLY GREASED SLOW COOKER STONEWARE**

2 cups	peaches, peeled and sliced, or 2 cans (14 oz/398 mL) sliced peaches, drained (see Tip, right)	500 mL
2 cups	blueberries, thawed if frozen	500 mL
½ cup	granulated sugar	125 mL
2 tbsp	all-purpose flour	25 mL
½ tsp	ground cinnamon	2 mL
2 tsp	lemon juice	10 mL
2 tbsp	Amaretto liqueur or ½ tsp (2 mL) almond extract	25 mL

Topping

½ cup	all-purpose flour	125 mL
¼ cup	granulated sugar	50 mL
1 tsp	baking powder	5 mL
Pinch	salt	Pinch
1 tbsp	lemon zest	15 mL
3 tbsp	butter	45 mL
⅓ cup	milk	75 mL

Tip

To peel peaches, drop in a pot of boiling water, leave for 1 minute, then run under cold water. The skins will slip off easily. You can also use canned sliced peaches, drained, and frozen blueberries, thawed. Add 1 tsp (5 mL) of lemon juice to compensate for the extra sugar in the canned peaches.

1. In prepared stoneware, combine peaches, blueberries, sugar, flour, cinnamon, lemon juice and Amaretto or almond extract. Cover and cook on **Low** for 4 hours or on **High** for 2 hours.

2. To make Topping: In a bowl, combine flour, sugar, baking powder, salt and lemon zest. Using your fingers or a pastry blender, cut in butter until mixture resembles coarse crumbs. Drizzle with milk and stir with a fork until a thick batter forms.

3. Drop batter by spoonfuls over hot fruit. Cover and cook on **High** for 45 minutes or until a toothpick inserted in the center comes out clean. Spoon into individual bowls and serve with vanilla ice cream or sweetened whipped cream, if desired.

Variations

Peach Cobbler: Use 4 cups (1 L) peaches instead of the blueberry-peach mixture.

Blueberry Cobbler: Use 4 cups (1 L) blueberries instead of the blueberry-peach mixture.

Blueberry-Rhubarb Spoonbread

I love this delicious variation on old-fashioned spoonbread. Serve over vanilla ice cream or with sweetened whipped cream and expect requests for seconds. • *SERVES 6 TO 8*

- LIGHTLY GREASED SLOW COOKER STONEWARE
- LARGE (MINIMUM 5 QUART) OVAL SLOW COOKER

2 cups	blueberries, thawed if frozen	500 mL
2 cups	rhubarb, cut into 1-inch (2.5-cm) chunks, thawed if frozen	500 mL
¼ cup	granulated sugar	50 mL
1 tsp	ground cinnamon	5 mL
	Zest and juice of 1 orange	

Cornbread

1 cup	cornmeal	250 mL
1½ tsp	baking powder	7 mL
Pinch	salt	Pinch
½ cup	softened butter	125 mL
½ cup	granulated sugar	125 mL
2	eggs	2
1 tsp	vanilla extract	5 mL

1. In a bowl, combine blueberries, rhubarb, sugar, cinnamon, orange zest and juice. Set aside.

2. To make Cornbread: In a separate bowl, combine cornmeal, baking powder and salt. In a mixing bowl, beat together butter and sugar until light and fluffy. Add cornmeal mixture. Add eggs, one at a time, and mix until well blended. Stir in vanilla.

3. Spread batter over bottom of stoneware. Spoon berries over top. Cover and cook on **High** for 3 hours, until batter is browning around the edges and spoonbread is set.

Variation

Blueberry Spoonbread: Use 4 cups (1 L) blueberries and reduce sugar to 2 tbsp (25 mL). Substitute 2 tbsp (25 mL) lemon juice and 1 tbsp (15 mL) lemon zest for the orange.

Rhubarb Betty

There are many different variations on this traditional dessert, which is basically baked fruit with a seasoned topping. This version, which relies on bread crumbs for its starch component, is particularly simple and good. It works equally well with a rhubarb-strawberry combination or with apples. Serve with sweetened whipped cream. • *SERVES 6*

- **LIGHTLY GREASED SLOW COOKER STONEWARE**
- **WORKS BEST IN A 3½-QUART SLOW COOKER (SEE TIP, RIGHT)**

⅓ cup	melted butter	75 mL
2 cups	fresh bread crumbs (see Tip, right)	500 mL
4 cups	rhubarb, cut into 1-inch (2.5-cm) chunks	1 L
1 cup	granulated sugar	250 mL
1 tbsp	all-purpose flour	15 mL
1 tsp	ground cinnamon	5 mL
	Zest and juice of 1 orange	

1. In a mixing bowl, combine butter and bread crumbs. Set aside.

2. In a separate bowl, combine rhubarb, sugar, flour and cinnamon.

3. In prepared slow cooker stoneware, layer one third of bread-crumb mixture, then one half of rhubarb mixture. Repeat layers of bread crumbs and fruit, then finish with a layer of bread crumbs on top. Pour zest and orange juice over top. Cook on **High** for 3 to 4 hours, until bubbly and brown.

Variations

Rhubarb-Strawberry Betty: Use 2 cups (500 mL) each of strawberries, quartered, and rhubarb, cut into 1-inch (2.5-cm) lengths. Reduce sugar to ¾ cup (175 mL) and omit cinnamon.

Apple Betty: Substitute apple slices for rhubarb and the juice and zest of one lemon for the orange. Reduce sugar to ½ to ¾ cup (125 to 175 mL), depending on preference.

Tip

If you have a large oval cooker, double the quantity. Refrigerate leftovers and reheat.

Tip

Fresh bread crumbs are far superior to the ready-made kind, which can be very dry. They are easily made in a food processor by removing the crust, if desired, cutting the bread into manageable chunks and then processing until the appropriate degree of fineness is achieved. Tightly covered, bread crumbs will keep for two or three days in the refrigerator.

Apple Charlotte with Apricot-Brandy Sauce

Served with a sophisticated sauce, this delicious old-fashioned dessert assumes an aura of elegance. This version is simple to make. For a more traditional approach, serve with sweetened whipped cream or vanilla ice cream. • *SERVES 6*

6	slices bread, crusts removed, buttered on one side, about ½ inch (1 cm) thick	6
6	cooking apples, peeled, cored and sliced	6
2 tbsp	melted butter	25 mL
3 tbsp	granulated sugar	45 mL
1 tsp	ground cinnamon	5 mL
½ tsp	ground ginger	2 mL
½ tsp	ground cloves	2 mL
¼ cup	brandy or Calvados or 1 tsp (5 mL) brandy extract (see Tip, right)	50 mL

Apricot-Brandy Sauce

⅓ cup	apricot jam	75 mL
2 tbsp	brandy or Calvados or ½ tsp (2 mL) brandy extract	25 mL
¾ cup	apple juice	175 mL
Pinch	ground ginger	Pinch
1 tsp	cornstarch, dissolved in 1 tbsp (15 mL) apple juice	5 mL

Tip

Calvados is apple brandy made in Normandy. It is quite strong, but can be a nice after-dinner drink in the right circumstances. I like to keep a bottle on hand as it is a great embellishment for many dishes made with apples.

1. Line bottom of stoneware with bread, buttered side to the bottom. Arrange apple slices on top.

2. In a bowl, combine butter, sugar, cinnamon, ginger, cloves and brandy. Pour mixture over apples. Cover and cook on **High** for 3 to 4 hours or until the edges of the bread are slightly browned.

3. To make Apricot-Brandy Sauce: In a saucepan, combine jam, brandy, apple juice and ginger. Bring to a boil and cook, stirring, for 1 to 2 minutes, until jam is completely dissolved. Add cornstarch mixture, stir well and remove from heat.

4. When ready to serve, spoon charlotte into individual bowls and top with sauce.

Bread Pudding with Raspberry Sauce

This easy-to-make version of bread pudding takes a comfort-food classic and, with the simple addition of a rich raspberry sauce, makes it into a much more sophisticated dessert. While it may not be like the one your mother used to make, expect your guests to request seconds. • *SERVES 6 TO 8*

• LIGHTLY GREASED SLOW COOKER STONEWARE

6 cups	stale bread, cut into 1-inch (2.5-cm) cubes	1.5 L
3 tbsp	melted butter	45 mL
4	eggs	4
¾ cup	granulated sugar	175 mL
4 cups	milk	1 L
½ tsp	ground cinnamon	2 mL
½ tsp	vanilla extract	2 mL

Raspberry Sauce

¼ cup	granulated sugar	50 mL
¼ cup	water	50 mL
2 cups	raspberries, thawed if frozen	500 mL
1 tsp	balsamic vinegar	5 mL

1. In prepared stoneware, combine bread and melted butter. Toss to mix thoroughly.

2. In a large bowl, beat eggs. Mix in sugar, milk, cinnamon and vanilla. Pour over bread cubes. Cover and cook on **High** for 4 hours, until top is golden brown.

3. To make Raspberry Sauce: In a saucepan, combine sugar and water. Bring to a boil. Cook for 1 minute or until sugar is thoroughly dissolved and mixture is becoming syrupy. Add raspberries. Return to a boil and cook until raspberries fall apart when crushed with a wooden spoon. (This will take several minutes, depending upon the size of the pot.) Remove from heat and stir in balsamic vinegar. If you prefer a smooth sauce, purée in a food processor.

4. Spoon pudding into individual bowls and top with sauce.

Old-Fashioned Rice Pudding

This recipe is adapted from a nineteenth-century English recipe that describes the secret to a deliciously creamy pudding as "very slow and prolonged baking on the outer edges of the fire." Today, the slow cooker eliminates the need for "fire" and takes all the guesswork out of the task. It's also remarkably easy. Just mix the ingredients together and turn the cooker on — you don't even have to precook the rice. The results are absolutely delicious. • *SERVES 6*

• **LIGHTLY GREASED SLOW COOKER STONEWARE**

¾ cup	long-grain rice	175 mL
3 cups	milk	750 mL
¾ cup	granulated sugar	175 mL
¾ tsp	ground cinnamon	3 mL
Pinch	salt	Pinch
⅓ cup	melted butter	75 mL
	Vanilla-flavored whipped cream	

1. In a colander, rinse rice thoroughly under cold water. Place in prepared stoneware. Add remaining ingredients, except for butter and whipped cream. Stir to combine. Pour butter over rice mixture. Cover and cook on **High** for 4 hours, until rice has absorbed the liquid.

2. When ready to serve, spoon into individual desert bowls and top with whipped cream flavored with vanilla.

Lemony Banana Custard

Just wait until you try this luscious combination of bananas and lemon in a creamy custard base. It's my idea of comfort food. Even better, it's so easy to make, you can enjoy it every day of the week. • *SERVES 4 TO 6*

• **LIGHTLY GREASED SLOW COOKER STONEWARE**

¾ cup	granulated sugar	175 mL
2 tbsp	lemon juice	25 mL
¼ cup	water	50 mL
⅓ cup	butter	75 mL
2	eggs	2
½ tsp	ground cinnamon	2 mL
8	bananas, mashed	8
	Finely chopped pecans or walnuts (optional)	
	Sweetened whipped cream (optional)	

1. In a saucepan, over medium heat, bring sugar, lemon juice and water to a boil. Cook, stirring until a light syrup forms, about 5 minutes. Set aside.

2. In a mixing bowl, using an electric mixer, if desired, cream together butter and eggs. Gradually fold into warm syrup. Add cinnamon and bananas and stir to combine. Pour mixture into prepared stoneware. Cover and cook on **High** for 3 hours, until mixture sets. When ready to serve, garnish with chopped pecans or walnuts, if using, and top with a dollop of sweetened whipped cream.

Crunchy Almond Crème Caramel

This creamy custard, Italian in origin and embellished with cinnamon-and-clove flavored caramel along with crunchy almonds, has a surprise ingredient — potatoes. Nevertheless, it is refreshingly light and lemony. Well chilled, it makes a lovely summer dessert. • *SERVES 6*

- **6-CUP (1.5-L) LIGHTLY GREASED SOUFFLÉ OR BAKING DISH**
- **LARGE (MINIMUM 5 QUART) OVAL SLOW COOKER**

Caramel

1 tbsp	lemon juice	15 mL
⅛ tsp	each ground cloves and cinnamon	0.5 mL
¾ cup	granulated sugar	175 mL
¼ cup	water	50 mL

Potato-Almond Custard

3	eggs	3
¾ cup	granulated sugar	175 mL
½ cup	blanched almonds, finely chopped	125 mL
2 tbsp	Amaretto liqueur or ½ tsp (2 mL) almond extract	25 mL
	Zest of 1 lemon	
2 cups	shredded cooked potato (see Tip, right)	500 mL
2 cups	milk	500 mL

1. In a small bowl, combine lemon juice, cloves and cinnamon. Stir well and set aside.

2. In a saucepan, over medium heat, combine sugar and water. Stirring constantly, cook until sugar is dissolved and mixture comes to a boil. Stop stirring and continue to cook for 3 to 4 minutes, until golden brown. Add lemon mixture, stir and, working quickly, pour into prepared dish, tilting to distribute syrup across the bottom and up the sides. (To make caramel in the microwave, see Tip, page 220.)

3. To make Potato-Almond Custard: In a large bowl, beat eggs with sugar until thickened and lemon-colored. Add almonds, Amaretto or almond extract and lemon zest, stirring to combine. Add potatoes and milk and mix thoroughly. Pour mixture into prepared dish. Cover with aluminum foil and secure with string or an elastic band. Place dish in slow cooker stoneware and pour in enough boiling water to come 1 inch (2.5 cm) up the sides of bowl. Cover and cook on **High** for 4 hours or until a toothpick inserted in center of custard comes out clean.

4. Chill thoroughly. To serve, run a sharp knife around edge of custard and invert onto serving plate.

Make ahead

This dish is best made early in the day or the night before it is served as it should be refrigerated for at least 4 hours before it is served.

Tip

To precook potatoes for this recipe, boil potatoes in their skins for 15 to 20 minutes or until almost tender. (You'll need 1 very large potato or 2 smaller ones for the required quantity.) Drain well. Set aside until cool enough to handle, then lift off the skins. Using the largest holes of a cheese grater, shred potato into a bowl. Measure correct amount and discard any excess.

Tip

I make this in a 7-inch (17.5-cm) square baking dish. Changing the proportions and using a smaller but deeper dish will increase the cooking time.

Chocolate Mocha Custard

For a deliciously decadent treat, spoon this dreamy custard into pretty glass dishes, top it with sweetened whipped cream and sprinkle with finely chopped walnuts or pecans. Serve your favorite vanilla wafers on the side. • *SERVES 6*

- **6-CUP (1.5-L) LIGHTLY GREASED BAKING OR SOUFFLÉ DISH**
- **LARGE (MINIMUM 5 QUART) OVAL SLOW COOKER**

1 cup	whipping cream	250 mL
1 cup	milk	250 mL
2 oz	unsweetened chocolate, grated	50 g
2 tbsp	strong coffee	25 mL
½ tsp	vanilla extract	2 mL
3	whole eggs, at room temperature	3
3	egg yolks, at room temperature	3
¾ cup	granulated sugar	175 mL
2 tbsp	coffee-flavored liqueur, such as Kahlua	25 mL

1. In a large pot, bring cream and milk to a boil, watching carefully to ensure liquid does not boil over the top of the pot. Remove from heat. Add chocolate and stir until melted. Stir in coffee and vanilla and set aside.

2. In a mixing bowl, using an electric mixer, if desired, beat eggs and yolks with sugar until fluffy. Add cream mixture and liqueur and stir well. Strain mixture into prepared dish. Cover with foil and secure with string or an elastic band. Place dish in slow cooker stoneware and pour in enough boiling water to come 1 inch (2.5 cm) up the sides of dish. Cover and cook on **High** for 3½ hours, until custard is set. Chill thoroughly and serve.

Make ahead

This dish is best made early in the day or the night before it is served as it should be refrigerated for at least 4 hours before it is served.

Tip

If, like me, you don't like the skin that forms on custard after it cools, spread plastic wrap directly over the surface of the custard as soon as you take the dish out of the slow cooker. This prevents the cream from being exposed to the air which causes a skin to form.

Tip

I make this in a 7-inch (17.5-cm) square baking dish. Changing the proportions and using a smaller but deeper dish will increase cooking time.

Elizabeth Raffald's Orange Custard

Many years ago I had the great pleasure of dining with Jane Grigson, the late food writer, at her seventeenth-century farmhouse in Wiltshire, England. Since I was interviewing her for an article I was writing on English food, she was keen to convince me that her native fare was as grand as any and cooked me a delicious meal that included this sophisticated custard. Elizabeth Raffald, who was born in 1748 and with whom this recipe originated, was a woman ahead of her time. Enjoying a remarkable career as a food retailer and domestic scientist, among other things, she was an eighteenth-century Martha Stewart. • *SERVES 6*

- 6-CUP (1.5-L) LIGHTLY GREASED BAKING OR SOUFFLÉ DISH
- LARGE (MINIMUM 5 QUART) OVAL SLOW COOKER

	Zest and juice of 1 orange, preferably Seville	
2 tbsp	orange-flavored liqueur, such as Grand Marnier or Cointreau, or 2 tbsp (25 mL) unsweetened orange juice concentrate, thawed	25 mL
¾ cup	granulated sugar	175 mL
4	egg yolks, at room temperature (see Tip, right)	4
2	whole eggs, at room temperature	2
1 cup	whipping cream	250 mL
1 cup	milk	250 mL

Make ahead

This custard can be served cold as well as warm, so it can be made ahead and chilled.

Tip

Since getting eggs to set before they scramble, particularly without adding starch, is tricky at the best of times, make sure the eggs are at room temperature and that the milk mixture is boiling when you add it to the egg mixture.

1. In a food processor or blender, combine orange zest and juice with liqueur or concentrate and process until peel is reduced to tiny particles. Add sugar, egg yolks and eggs and process until smooth.

2. In a pot, over medium heat, bring cream and milk to a boil, watching carefully to ensure mixture doesn't boil over. Add gradually to orange mixture, pulsing to combine.

3. Pour mixture into prepared dish. Cover with aluminum foil and secure with string or an elastic band. Place dish in slow cooker stoneware and pour in enough boiling water to reach 1 inch (2.5 cm) up the side of dish. Cover and cook on **High** for 3½ hours, until top is set. Serve over fresh fruit, warm or chilled.

Variation

Lemon Custard: Substitute the zest and juice of 1 lemon for the orange and 1 tbsp (15 mL) vodka or gin, for the orange-flavored liqueur, if desired.

Maple Surprise

Served over vanilla ice cream, this delicious sauce makes a great way to finish a meal. If you don't identify the key ingredient for your guests, they'll enjoy guessing. Most will think it's a particularly good applesauce, but won't be able to pinpoint the unusual flavoring. You can also serve this on its own with a good dollop of whipped cream. • *SERVES 6*

4 cups	squash or pumpkin, peeled and cut into 1-inch (2.5-cm) cubes	1 L
¼ cup	melted butter	50 mL
Pinch	salt	Pinch
1 tbsp	dark or amber rum or ½ tsp (2 mL) vanilla extract	15 mL
1 cups	maple syrup	250 mL
3 tbsp	walnuts, finely chopped	45 mL
3 tbsp	candied ginger, finely chopped (see Tip, right)	45 mL
	Vanilla ice cream (optional)	

Tip

Candied ginger is usually available in the bulk food section of supermarkets.

1. In slow cooker stoneware, combine squash or pumpkin, butter, salt, rum or vanilla extract and maple syrup. Cover and cook on **Low** for 8 hours or on **High** for 4 hours, until squash is very tender.

2. With a wooden spoon or potato masher, crush mixture to a smooth purée. Spoon over vanilla ice cream, if desired, and top with walnuts and ginger.

Spiced Pears Baked in Red Wine

This classic light dessert, which makes an elegant finish to any meal, fills your house with a wonderful aroma as it cooks. It's a snap to make and festive enough for any celebration. Although it's tasty enough to serve solely with vanilla wafers, for special occasions, I like to serve a cheese course as an accompaniment. • *SERVES 6 TO 8*

• **WORKS BEST IN A 3½-QUART SLOW COOKER, WHICH ENSURES THAT THE PEARS WILL BE APPROPRIATELY SUBMERGED IN THE WINE**

6 to 8	pears, peeled, cored and cut in half lengthwise	6 to 8
2 cups	dry red wine, or more, if necessary, to cover pears	500 mL
½ cup	granulated sugar	125 mL
1	cinnamon stick piece, about 2 inches (5 cm)	1
4	whole cloves	4
	Zest of 1 orange	

1. Place pears in slow cooker stoneware. Add wine (enough to cover pears), sugar, cinnamon, cloves and orange zest. Cover and cook on **Low** for 6 to 8 hours, until pears are tender. Chill well and serve.

Make ahead

This should be made early in the day or the night before so it can be well chilled before serving.

Tip

Rub pears with lemon juice after they are peeled to prevent discoloring or place a piece of parchment directly on top of pears to ensure more even color.

Old-Fashioned Gingerbread

This delicious cake is wonderful with applesauce, stewed rhubarb or butterscotch sauce. Since I almost always have the ingredients on hand, I most often serve it with whipped cream flavored with candied ginger, which is usually available in the bulk food sections of supermarkets. Simply whip the cream and add finely chopped candied ginger, to taste. Expect requests for seconds. • *SERVES 6 TO 8*

- **LIGHTLY GREASED BAKING PAN OR SLOW COOKER STONEWARE (SEE TIP, RIGHT)**
- **LARGE (MINIMUM 5 QUART) OVAL SLOW COOKER, IF USING BAKING PAN**

1 cup	milk	250 mL
2 tsp	baking soda	10 mL
1 tbsp	ground ginger	15 mL
½ cup	butter	125 mL
½ cup	packed brown sugar	125 mL
1 cup	corn syrup	250 mL
2 cups	all-purpose flour	500 mL
1	egg, beaten	1
	Zest of 1 lemon	

1. In a saucepan, over low heat, warm milk. Remove from heat. Stir in baking soda and ginger. Set aside.

2. In a large saucepan, over low heat, melt butter. Add brown sugar and stir until dissolved. Add corn syrup and stir to combine.

3. Stir flour into syrup mixture, mixing well. Stir in egg, milk mixture and lemon zest, mixing to combine thoroughly. Pour into prepared pan and place in slow cooker. Place two clean tea towels, each folded in half (so you will have four layers) over top of the stoneware. Cover and cook on **High** for 4 hours or until a toothpick inserted in the center of the cake comes out clean. Serve warm.

Tip

One challenge with making cakes in a slow cooker is finding a baking pan that will fit. I make this recipe in a 5-quart slow cooker using a 6-cup (1.5-L) oval baking dish which measures 10¼ inches (26 cm) end to end. You can also bake this directly in the stoneware that fits a smaller slow cooker. However, the baking time will be significantly reduced. In that case, begin checking doneness at the 2-hour mark.

Lemon Cheesecake

The refreshing lemon taste combined with its rich cheese base makes this cake one of my favorites. Since almonds and lemons have a great affinity, I'm particularly fond of the Variation with almonds in the crust. In summer, I serve this with fresh blueberries. • *SERVES 8 TO 10*

- 7-INCH (17.5-CM) WELL-GREASED SPRINGFORM PAN
  OR BAKING DISH LINED WITH GREASED HEAVY-DUTY FOIL
- LARGE (MINIMUM 5 QUART) OVAL SLOW COOKER

Crust

1 cup	vanilla wafer crumbs	250 mL
2 tbsp	granulated sugar	25 mL
Pinch	salt	Pinch
3 tbsp	melted butter	45 mL
1 tsp	lemon zest	5 mL
¼ tsp	vanilla extract	1 mL

Cheesecake

2	packages (8 oz/250 g) cream cheese, softened	2
¾ cup	granulated sugar	175 mL
2	eggs	2
1 tsp	each vanilla extract and lemon zest	5 mL
Pinch	salt	Pinch
¼ cup	freshly squeezed lemon juice	50 mL
½ cup	sour cream	125 mL

1. In a bowl, combine vanilla wafer crumbs, sugar, salt, butter, lemon zest and vanilla. Press the mixture into the bottom of prepared pan. Place in freezer until ready for use.

2. To make Cheesecake: In a food processor, combine cream cheese and sugar until smooth. Add eggs, one at a time, mixing well after each addition. Add vanilla, lemon zest and salt and mix well. Blend in lemon juice and sour cream.

3. Spoon mixture over crust and cover tightly with aluminum foil, securing with a string. Place pan in stoneware and pour in enough boiling water to come 1 inch (2.5 cm) up the sides. Cover and cook on **High** for 3 to 4 hours or until edges are set and center is just slightly jiggly. Remove from slow cooker and chill thoroughly, preferably overnight, before serving.

Variation

Lemon Cheesecake with Crunchy Almond Crust: Reduce vanilla wafer crumbs to ½ cup (125 mL) and add ½ cup (125 mL) ground almonds, blanched and toasted (see Tip, right). Increase sugar to ¼ cup (50 mL).

Make ahead

This cake is best made a day ahead and allowed to chill in the refrigerator overnight.

Tip

To blanch, grind and toast almonds: Drop almonds in their skins in rapidly boiling water for 1 minute. Drain in a colander and rinse thoroughly in cold water. The almonds will pop out of their skins. Allow to dry, then process until fine in a food processor. Spread on a baking sheet and toast until lightly browned.

Chocolacinno Cheesecake

This is a rich, delicious cheesecake, appropriate to any occasion, and it's a cinch to make in your slow cooker. I like to serve this to guests on warm summer evenings when we're having dinner in the garden. Place a slice on a plate and accompany with fresh raspberries that have been tossed with sugar and a tiny bit of good quality balsamic vinegar. • *SERVES 8 TO 10*

- 7-INCH (17.5-CM) WELL-GREASED SPRINGFORM PAN
  OR 7-INCH (17.5-CM) 6-CUP (1.5-L) SOUFFLÉ DISH LINED
  WITH GREASED HEAVY-DUTY FOIL
- LARGE (MINIMUM 5 QUART) OVAL SLOW COOKER

Crust

¾ cup	chocolate wafer crumbs	175 mL
3 tbsp	melted butter	45 mL
¼ cup	granulated sugar	50 mL

Cheesecake

2	packages (8 oz/250 g) cream cheese, softened	2
½ cup	granulated sugar	125 mL
2	eggs	2
¼ cup	whipping cream	50 mL
1 tsp	vanilla extract	5 mL
2 tbsp	strong coffee	25 mL
1 cup	semisweet chocolate chips	250 mL
¼ cup	coffee-flavored liqueur, such as Kahlua	50 mL

Make ahead

This cake is best made a day ahead and allowed to chill in the refrigerator overnight.

Tip

To ensure that the cake lifts off the pan intact, spray pan with nonstick vegetable spray. For added insurance, cover the bottom of the pan with a parchment circle, cut to size.

1. In a bowl, combine chocolate wafer crumbs, melted butter and sugar. Press the mixture into the bottom of prepared pan. Place in freezer until ready for use.

2. To make Cheesecake: In a large bowl, using an electric mixer, beat cream cheese and sugar until smooth. Beat in eggs, one at a time, until incorporated. Beat in whipping cream and vanilla.

3. In a saucepan, over low heat, combine coffee, chocolate chips and Kahlua. Cook, stirring, until melted. Pour into cheese mixture and beat until thoroughly combined. Spoon over prepared crust and cover tightly with aluminum foil, securing with a string.

4. Place pan in slow cooker stoneware and pour in enough boiling water to come 1 inch (2.5 cm) up the sides. Cover and cook on **High** for 3 to 4 hours or until edges are set and center is just slightly jiggly. Remove from slow cooker and chill thoroughly, preferably overnight, before serving.

Apple Sponge Pudding

This simple old-fashioned dessert is a mouth-watering combination of aromatic fruit and crumbly cake with a hint of creamy pudding. All it needs is sweetened whipped cream to make a perfect finish for any meal. • *SERVES 8 TO 10*

• **LIGHTLY GREASED SLOW COOKER STONEWARE**

1 tbsp	butter	15 mL
1 cup	packed brown sugar	250 mL
1 to 2 tbsp	dark rum (optional)	15 to 25 mL
6	apples, peeled, cored and sliced	6
1 tbsp	lemon juice	15 mL
3	eggs, separated	3
1 cup	granulated sugar	250 mL
1 tsp	vanilla extract	5 mL
1 cup	all-purpose flour	250 mL
½ tsp	salt	2 mL
1 tsp	baking powder	5 mL
¼ cup	water	50 mL

1. In a saucepan, over medium heat, melt butter. Add brown sugar and stir until melted. Add rum, if using. Spread mixture over bottom of prepared stoneware. Spread apples over mixture and drizzle lemon juice over top.

2. In a mixing bowl, using an electric mixer, beat egg yolks and sugar until light. Stir in vanilla.

3. In another bowl, combine flour, salt and baking powder. Add to egg mixture, alternately with water, making three additions of flour and two of water, beating thoroughly after each addition.

4. In another bowl, beat egg whites until stiff. Gently fold into batter and spoon over apples. Cover and cook on **High** for 3½ to 4 hours, until top is firm and fruit is bubbly. Serve warm.

Ginger Sponge Pudding

This light and delicious sponge-like pudding cake is wonderful on its own, topped with a dollop of whipped cream or as an accompaniment for fresh berries. It's easy to make, and so long as you have candied ginger on hand, it can be assembled with pantry ingredients. Candied ginger is usually available in the bulk food section of supermarkets and we always have some in the house as my husband keeps it around to nibble on as a digestive aid. • *SERVES 6 TO 8*

- **6-CUP (1.5-L) LIGHTLY GREASED PUDDING MOLD, BAKING OR SOUFFLÉ DISH**
- **LARGE (MINIMUM 5 QUART) OVAL SLOW COOKER**

¼ cup	butter	50 mL
¼ cup	granulated sugar	50 mL
3	eggs, separated	3
½ tsp	vanilla extract	2 mL
½ cup	all-purpose flour	125 mL
1 tsp	baking powder	5 mL
½ tsp	ground ginger	2 mL
Pinch	salt	Pinch
1 cup	milk	250 mL
¾ cup	candied ginger, finely chopped	175 mL

Tip

"Chop" the ginger in a food processor. Combine with milk and process until the desired fineness is achieved.

Tip

I make this in a 7-inch (17.5-cm) square baking dish. The cooking times will vary in a differently proportioned dish.

1. In a mixing bowl, using an electric mixer, if desired, cream butter and sugar, until fluffy. Add egg yolks one at a time and beat until smooth. Add vanilla and stir to combine thoroughly.

2. In a separate bowl, combine flour, baking powder, ground ginger and salt. Add to butter mixture alternately with milk, mixing well after each addition. Stir in chopped ginger. Alternately, add candied ginger with milk, if chopped in food processor (see Tip, right).

3. In a separate bowl, beat egg whites until stiff. Gently fold into flour mixture to make a smooth batter. Spoon into prepared dish. Cover with lid or foil and secure with string or an elastic band.

4. Place in dish in slow cooker stoneware and pour in enough boiling water to come 1 inch (2.5 cm) up the sides of bowl. Cover and cook on **High** for 2½ to 3 hours or until a toothpick inserted in center of cake comes out clean. Turn out on a plate and serve with sweetened whipped cream or fresh berries.

Steamed Strawberry Pudding

Fresh, locally picked strawberries, served simply with a bit of sugar, a splash of good balsamic vinegar and cream, are one of life's great treats. But there can be times during strawberry season — for instance, when my husband returns from the farmers' market with an entire flat of berries because they were such a bargain — when what to do with them all becomes a concern. This remarkably light pudding-cake is a perfect solution. I think it's every bit as delicious as strawberry shortcake, with fewer calories and fat. • *SERVES 4 TO 6*

- 6-CUP (1.5-L) LIGHTLY GREASED PUDDING MOLD, MIXING BOWL OR SOUFFLÉ DISH
- LARGE (MINIMUM 5 QUART) OVAL SLOW COOKER

Pudding

¼ cup	butter	50 mL
¼ cup	granulated sugar	50 mL
4	eggs, separated	4
¾ cup	all-purpose flour	175 mL
2 cups	sliced strawberries	500 mL

Strawberry Sauce

¼ cup	granulated sugar	50 mL
¼ cup	water	50 mL
2 cups	strawberries	500 mL
1 tbsp	balsamic vinegar	15 mL

Tip
Substitute individually frozen, unsweetened berries, thawed, if desired.

1. In a mixing bowl, cream butter and sugar until light and fluffy. Beat in egg yolks, one at a time. Gradually add flour, beating to combine thoroughly. Gently fold in strawberries.

2. In a separate bowl, beat egg whites until stiff. Gently fold into strawberry mixture to make a smooth batter. Spoon into prepared dish. Cover with lid or foil and secure with string or an elastic band. Place in dish in slow cooker stoneware and pour in enough boiling water to come 1 inch (2.5 cm) up the sides of bowl. Cover and cook on **High** for 2½ to 3 hours or until a toothpick inserted in center of cake comes out clean.

3. To make Strawberry Sauce: In a saucepan, combine sugar and water. Bring to a boil and cook for 1 minute. Add strawberries, return to a boil and cook for several minutes, until strawberries begin to lose their juice. Remove from heat and stir in balsamic vinegar. Spoon pudding into individual bowls and top with sauce.

Variations

Substitute blueberries or raspberries, when in season.

Rich Chocolate Pudding

If you love chocolate, you'll love this simple steamed pudding — it's deliciously rich and decadent. For optimum results, use good quality chocolate and finish with a healthy dollop of sweetened whipped cream. • *SERVES 6*

- **6-CUP (1.5-L) LIGHTLY GREASED PUDDING MOLD, BAKING OR SOUFFLÉ DISH**
- **LARGE (MINIMUM 5 QUART) OVAL SLOW COOKER**

4	eggs, separated	4
¼ cup	granulated sugar	50 mL
10 oz	bittersweet chocolate, grated, about 1 cup (250 mL)	300 g
1 tbsp	all-purpose flour	15 mL
½ tsp	baking powder	2 mL
Pinch	salt	Pinch
½ tsp	vanilla	2 mL

1. In a mixing bowl, using an electric mixer, if desired, cream egg yolks and sugar. Melt chocolate (see Tip, right) and beat into egg mixture. Blend in flour, baking powder, salt and vanilla.

2. In a clean bowl, with an electric mixer, beat egg whites until stiff. Gently fold into chocolate mixture. Pour into prepared dish. Cover with aluminum foil and tie tightly with string or an elastic band. Place dish in slow cooker stoneware and add boiling water to come 1 inch (2.5 cm) up the sides of dish. Cover and cook on **High** for 2½ hours, until toothpick inserted in center of pudding comes out clean.

Tip

The only challenging part of this recipe is melting the chocolate, as it has a tendency to "seize" and become grainy. To avoid this problem, grate the chocolate first by pulsing it in a food processor and then melt it in a double boiler over hot water, stirring constantly. Or place half the quantity of grated chocolate in a microwaveable bowl, cover and cook at full power for 45 seconds per ounce (25 g) of chocolate. Stir in remaining chocolate and use immediately.

Pineapple Upside-Down Spice Cake

This recipe is an old favorite, remembered from my childhood. I still love it, topped with a big scoop of vanilla ice cream. • SERVES 6 TO 8

• **LIGHTLY GREASED SLOW COOKER STONEWARE**

Fruit

¼ cup	melted butter	50 mL
½ cup	firmly packed brown sugar	125 mL
10	slices fresh pineapple or 1 can (19 oz/540 mL) sliced pineapple, drained	10

Cake

¾ cup	all-purpose flour	175 mL
1 tsp	baking powder	5 mL
¼ tsp	salt	1 mL
¼ cup	butter	50 mL
1 cup	granulated sugar	250 mL
1	egg	1
½ cup	milk	125 mL
1 tsp	each ground cinnamon and ground allspice	5 mL
½ tsp	each ground cloves and ground nutmeg	2 mL
1 tsp	vanilla extract	5 mL

Tip

To prevent accumulated moisture from dripping on the cake batter, place two clean tea towels, each folded in half (so you will have four layers), across the top of the stoneware before covering. The towels will absorb the moisture generated during cooking.

1. In a small bowl, combine butter and brown sugar. Spread over bottom of prepared stoneware. Arrange pineapple on top.

2. To make Cake: In a bowl, combine flour, baking powder and salt. In a mixing bowl, using an electric mixer, if desired, cream butter and sugar until light and fluffy. Beat in egg. Add milk and flour mixture alternately, making three additions of flour and two of milk, beating well after each addition. Blend in cinnamon, allspice, cloves, nutmeg and vanilla. Pour mixture over pineapple slices.

3. Place tea towels over top of stoneware (see Tip, right). Cover and cook on **High** for 3 hours or until a toothpick inserted in center of cake comes out clean. To serve, slice and invert on plate. Top with vanilla ice cream.

Variation

Peach Upside-Down Spice Cake: For the pineapple, substitute 6 peaches, sliced, or 2 (14 oz/398 mL) cans of peach slices, drained.

National Library of Canada Cataloguing in Publication Data

Finlayson, Judith
The 150 best slow cooker recipes

Includes index.
ISBN 0-7788-0039-3 (bound) — ISBN 0-7788-0041-5 (Canada: pbk.)
ISBN 0-7788-0038-5 (USA: pbk.)

1. Electric cookery, Slow.
I. Title   II. Title: One hundred fifty best slow cooker recipes.

TX827.F55 2001   641.5'884   C2001-900966-6

Index